Grade
2

The Complete Year in Reading and Writing

Daily Lessons • Monthly Units • Yearlong Calendar

Patty Vitale-Reilly and Pam Allyn

SCHOLASTIC

NEW YORK • TORONTO • LONDON • AUCKLAND • SYDNEY
MEXICO CITY • NEW DELHI • HONG KONG • BUENOS AIRES

To all second grade teachers, who care so much, and:

To my father, Charles Joseph Vitale Sr., whose conversations
about education forever changed the course of my life.
~ *Patty Vitale-Reilly*

To Lois Bridges and Danny Miller
~ *Pam Allyn*

Cover design by Jay Namerow

Interior design by Maria Lilja

Photos by LitLife Archives (interior and cover), Maria Lilja (inside cover)

Acquiring Editor: Lois Bridges

Development and Production Editor: Danny Miller

Copy Editor: Erich Strom

ISBN 13: 978-0-545-04636-7

ISBN 10: 0-545-04636-X

Copyright © 2008 by LitLife Publishing LLC

Contents

● As a bonus, use our Spotlight Units to journey through day-by-day lessons in all the Complete 4 components.

Acknowledgments

We would like to thank the teachers, the children and our colleagues in the LitLife network of schools who believe in the power of words.

There was a team of people who gave of themselves in the deepest and most generous of ways to this project. We are full of gratitude for the wise and thoughtful Delia Coppola, Janet Knight, Debbie Lera, and Michelle Yang. Their insights, feedback, and creations glow brightly throughout this series.

We are grateful for the support of our extraordinary LitLife team: the remarkable and talented Jenny Koons who understands life and people and kids and curriculum, and enriched the books with her careful eye, and the marvelous Rebekah Coleman whose spirit kept us going and whose wise attention completed us. With thanks to our dedicated interns Jen Estrada and Alyssa McClorey, and to Deb Jurkowitz, LitLife grammarian and in-house linguist. We deeply appreciate our agent, the magical Lisa DiMona, for shining the light that guides our way.

Danny Miller may very well be one of the funniest people on earth. He is also a brilliant editor. His dedicated efforts to this series are appreciated beyond compare by us all. Lois Bridges: inspiration, mentor, friend, champion of children and humanistic education, connector of all dots, editor extraordinaire, we thank you. All our appreciation to the team at Scholastic: the creative Maria Lilja, and Terry Cooper for her vision and dedication to the work of supporting teachers. In addition, we thank Eileen Hillebrand for her genius way of getting the word out there, and Susan Kolwicz for her genius in getting the message heard.

This experience of writing six books together has been by turns precious, wild, funny, exhausting, scary, joyous, and deeply satisfying. We collectively gave birth to three babies during this process, visited hundreds of schools, took our own kids to school, and tried to have dinner with our husbands once in awhile. From the beginning, we committed to one another that when the work felt hard we would always remember that relationships come first. We are most proud of this and hope our readers can feel the power of our bonds in every page of every book in this series. We thank one another, always.

Pam Allyn sends her boundless gratitude to Jim, Katie, and Charlotte Allyn for their love and for their countless inspirations. She would also like to thank her co-author Patty Vitale-Reilly for her huge heart, enormous energy, and deep integrity, in friendship and in work, forever.

Patty Vitale-Reilly would like to first thank co-author Pam Allyn for her vision, inspiration, partnership, and friendship that have made this book and so much in her life possible. Thank you as well to Jim Allyn for his integrity, intelligence, and commitment to LitLife and the work we do. She would also like to thank the extraordinary LitLife community of clients with a special thank you to the Ramapo Central School District. Special thanks to the colleagues in her former learning communities: the Teachers College Reading and Writing Project and the Smith School, Tenafly, New Jersey. To all of her former students and to the teachers who have over the years opened their classrooms and teaching lives to her and to LitLife, but most especially the second-grade teachers whose classrooms and children have had a special impact on this book: Jay Auerfeld, Catherine Danzuso, Jeanne Ferraro, Jayne Levin, Kristin Nicholson, Val Palacio, and Meredith Sellitti; she truly thanks you. To her parents, John and Pat Hoy, all her gratitude for all that they do for her and for her family. Thank you to the Vitale clan, her eight siblings, nieces, and nephews as "what you know first" is with her each and every day. Love and thanks to Rhiannon and Jack Reilly, the children of her heart, for the incredible joy they bring to her life. And most especially she thanks her husband, Kevin Reilly, for all that he does for their family, and whose unwavering love and support allowed this project to happen!

Chapter 1

All About the Complete Year

Dear Second-Grade Teacher,

The second grader, with his gap-toothed smile, is a physical marvel. He stumbles running across the playground, because his legs probably grew while he slept last night! He is growing new teeth and losing old ones at such a rapid rate that he looks slightly different every day. Suddenly, he is able to think outside the concrete experience of his in-the-moment life, and to plan ahead. He can envision what is not yet there. As a result, he worries about things more than ever before. What will happen if Mom is not there to meet him when he gets off the school bus? What if his playdate goes badly? Second graders worry, but they also revel in the life-rich moments that are special to that age. An ice cream cone with a grandparent, a subway ride with mom: these moments are grand adventures. Second graders are cuddly and cozy, and inch closer and closer to you as the read-aloud begins. They are just learning the pleasures of a good joke, and no one will laugh harder or louder at the funny parts in a book. They are your best buddies and true companions. They are wondering about virtually everything, and so we have woven in a theme of questioning and wondering throughout the year, as they forge their reading and writing identities, explore nonfiction, and dream of imaginary worlds.

These are the ones who want so much to write like the big kids, who carry their official writers' notebooks everywhere, who can read chapter books and are proud to carry their books between home and school. We want to encourage our second graders to make wise book choices, reread books for many reasons, and build stamina as they read and write. These are all critical process skills to learn this year. We are giving our second graders various tools for gaining their own autonomy and independence.

Our second graders are captivated by a love of story: They are learning that it anchors them, gives them a way to identify with their daily challenges, and transports them to magical lands. This year, the genre work includes fairy tales, nonfiction, and poetry. Second graders live somewhere between the real world and the world in their imaginations. They hold tightly to magic and perfect endings, but they are equally fascinated by the world of science. Poetry is hidden everywhere: inside the petal of a flower, inside the story of Sundays at Grandma's house.

Second graders are learning how to be strategic. They make plans with their friends, and recess games can go on for days. The skills of rereading and revising are part of the very fabric of their lives at this age—they are masters at reseeing. Where we all rush by, the second grader will tug at your hand to bend down and take another look. They want to keep that much loved book by their bed and in the basket near your chair because the act of rereading feels important, soothing, and instructive. And how right they are! They are building their reading muscles by rereading, increasing their fluency, stamina, and comprehension.

Their understanding of conventions is exploding—they can use them like never before. They are both eager to do what the big kids are doing, but they are still happily silly about their love for a question mark or an ellipsis. This year marks big turning points in their understanding of the way grammar and conventions affect meaning. They can see how words and white space work together build ideas—just like when they build a fort or make a castle out of blocks. They are in the world of words, and they feel the power of it, awesome and sometimes intimidating, but also joyful and energizing.

Second graders want to feel the closeness of us, of their friends, of cherished texts and authors. And yet, they are stepping out, exploring relationships, and growing up.

Warmly,

Patty Vitale-Reilly   Pam Allyn

At-a-Glance Overview of the Complete Year

Organized around the Complete 4 components (Process, Genre, Strategy, and Conventions) and four unit stages (Immersion, Identification, Guided Practice, and Commitment), each book in the Complete Year series features a year's worth of integrated reading and writing curriculum. Because we honor your professional decision-making, you will find that the Complete Year provides a flexible framework, easily adapted to your state standards and to the needs and goals of your community, your students, and your teaching style.

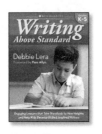

Pam Allyn's *The Complete 4 for Literacy* and Debbie Lera's *Writing Above Standard* are foundational texts for the Complete Year. LitLife and RealeBooks provide innovative professional and technological support for the Complete Year.

What Will You Find Inside the Complete Year Series?

Yearlong Curricular Calendar

Units of Study

- Over 25 detailed unit outlines spanning every season of the school year.
- 8 Spotlight Units including more than 100 day-by-day lessons
- 2 ARCH units to start your year right
- 2 reflective units to end your year on a powerful note

Assessment

- Individualized assessments for every unit
- Complete 4 Assessment (C4A)

Lists of Anchor Texts for Each Unit

Parent Letters

Resource Sheets and Homework Assignments

Professional Reading Lists

Glossary of Terms

DVD that features Pam Allyn sharing the benefits of the Complete 4 for the Complete Year as well as ALL downloadable assessment forms and resources. You will also find helpful links to professional development support from LitLife and easy-to-use technological support from RealeBooks to help you publish your students' work.

The Complete Year Supports...

Individual teachers wanting a clear road map and detailed lessons for reading and writing and for reading/writing connections.

School or district teams wanting to plan a continuum together with specific lessons and units that address the needs of all students—ELL, gifted, and special needs.

Administrative leaders and literacy coaches wanting to guide their school to a consistent, standards-rich plan for reading and writing instruction.

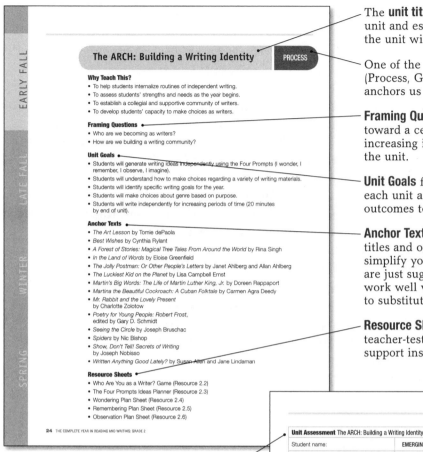

The ARCH: Building a Writing Identity — PROCESS

Why Teach This?
- To help students internalize routines of independent writing.
- To assess students' strengths and needs as the year begins.
- To establish a collegial and supportive community of writers.
- To develop students' capacity to make choices as writers.

Framing Questions
- Who are we becoming as writers?
- How are we building a writing community?

Unit Goals
- Students will generate writing ideas independently using the Four Prompts (I wonder, I remember, I observe, I imagine).
- Students will understand how to make choices regarding a variety of writing materials.
- Students will identify specific writing goals for the year.
- Students will make choices about genre based on purpose.
- Students will write independently for increasing periods of time (20 minutes by end of unit).

Anchor Texts
- *The Art Lesson* by Tomie dePaola
- *Best Wishes* by Cynthia Rylant
- *A Forest of Stories: Magical Tree Tales From Around the World* by Rina Singh
- *In the Land of Words* by Eloise Greenfield
- *The Jolly Postman: Or Other People's Letters* by Janet Ahlberg and Allan Ahlberg
- *The Luckiest Kid on the Planet* by Lisa Campbell Ernst
- *Martin's Big Words: The Life of Martin Luther King, Jr.* by Doreen Rappaport
- *Martina the Beautiful Cockroach: A Cuban Folktale* by Carmen Agra Deedy
- *Mr. Rabbit and the Lovely Present* by Charlotte Zolotow
- *Poetry for Young People: Robert Frost,* edited by Gary D. Schmidt
- *Seeing the Circle* by Joseph Bruschac
- *Spiders* by Nic Bishop
- *Show, Don't Tell! Secrets of Writing* by Joseph Nobisso
- *Written Anything Good Lately?* by Susan Allen and Jane Lindaman

Resource Sheets
- Who Are You as a Writer? Game (Resource 2.2)
- The Four Prompts Ideas Planner (Resource 2.3)
- Wondering Plan Sheet (Resource 2.4)
- Remembering Plan Sheet (Resource 2.5)
- Observation Plan Sheet (Resource 2.6)

24 THE COMPLETE YEAR IN READING AND WRITING: GRADE 2

The **unit title** clarifies the purpose of the unit and establishes the placement of the unit within a larger K–5 continuum.

One of the **Complete 4 components** (Process, Genre, Strategy, or Conventions) anchors us inside the Unit Template.

Framing Questions guide students toward a central understanding with increasing independence throughout the unit.

Unit Goals focus your instruction within each unit and give you measurable outcomes to help you focus assessment.

Anchor Texts list children's literature titles and other resources that will simplify your planning process. They are just suggestions that we feel would work well with the unit. You are free to substitute your favorites.

Resource Sheets provide you with teacher-tested graphic organizers that support instruction.

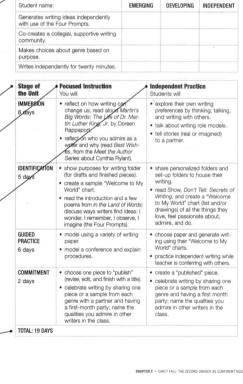

Unit Assessment The ARCH: Building a Writing Identity			PROCESS
Student name:	EMERGING	DEVELOPING	INDEPENDENT
Generates writing ideas independently with use of the Four Prompts.			
Co-creates a collegial, supportive writing community.			
Makes choices about genre based on purpose.			
Writes independently for twenty minutes.			

Stage of the Unit	Focused Instruction You will	Independent Practice Students will
IMMERSION 6 days	• reflect on how writing can change us; read aloud *Martin's Big Words: The Life of Dr. Martin Luther King, Jr.* by Doreen Rappaport. • reflect on who you admire as a writer and why (read *Best Wishes,* from the *Meet the Author Series* about Cynthia Rylant).	• explore their own writing preferences by thinking, talking, and writing with others. • talk about writing role models. • tell stories (real or imagined) to a partner.
IDENTIFICATION 5 days	• show purposes for writing folder (for drafts and finished pieces). • create a sample "Welcome to My World" chart. • read the introduction and a few poems from *In the Land of Words;* discuss ways writers find ideas: I wonder, I remember, I observe, I imagine (the Four Prompts).	• share personalized folders and set-up folders to house their writing. • read *Show, Don't Tell: Secrets of Writing,* and create a "Welcome to My World" chart (list and/or drawings) of all the things they love, feel passionate about, admire, and do.
GUIDED PRACTICE 6 days	• model using a variety of writing paper. • model a conference and explain procedures.	• choose paper and generate writing using their "Welcome to My World" charts. • practice independent writing while teacher is conferring with others.
COMMITMENT 2 days	• choose one piece to "publish" (revise, edit, and finish with a title). • celebrate writing by sharing one piece or a sample from each genre and having a first-month party; name the qualities you admire in other writers in the class.	• create a "published" piece. • celebrate writing by sharing one piece or a sample from each genre and having a first month party; name the qualities you admire in other writers in the class.
TOTAL: 19 DAYS		

CHAPTER 2 • EARLY FALL: THE SECOND GRADER AS CONFIDENT READER AND WRITER 25

Unit Assessments are linked to unit outcomes and evaluate individual student progress. You can print out copies of these assessments from the accompanying DVD.

Stages of the Unit organize your instruction, guiding your students from inquiry to application.

Focused Instruction provides day-by-day direction for teaching throughout the unit. Each bullet reflects approximately one day of instruction.

Independent Practice links student engagement to Focused Instruction.

Total Days are based on suggested lessons. Numbers of days can be adjusted to meet the needs of your class.

How This Book Will Support You

The Complete Year in Reading and Writing: Grade 2 is written by two authors: Patty Vitale-Reilly, the executive director of LitLife West Hudson, and Pam Allyn, the executive director of LitLife. Together, we have spent thousands of hours in second-grade classrooms, pondering the unique experience that comprises this year.

LitLife is a global organization dedicated to teacher training in the area of literacy education. Every lesson in this book has been field tested in a wide variety of classrooms. LitLife team leaders coach teachers and work alongside students to create a practical, meaningful curriculum that is well-suited to each grade level because it exists inside a broader continuum. See this book as a compass you can use to chart a course in reading and writing instruction that feels true to your beliefs about the developmental needs and interests of second graders.

Many programs do not differentiate sufficiently by grade level. Second-grade teachers are often combined into a K–2 grouping in professional literature and workshops. And yet the span between these grades is gigantic psychologically, socially, and intellectually. A curriculum for second grade needs to match the development of the learner and the uniqueness of this age student.

In creating this book for you, we also keep in mind the entirety of the child's learning experience throughout the elementary grades. While specifically written for second graders, the units presented here were created with the big picture in mind, children's entire K–5 experience.

The Complete 4

The Complete 4 was devised in response to the need expressed to us by teachers for balance in literacy instruction. We believe students should be well-rounded readers and writers. This means they should learn about reading and writing strategies. They should also develop a strong understanding of genre and a working knowledge of the conventions of the English language and begin to take on the passions, habits, and behaviors of lifelong readers and writers. The Complete 4 includes four key components of literacy instruction that will help us teach into these varied expectations: Process, Genre, Strategy, and Conventions.

The Complete 4 components help us to plan the school year by balancing the types of units across the year. Knowing whether a unit falls under the category of Process, Genre, Strategy, or Conventions, helps us to focus the unit so that all our lessons lead up to several key understandings.

Here is what we mean by the Complete 4:

Fluency, Stamina, independence

Process	Your students will practice the processes shared by all successful readers and writers, at an appropriate developmental level. These include fluency, stamina, and independence.
Genre	Your students will learn to identify and use various literary containers, including narrative, nonfiction, poetry, and standardized tests.
Strategy	Your students will learn to be strategic readers and writers, practicing how writers make plans on a page, and how readers approach text differently depending on their needs.
Conventions	Your students will learn grammar and punctuation in contexts that are real, practical, and relevant to their reading and writing experiences.

In planning a Complete Year of literacy instruction for second grade, we have created reading and writing units that reflect a deep balance. All four Complete 4 components are represented. Take a look at the color calendar on the inside front cover of this book to see how these units are organized across the year. We have arranged them so that they build on one another.

Will this book help me connect other aspects of the curriculum to the Complete 4?

Absolutely! One of the best features of the Complete 4 system is its flexibility. It has the capacity to help you integrate all these areas of your curriculum. For example, in second grade your students are studying history and science topics of all kinds. They are expanding their research skills. Units on nonfiction reading and writing support cross-content work. You can teach the skills and strategies for reading and writing in the content areas inside one or more of these units.

Alignment to standards is critical, and these units are constructed in such a way as to reflect the standards and to allow for your adjustments for your state standards.

Can this book help me if I have other demands in my day and cannot teach all the units?

Yes, it can. Here are three suggestions for how you could adapt this calendar to your particular situation:

- You can choose one reading and one writing unit from each Complete 4 component to teach during the year.
- You can focus on the units of study that pair well with your existing themes.
- You can teach only the reading or writing strand.

Will the Complete 4 help me forge reading and writing connections with my students?

This is another great aspect of the Complete 4 program: we link reading and writing units as "companions." Although the instruction may not always be identical, the units should be "talking" to one another. You will see how we take special care to make sure reading and writing units echo and parallel each other, or to stagger them so students see, feel, and understand those essential connections. Indeed, reading and writing are interrelated processes that are mutually supportive when taught together. You may have noticed that your strongest writers are typically your most passionate readers.

Can I use this book to support just my writing instruction since I already use another reading program?

Yes. You can use this book to guide you in either reading or writing. Take a look at the writing calendar only; with your grade-level team, you can look into your reading program and see where you can link the writing units into your instruction. For example, if your reading program has a set of stories on friendship, you could link that set to our Enhancing Comprehension Strategies Through Series Books unit in the late fall. This calendar is designed so that you can use it flexibly—you can use either the reading calendar or the writing calendar on its own, or, if you want the "complete" package, you can use both of them together. And the Complete 4 is also a way to reintroduce quality children's literature into your classroom even if you use a core reading program.

Can I still benefit from this yearlong approach if my school has commitments that must be addressed at different times of the year?

One of the most exciting aspects of the Complete 4 is that the reading and writing units are interconnected and follow a logical sequence. However, we have also constructed the calendars to allow for flexibility. If, for example, your standardized testing comes earlier in the year, you can easily move units around to suit your test-preparation schedule. Or if your entire school studies poetry together in the fall rather than the spring, you can move the units to accommodate that. The calendar is designed to be used either as a whole unit, as a step by step program, or as building blocks to construct your own unique program.

Will the Complete 4 help me meet the needs of all learners in my classroom?

The range of ability levels and learning modalities in each of our classrooms reminds us to balance our own teaching. The Complete 4 can help us accomplish this. For example, we tend to work with our English language learners mostly on conventions of print, while we work with writers whose first language is English more on strategies or genre. The Complete 4 reminds us that our English language learners flourish with exposure to the habits and passions of readers and writers, the study of different genres, and practice with complex strategies. Similarly, your students who have a comparatively strong sense of conventions are often not given intensive instruction in that area, but they too would enjoy and benefit greatly from inspiring lessons on the construction of a sentence or the artful use of a punctuation mark. The Complete 4 guides us to teach with an eye to creating a Complete Year for all students.

Will this book help me with the flow of my day?

Yes! We are very aware of your time constraints and the benefits of predictable routines. We have created a very simple, easy-to-follow outline for each day's work during reading and writing time that follows a whole/small/whole pattern. These are the three parts of every lesson:

- Focused Instruction: the whole-class lessons
- Independent Practice: individualized or small-group work
- Wrap-Up: more whole-class teaching with planning for the next day's lesson

Focused Instruction	Students gather for a period of Focused Instruction for 5 to 15 minutes.
	• Warm up your students with a reference to prior teaching and learning.
	• Teach one clear point.
	• Ask students to quickly try your point.
	• Clarify your teaching point.
	• Set the stage for Independent Practice.
Independent Practice	Students practice independently while you confer with students and/or conduct small instructional groups.
	• Encourage students to read or write independently (at their level).
	• Have students practice your teaching point as they read and write.
	• Meet with individual students, partnerships, and/or groups regularly for informal assessment and instruction.
	• Look for future teaching points or an example to use in the Wrap-Up.
Wrap-Up	Students return for a focused, brief discussion that reflects on the day's learning.
	• Restate your teaching point.
	• Share examples of students' work or learning.
	• Set plans for the next day and make connections to homework.

What are my students actually doing during Independent Practice?

As you will see from the scripted lessons in our Spotlight Units, during Independent Practice students practice a skill you have demonstrated. In addition, they are doing something that seems fairly simple on the surface but in fact is the heart of our work and the driving energy for all the lessons in this book: **They are reading and writing independently**, every day. We suggest that 50 percent of all reading and writing time should be Independent Practice. Of this time, approximately 20 percent should be spent practicing a specific skill associated with their reading, and 80 percent of the time should be spent actually reading and writing! Students should be given time every day to read and write in a comfortable manner, at their reading and writing levels, and in books and topics that are of great personal interest to them. Here are the approximate amounts of time your students can and should be reading and writing for each day (you may have to work toward these minutes as the year unfolds):

Grade Level	Actual Reading Time	Actual Writing Time
KINDERGARTEN	10–15 minutes	10–20 (writing/drawing)
FIRST GRADE	10–20	10–20
SECOND GRADE	20–30	20–25
THIRD GRADE	30–40	25–30
FOURTH GRADE	35–45	25–30
FIFTH GRADE	40–45	30–40

Are there essential materials I must use in order to make the Complete 4 program a success?

You can use any of your support materials, including a core reading program or a phonics program, alongside the Complete 4 approach. The heart of our approach is that every child has time to practice skills, strategies, and processes through reading and writing that is at his level and is as authentic as possible. A seminal National Endowment for the Arts study (2007) found, not surprisingly, that "students who read for fun nearly every day performed better on reading tests than those who reported reading never or hardly at all." The study points to the "failure of schools and colleges to develop a culture of daily reading habits." In addition, an analysis of federal Department of Education statistics found that those students who scored lower on all standardized tests lived in homes with fewer than ten books. (Rich, 2007). This study then points to two pivotal factors in ensuring lifelong literacy: Children must have time to read a lot, and children must have easy, continual access to books.

Our work throughout this book and this series is designed to focus on daily Independent Practice: Students are reading authentic literature and reading a lot, every day, at their own level. Students are writing about topics of authentic interest and writing a lot, every day, at their own level. Students are navigating texts and have easy access to understandable texts throughout the day, especially during literacy time. These then are the two keys to our work: giving students time to practice reading and writing and giving them access to texts that inspire them both as readers and as writers.

The access is critical and is best accomplished by establishing a well-stocked classroom library. Your library should have a variety of genres: nonfiction, fiction, and poetry. Approximately 20 to 30 percent of your library should be leveled through a clearly organized system in which children can find books that are truly comfortable for them to read at their independent reading levels.

Your students should have a way to bring their books between home and school, and to store the stack of books they have been reading most recently, either in bags or baskets. Organization is one of two keys to life (the other being passion!). Don't let disorder get in the way of helping your children do a lot of reading in your classroom. They can help you organize your library, too.

It is also crucial for students to have a way to record thinking about reading, either in a reading notebook, a folder, or even a binder. The important thing to remember is that this should be a system that works for you and your students. It does not matter so much what you select or what you call it, as long as you know your children can easily access it and that they feel comfortable writing or drawing in it.

During writing time, your students need order as well. Keep a separate writing area neat and stocked, equipped with all the helpful tools a writer loves: sticky notes, staplers, tape, and date stamps. And as with reading time, your students should have a clearly identified, easy-to-use container to capture their writing. In this series we use writing notebooks with our students at some point from mid-second grade to fifth grade, and writing folders with students in kindergarten and first grade. Using folders at the beginning of second grade allows us to provide our students with a variety of paper choices if they need them. The key to keeping containers for students' writing work is that it is easy for them to revisit, reread, and reflect upon, and it is easy for you to review before conferences and to assess on an ongoing basis. Again, it does not matter what you call these containers, or which ones you choose, as long as they are truly useful for both you and your students.

I don't have access to all the anchor texts you recommend in this book, or there are other texts I prefer to use instead. Will my units be as effective if my anchor-text selections are somewhat different from yours?

We want to give you as many specific suggestions as we can, and so we have recommended many anchor texts for each unit. You can find them both in the unit templates and also in the back of the book in a seasonally organized bibliography so you can order all of them for your classroom library if you wish. However, if you can't find them all, or you have others you wish to use instead, you are more than welcome to use other texts, and the units will absolutely be as successful. Take a close look at why we chose the texts we did so you can replace them with selections that will still match the outcomes for the units and will feel comfortable for you.

I use the elements of balanced literacy: shared reading, guided reading, read-aloud, and more. Where do they fit in to the Complete 4 system?

See your elements of balanced literacy as the "how" of your teaching and the Complete 4 as the "what." Teachers who use balanced literacy elements are still asking: But WHAT do I teach tomorrow? The Complete 4 answers that age-old question. Your balanced literacy structures, then, can truly become the engines that drive your content home. For example, shared reading and the read-aloud are structures you can use to present your content, both in the Focused Instruction and in the Wrap-Up. Guided reading is a structure you can use to practice content with smaller groups of children. This can be done during Independent Practice, so while some of your children are reading independently, others are meeting with you in small groups.

What if I've never taught in units like this before?

In a Complete Year unit of study, students learn about one aspect of reading or writing (Process, Genre, Strategy, or Conventions) in a one- to six-week cycle of learning. Inside this book you will find all the units for a Complete Year of reading and writing instruction. In each unit, we have set a specific focus for instruction and created framing questions to guide you and your students. We have set a time frame and established goals for each unit and put together a list of anchor texts that you can use to teach the lessons. Most important, we have provided helpful templates to take you through *all* the units.

To help you implement and pace your instruction, we have divided the instruction in each unit into four key lesson stages: Immersion, Identification, Guided Practice, and Commitment. The premise behind this concept was inspired by the work of Pearson and Gallagher (1983). They delineated a gradual release of responsibility from teacher to student as the ideal condition for learning. These stages help us make the necessary turns in our teaching so that we move in an efficient and effective way through any unit of study and our students have the best chance for success.

Immersion	We immerse our students in a topic of study.
Identification	We name or define what students must know about the topic by the end of the unit.
Guided Practice	We model reading and writing for our students and give them time for practice, so that we can guide them toward the goals of the unit.
Commitment	We ask students to reflect on their learning and commit to the use of this knowledge in their future reading and writing.

You use specific language to identify the parts of a unit and the parts of a lesson. How can I be sure I can follow along easily?

The language in this book is extremely user-friendly. We try to steer clear of jargon as much as we can. To best help teachers plan units and teach lessons, we have identified terms that help us all move forward easily. We have included a helpful Glossary of Terms for you on page 233.

What is the role of the Spotlight Units in the Complete Year books?

Each Complete Year book features eight bonus Spotlight Units, designed to help you understand what each unit of study can look and feel like in your classroom—both in terms of the concrete day-to-day details as well as the "learning energy" that you create through your instructional language and strategies. During the Spotlight Units, we invite you into our classrooms to sit by our sides and listen as we interact with our students. While we know you'll use your own language that reflects your unique teaching personality, we provide examples of language we use in our classrooms as a model for you to adapt. Learning how to craft our teaching language in artful ways that encourage active student participation takes practice; for example, knowing how to design open-ended questions rather than questions that just elicit a yes–no response is an art, typically learned through classroom-tested trial and error. Sometimes, it's helpful to listen in on another teacher and notice how she uses language to frame each teaching moment.

Inside the Spotlight Units, you'll find one reading unit and one writing unit in each of the Complete 4 components (Process, Genre, Strategy, and Conventions). Our Spotlight Units also include unit templates, so you can see how we translate the templates into day-by-day lesson plans. You'll notice that not all bullets are translated directly into lessons and that the flow of the unit is fluid and flexible so you can adapt it in ways that fit your students' unique needs and interests.

How do I use the unit templates?

We envision teachers taking the templates we provide for each unit and adapting them to their students' needs. Perhaps you have favorite books you love to read in your nonfiction unit. Or perhaps your students need more than one day on a bulleted lesson. Although the templates offer guidelines for the overall structure of a unit and suggestions for how the unit might be paced, we see them as a road atlas, a guide that leads you toward your goal but also gives you the opportunity to add your own special touches along the way. Many teachers like to keep these unit templates on their desks as a reminder of where they are going, to help them plan each day's lesson.

How will I assess my students through the Complete Year?

The structure of the Complete 4 classroom gives you a rich opportunity to assess your students during their Independent Practice. Units of study give you regular, frequent opportunities to take stock of your students' progress. At the end of each unit is an assessment form for you to use.

Chapter 6 is dedicated to the C4 Assessment: a comprehensive tool designed for your grade level. You can use the C4 A three times a year for both reading and writing. Quick and easy, the C4 A will provide valuable information on your students' progress in all areas of reading and writing instruction.

The Complete Year in Grade 2

These books are organized around the seasons of the year. Our learning time with our students, bound by the parameters of the school year, is also organized by seasons and so we thought it would be helpful to organize our books that way, too.

As the year begins, second graders still feel very young in so many ways, but have gained confidence about their place in school: They know where everything is, and they walk the halls with an air of confidence. Winter brings some hesitation: They see some of their friends reading at much different levels than others; their writing is developing at varying rates, too. At the same time, they are hungry to communicate through print. There is a newfound power in it for them. The spring brings with it more possibilities for blooming as students develop affinities for authors and book titles. They love to reread books, and their capacity for reading for longer periods of time is growing monumentally. At the end of the year they are amazed by their capacity to write and read more, longer, and stronger. They are making good friends and are able to sustain talk in ways we could not have imagined earlier in the year. By springtime, their faces are changing: We can see glimmers of their more mature selves to be. They are no longer so young and vulnerable. They are growing up.

Get ready now for the Complete Year experience: It's timely and timeless (and won't cost YOU time). Flexible and friendly (and fun). Easy to use and easy to navigate (and easy to explain to parents). Standards-based and field-tested (in hundreds of classrooms). Made for you (to simplify your teaching life and to reconnect you with the joy of teaching). Made for your second graders (especially).

Have a great year!

Chapter 2

EARLY FALL

The Second Grader as Confident Reader and Writer

"But the sea was full of wonderful creatures, and as he swam from marvel to marvel, Swimmy was happy again."

—from *Swimmy* by Leo Lionni

The second grader is proud. He is proud of his backpack and his zipped jacket, his new sneaks and his homework. This first season is rich with new skill building in reading and writing. Join us as we enter the world of second grade through units that support skills and passions for language all at the same time.

EARLY FALL UNITS

SPOTLIGHT UNITS

EARLY FALL

LATE FALL

WINTER

SPRING

Beginning the Year With the ARCH

Our first units, known as the ARCH, are designed to bring our students together into a reading and writing community. This acronym stands for Assessment, Routines, Choice, and Healthy Community. The units balance the need to assess students as readers and writers with lessons on the routines of reading and writing time, the community-building aspects of reading and writing time, and how to make choices both in terms of topics and texts.

We must actively construct this community by establishing the daily routines for reading and writing time, discovering personal and shared interests, and introducing our students to our libraries and writing tools. Fountas and Pinnell (2001) remind us that during the first month of school you have two important goals: to help your students think of themselves as readers and to establish roles and routines. They remind us to repeat key lessons, chart the routines and roles of the reader and writer, and refer our students back to these reference points regularly.

As teachers, we are always a bit uncertain about how to begin the year in terms of content. We want to get to know our students, and we know we need to establish these routines, but we wonder what the content and outcomes are for this work. The ARCH is designed to blend both process and products: the beautiful work we do in coming together for the first time, as well as the important work we do in generating products that represent our students and move them forward at the very beginning of this school year's journey.

Each Complete 4 year begins with an ARCH unit at every grade level, but each year should feel different because of your students' changing developmental needs. (See page 112 of *The Complete 4 for Literacy* to see all the ARCH articulations for each grade level.) In second grade, our ARCH focus is Building a Reading and a Writing Identity. In the reading and writing units that follow, we continue to build upon that theme with units that help our students discover the value of thinking and working across text.

The ARCH units set the foundation for the entire year. The ARCH incorporates teaching of all of those routines and habits you long for and need when you are in the midst of your work with your students. If you set the stage now, you are guaranteed a happy, truly productive year in the teaching of reading and writing.

Assessment
Routines
Choice
Healthy Community

The ARCH: Building a Reading Identity

PROCESS

Why Teach This?
- To help students internalize the routines of independent reading.
- To assess students' strengths and needs as the year begins.
- To establish a collegial and supportive community of readers.
- To develop students' capacity to make choices about what they read.

Framing Questions
- Who are we becoming as readers?
- How are we building a reading community?

Unit Goals
- Students will recognize the varied purposes for reading.
- Students will identify qualities they have as readers and ones they want to nurture in themselves as readers.
- Students will make book choices that represent interest, level, and purpose.
- Students will read independently for increasing periods of time.

Anchor Texts
- *Abe Lincoln: The Boy Who Loved Books* by Kay Winters
- *Chrysanthemum* by Kevin Henkes
- *Donovan's Word Jar* by Monalisa Degross and Cheryl Hanna
- *The House of Joyful Living* by Roni Schotter
- *Max's Words* by Kate Banks
- *Swimmy* by Leo Lionni
- *Tomás and the Library Lady* by Pat Mora
- *Wonderful Words: Poems about Reading, Writing, Speaking and Listening*, edited by Lee Bennett Hopkins and Karen Barbour
- *Zen Shorts* by Jon Muth

Resource Sheet
- Who Are You as a Reader? (Resource 2.1)

Unit Assessment The ARCH: Building a Reading Identity			PROCESS
Student name:	EMERGING	DEVELOPING	INDEPENDENT
Follows routines of reading time.			
Makes book selections independently.			
Identifies personal reading goals.			
Actively participates in a collegial, vibrant community of readers.			

Stage of the Unit	Focused Instruction You will	Independent Practice Students will
IMMERSION 6 days *Jake Carly*	• share how together you will build a community of readers and read *The House of Joyful Living* to support the idea of community building. • share reading memories. • read aloud *Max's Words* or *Donavan's Word Jar.* • discuss how readers read by interest, by purpose, and with a good fit. • invite guests in to talk about who they are as readers and what their own "short stack" of favorite books is. • demonstrate how to play the "Who Are You as a Reader?" game.	• write: "My ideal reading community would be…" • write about/sketch a special reading memory. • share a time when words felt important and powerful to them. • explore their own preferences and habits by touring the library and talking to other readers. • collect a "short stack" of books to read independently. • play the "Who Are You as a Reader?" game (see Resource 2.1 survey and ask children to fill it out; then have them find someone in the class who answers the questions most similarly).
IDENTIFICATION 5 days	• name the importance of "one-inch voices" during reading time (quiet reading voices); name the importance of sitting in a "quiet bubble." • read selections from *Wonderful Words*; talk about how words inspire us; model creating a reading self-portrait. • Read *Zen Shorts* by Jon Muth; talk about how words and stories bring us closer together. • model selecting books for interest and level. • identify what makes people strong as readers (their habits, environments, choices).	• read. • draw/write a "reading self-portrait." • discuss how words have brought them closer to someone; add to their self-portrait. • add to short stack of books to read independently. • draw/write a list of "reading dreams" (plans for oneself as a reader going forward).

GUIDED PRACTICE 4 days	• read *Swimmy* and demonstrate what readers do when they are finished with a book (reread, find a favorite part, share with partner, choose a new book from their "short stack"); introduce egg timer. • model what readers do when they share ideas about books (put a card on the sharing board, talk with partner). • read aloud *Abe Lincoln: The Boy Who Loved Books* and talk about how reading influences people. • read aloud *Chrysanthemum*; discuss genre choices (fiction, nonfiction, poetry).	• practice daily routines, increasing reading time on the egg timer. • practice sharing book suggestions with others. • practice talking with a partner about what they are reading; share: how does reading influence me? • practice reading in a variety of genres.
COMMITMENT 2 days	• model goal setting (will read in different genres, will read for a certain amount of minutes each day, will read for different purposes). • model how you continue to develop your own reading identity by trying new kinds of reading, new genres, talking with different people about books.	• draw or write a list of reading goals. • draw or write how they see themselves as readers at the end of this unit; celebrate reading goals.
TOTAL: 17 DAYS		

The ARCH: Building a Writing Identity

PROCESS

Why Teach This?

- To help students internalize the routines of independent writing.
- To assess students' strengths and needs as the year begins.
- To establish a collegial and supportive community of writers.
- To develop students' capacity to make choices as writers.

Framing Questions

- Who are we becoming as writers?
- How are we building a writing community?

Unit Goals

- Students will generate writing ideas independently using the Four Prompts (I wonder, I remember, I observe, I imagine).
- Students will understand how to make choices regarding a variety of writing materials.
- Students will identify specific writing goals for the year.
- Students will make choices about genre based on purpose.
- Students will write independently for increasing periods of time (20 minutes by end of unit).

Anchor Texts

- *The Art Lesson* by Tomie dePaola
- *Best Wishes* by Cynthia Rylant
- *A Forest of Stories: Magical Tree Tales From Around the World* by Rina Singh
- *In the Land of Words* by Eloise Greenfield
- *The Jolly Postman: Or Other People's Letters* by Janet Ahlberg and Allan Ahlberg
- *The Luckiest Kid on the Planet* by Lisa Campbell Ernst

- *Martin's Big Words: The Life of Martin Luther King, Jr.* by Doreen Rappaport
- *Martina the Beautiful Cockroach: A Cuban Folktale* by Carmen Agra Deedy
- *Mr. Rabbit and the Lovely Present* by Charlotte Zolotow
- *Poetry for Young People: Robert Frost*, edited by Gary D. Schmidt
- *Seeing the Circle* by Joseph Bruchac
- *Show, Don't Tell! Secrets of Writing* by Josephine Nobisso
- *Spiders* by Nic Bishop
- *Written Anything Good Lately?* by Susan Allen and Jane Lindaman

A writing notebook demonstrating "Who I am" as a writer.

Resource Sheets

- Who Are You as a Writer? (Resource 2.2)
- The Four Prompts Ideas Planner (Resource 2.3)
- Wondering Plan (Resource 2.4)
- Remembering Plan (Resource 2.5)
- Observing Plan (Resource 2.6)
- Imagination Plan (Resource 2.7)

Unit Assessment The ARCH: Building a Writing Identity			PROCESS
Student name:	EMERGING	DEVELOPING	INDEPENDENT
Generates writing ideas independently with use of the Four Prompts.			
Co-creates a collegial, supportive writing community.			
Makes choices about genre based on purpose.			
Writes independently for 20 minutes.			

Stage of the Unit	Focused Instruction You will	Independent Practice Students will
IMMERSION 7 days	• reflect on how writing can change us; read aloud *Martin's Big Words: The Life of Dr. Martin Luther King, Jr.* by Doreen Rappaport. • reflect on who you admire as a writer and why (read *Best Wishes*, from the *Meet the Author Series* about Cynthia Rylant). • read *Martina the Beautiful Cockroach* and discuss the importance of storytelling for building writing ideas. • demonstrate how you personalize your writing folder or notebook. • read a story from *A Forest of Stories* and discuss how words can create magic. (More stories can be read at other times of the day during this unit.) • discuss the Four Prompts: I wonder, I remember, I observe, I imagine; ask students to generate a piece of writing. • read *Seeing the Circle* by Joseph Bruchac and discuss writing identity: What kind of writer is Joseph Bruchac?	• explore their own writing preferences by thinking, talking, and writing with others. • talk about writing role models. • tell stories (real or imagined) to a partner. • personalize writing folders or notebooks. • practice routines of writing time. • generate a baseline writing piece using the Four Prompts: I wonder, I remember, I observe, I imagine. • play the "Who are You as a Writer?" game (have children fill out the survey on Resource 2.2; then have them find someone in the class who answers the questions most similarly).

IDENTIFICATION 5 days	• show purposes for writing folder (for drafts and finished pieces). • read *Show, Don't Tell: Secrets of Writing*, and create a sample "Welcome to My World" chart. • read the introduction and a few poems from *In the Land of Words*; discuss ways writers find ideas: I wonder, I remember, I observe, I imagine (the Four Prompts). • name the ways writers you admire write and what they write about: read *The Luckiest Kid on the Planet* and discuss what might have been Lisa Campbell Ernst's writing inspiration. • read *Written Anything Good Lately?* and demonstrate purposes for writing (read *The Jolly Postman* for communication and *The Art Lesson* for self-expression) and discuss possible genres to write in.	• share personalized folders and set-up folders to house their writing. • create a "Welcome to My World" chart (list and/or drawings) of all the things they love, feel passionate about, admire, and do. • share stories, wonderings, and observations with one another. • discuss what could be on Lisa Campbell Ernst's "Welcome to My World" chart; share their own "Welcome to My World" charts and compare. • discuss purposes and genres for writing: letters, narrative stories, poetry; share favorite genres and discuss what genres you have written in.
GUIDED PRACTICE 6 days	• model using a variety of writing paper. • model a conference and explain procedures. • discuss and explain what you can do when the teacher is busy in a conference (continue on to a new piece, share with a partner, read an anchor text, reread writing and add to it). • read *Spiders* by Nic Bishop; talk about how nonfiction writers write to share facts. • read *Poetry for Young People*; talk about poets writing to share feelings and observations. • read *Mr. Rabbit and the Lovely Present*; talk about how fiction writers write to create a world from the imagination.	• choose paper and generate writing using their "Welcome to My World" charts. • practice independent writing while teacher is conferring with others. • practice independent writing using their charts and if they get stuck, use one of the strategies discussed during Focused Instruction. • practice independent writing and try writing a nonfiction piece (sharing facts). • practice independent writing and try writing a poem (sharing feelings and observations). • practice independent writing and try writing a narrative (telling a story and/or sharing ideas from their imaginations).
COMMITMENT 2 days	• choose one piece to "publish" (revise, edit, and finish with a title). • celebrate writing by sharing one piece or a sample from each genre with a partner and having a first-month party; name the qualities you admire in other writers in the class.	• create a "published" piece. • celebrate writing by sharing one piece or a sample from each genre and having a first month party; name the qualities you admire in other writers in the class.
TOTAL: 20 DAYS		

Word Power

The second grader is paying attention to everything—she is ready for more challenge on the page, and mostly welcomes it. She loves the idea of carrying a big book around and writing a long story. She is literally counting the words she can read and the words she can write! If you see, on the other hand, that she is not embracing words in this way, that reading and writing continue to feel like a struggle, do not hesitate to use all the resources you have in your school to get your students all the help they need. Do not wait until later in the year. This year, your second graders should be decoding print wherever they go, but also internalizing the strategies they practiced so carefully the year before. These paired units support these investigations: helping students to build their understanding of what will help them decode words and synthesize strategies so as to move toward chapter books and topical books, and to construct the ideas welling up inside of them that they are longing to share.

Synthesizing Word-Attack Strategies   CONVENTIONS

Why Teach This?
- To enable students to use strategies to decode unknown words.
- To give students a variety of word-attack strategies.
- To support students as they approach new and more challenging texts.

Framing Questions
- How do readers approach unknown words?
- How do readers synthesize and cross-reference strategies for approaching unknown words?

Unit Goals
- Students will identify and revisit strategies for approaching print.
- Students will practice blending sounds within words.
- Students will practice reading "chunks" of words, using known words or spelling patterns to read unknown words.
- Students will use rereading as a strategy to figure out unknown words.

Anchor Texts
- *Diary of a Worm* by Doreen Cronin
- *Dinosaurumpus!* by Tony Mitton
- *My Friend John* by Charlotte Zolotow
- "Sliding Board" from *Did You See What I Saw? Poems About School* by Kay Winters
- "Snow City" from *Good Rhymes, Good Times* by Lee Bennett Hopkins

Unit Assessment Synthesizing Word-Attack Strategies			CONVENTIONS
Student name:	EMERGING	DEVELOPING	INDEPENDENT
Recognizes the need to employ various strategies to read words.			
Uses knowledge of blends to attack and approach a word.			
Uses knowledge of words and spelling patterns to figure out unknown words.			
Rereads a sentence, using meaning to determine an unknown word.			
Applies various strategies until word is read.			
Applies multiple strategies to read an unfamiliar word.			

Stage of the Unit	Focused Instruction You will	Independent Practice Students will
IMMERSION 2 days	• read aloud from *Diary of a Worm* by Doreen Cronin; model getting stuck on a word and ask students what you could do to figure out the word (for example, use your knowledge of sounds to read a word: "*Ground* is the blend *gr* with *ou*; we know that *ou* is pronounced "ow" when read; the word is *ground*"); ask students to name what you did. • reread a favorite class text such as *My Friend John* by Charlotte Zolotow; pause at a word, saying that it's unfamiliar; try sounding out the word by blending sounds and then look for the a little word in the big word; ask students to name what you did to read the word.	• read independently, practicing the strategies modeled during the Focused Instruction; put a sticky note on a word they read using a modeled strategy. • read independently using a modeled strategy and put a sticky note on an unfamiliar word; discuss with a reading partner what strategy they used to read the word.

IDENTIFICATION 2 days	• generate a chart of strategies that a reader uses when he comes to an unfamiliar word. • put a sentence on the chart from a favorite text, such as *Diary of a Worm* by Doreen Cronin; model reading the sentence and then thinking aloud about yourself as a reader, examining which strategies on the list you used to read the sentence.	• read with a partner from an independent text, practicing strategies on the chart. • name and discuss the strategies they are using a lot and the kinds of words they are getting stuck on.
GUIDED PRACTICE 4 days	• model how a reader uses blending of sounds to read an unfamiliar word; use a text with many words with beginning consonant blends, such as "Snow City" by Lee Bennett Hopkins. • read *Dinosaurumpus!* by Tony Mitton and model rereading a sentence and decoding unfamiliar words. • demonstrate how a reader chunks a word to segment it and find known words or spelling patterns inside it. • read "Sliding Board" and model using multiple strategies when a word does not make sense; demonstrate how good readers may need to try a few strategies to read an unknown word.	• practice blending consonants when reading an unknown word. • use strategies to read unknown words. • read independent texts using what they know about word families or chunks within a word to read words that they do not know. • read and discuss with a partner places in their books where the first strategy they used did not help them figure out an unfamiliar word.
COMMITMENT 2 days	• discuss the strategies good readers use when they approach unknown words. • ask students to create a bookmark listing word-attack strategies that will help them as they read.	• share which strategies helped them most as a reader. • work on their bookmark, listing the strategies a reader can use to attack unknown words.
TOTAL: 10 DAYS		

Synthesizing Spelling Strategies

CONVENTIONS

Why Teach This?

- To enable students to use various strategies when they're encoding words.
- To reinforce how a writer uses knowledge of sounds, letters, and syllables to write words.
- To help students use resources for spelling words as they write.

Framing Questions

- How can we teach writers to use their knowledge of letters, sounds, and spelling rules in order to write words on the page?
- How can we use spelling resources to determine the correct spelling of words?

Unit Goals

- Students will use the strategy of chunking and clapping out syllables in order to spell words.
- Students will circle incorrect words and attempt to spell them correctly using their knowledge of word families (e.g., ate, gate, mate, date).
- Students will use a personal word wall to record words that they need to know quickly.

Resource Sheet

- Individual Student Word Wall (Resource 2.8)

Unit Assessment Synthesizing Spelling Strategies			CONVENTIONS
Student name:	EMERGING	DEVELOPING	INDEPENDENT
Uses letter, sound, and word family knowledge to encode words.			
Uses the strategy of chunking and clapping out syllables to write words.			
Identifies misspelled words.			
Uses the "write it two or three times" strategy to write a word correctly or to come up with a better approximation.			
Uses class word wall to find the spelling of words.			
Uses individual word wall to find the spelling of words.			

Stage of the Unit	Focused Instruction You will	Independent Practice Students will
IMMERSION 2 days	• model what you do when you come across words that are challenging to spell. • invite other writers (students from another class, parents, or teachers) into the class to interview them and ask them what they do to spell challenging words.	• look through their own writing and put a sticky note on places where spelling words was difficult or challenging. • work with a partner to look at their writing to find words they would like to learn how to spell conventionally.

IDENTIFICATION 1 day	• chart strategies for spelling (possibilities include closing your eyes and recalling, spelling, stretching sounds, chunking parts of a longer word, and spelling smaller parts one at a time); list spelling resources (word wall, words in personal writing tools, list of sight words, dictionaries).	• work with a partner and discuss what spelling strategies or resources they use.
GUIDED PRACTICE 4 days	• introduce/review class word wall, which identifies the words students should be spelling conventionally; demonstrate how to find a word on the word wall using the alphabetical system and scanning words in that letter box to find the needed word. • introduce students to the routine of leaving time at the end of Independent Practice for editing; divide Independent Practice into generating time and editing time, saving the last three to five minutes to give attention to spelling; model for students what a writer does during the time when she is no longer generating writing but looking at spelling of words. • demonstrate the use of chunking words and clapping or tapping out syllables; model for students how to not just segment sounds but clusters sounds into a chunk to spell. • demonstrate for students how a speller will frequently write a word two or three times (perhaps in the margin) to figure out the correct spelling or a close approximation.	• use the word wall (either during the writing or editing stage) to spell at least one word in their writing. • spend the last three to five minutes of writing time rereading their work and paying attention to the spelling of words. • use the chunking strategy to write multisyllabic or more challenging words. • generate writing and then find three words that they want to try spelling two or three times in the margin in order to create the best spelling of the word.
COMMITMENT 2 days	• introduce students to a personal spelling word wall that will hold the words that students need to know quickly and are still learning to spell (see Resource 2.8). • model reflection by responding to the question "What kind of speller am I now?" and record answers on class chart.	• create a personal word wall consisting of words that they still find challenging. • reflect on learning and discuss the kind of speller they think they are; have a "spelling celebration"— each student will select one really challenging word he or she learned to spell this week and hang it up on the wall.
TOTAL: 9 DAYS		

SPOTLIGHT on Process

- Building Stamina: Reading Long and Strong
- Building Stamina: Writing Long and Strong

In my book *The Complete 4 for Literacy*, I explain in detail how process units are designed to build identity, capacity, collaboration, and responsibility. Although these form the foundations upon which readers and writers grow, they are so intangible that they often take a back seat in our instructional plans. A student's understanding of herself and the actions that move her forward as a reader and writer are all such an important part of her growth as a second grader. Establishing a strong understanding of processes now will help us move forward smoothly, rather than having to grapple with management issues later on in the year. Our explicit instructions for working with a partner give our students a structure for growing ideas and supporting one another. Lessons on building community will create a spirit of joy and collaboration that is indispensable in sustaining the atmosphere of safety and trust in your room. In these units students learn how to develop the essential process skills of reading and writing stamina. These capacities are critical to establishing lifelong independence as readers and writers, and so we have created lessons that take our students through the experience of choice in a supported, layered approach.

For more information on process units, please see pages 37–47 of my book *The Complete 4 for Literacy*.

Pam Allyn

Building Muscles for Reading and Writing Longer and Stronger

Reading instruction tends to emphasize phonemic awareness, comprehension strategies, and fluency. While these are all important, a fourth component is often ignored—stamina. Especially in second grade, our students need our help in building those muscles that will allow them to read longer and stronger.

Remember the old days, when some of us sat in our classrooms and watched Evelyn Wood-like filmstrips that were supposed to help us read faster? Perhaps those did not work, but there are ways to teach our students how to read faster and to become more adept at getting through text in a sustained way.

Some of your students will naturally read very quickly, while others will not. We want to create an environment that lets them take risks as readers and push themselves. If they are worried that they read more slowly than someone else, we can assure them that the slower reader is often the most thoughtful reader, pausing at interesting spots, reflecting and musing on what she's read. At the same time, we can discuss techniques to build reading fluency and stamina: skimming, reading words in chunks, getting the gist of a big idea from chapter headings. All of these are tremendously valuable for the growing reader.

Building Stamina: Reading Long and Strong

PROCESS

Why Teach This?
- To strengthen students' reading stamina so they can read for longer periods of time.
- To build students' capacity for comprehension.
- To teach students that reading is possible in many different circumstances.

Framing Questions
- How can we increase our reading stamina?
- How does reading stamina help with comprehension?

Unit Goals
- Students will increase time spent reading.
- Students will learn how reading longer can help with comprehension.
- Students will understand that reading is possible under a variety of conditions and circumstances.

Students read at their independent levels to build stamina.

Anchor Texts
- *Catwings* by Ursula LeGuin
- *Danny and the Dinosaur* by Syd Hoff

Resource Sheet
- Stamina Observation (Resource 2.9)
- Student Stamina Reading Rubric (Resource 2.10)

Unit Assessment Building Stamina: Reading Long and Strong			PROCESS
Student name:	EMERGING	DEVELOPING	INDEPENDENT
Reads for increasing periods of time.			
Identifies and reads texts at a comfortable level that will help him or her sustain and increase stamina.			
Sustains independent reading for 20 minutes.			
Understands the value of rereading to build stamina and quicken pace.			
Uses comprehension strategies to move through the hard parts of text and sustain stamina.			

Stage of the Unit	Focused Instruction You will	Independent Practice Students will
IMMERSION 3 days	• describe what stamina feels like in other areas (riding a bike, walking). • watch older readers reading (through video or visits to another classroom); model how to complete the Stamina Observation sheet (Resource 2.9). • model what you notice about yourself as a reader when your reading feels strong (you are in a level book, you are in a familiar genre, you are in a comfortable spot, you are understanding what you're reading).	• talk to a partner about what activities they can sustain over time and what that feels like. • record what they notice about readers engaged with their reading (the conditions under which they are reading, the kinds of books they are reading) on the Stamina Observation sheet (Resource 2.9). • think about what they need to have in place for reading to feel good; begin to use their Student Stamina Reading Rubrics (Resource 2.10).

IDENTIFICATION 2 days	• identify ways you have been able to read longer and stronger as a class through a read-aloud; discuss the conditions that allowed you to sustain your interest (the book's content, the level of the book, strategies for getting through the hard parts). • discuss how important it is to choose the right books; model with students finding a whole-class read-aloud that will build stamina.	• talk to a partner about ways to read longer and stronger. • fill book bags with books that will build stamina.
GUIDED PRACTICE 3 days	• demonstrate reading longer and stronger by taking a picture walk using *Danny and the Dinosaur* by Syd Hoff, showing how a reader goes through the pages; demonstrate how you reread a book you love, and how when you do you can read it faster; discuss how reading nonfiction or poetry, or a familiar series can help a reader read longer and stronger. • chart the many different environments readers read in and discuss what gets us through the challenges and what behaviors might affect stamina. • demonstrate strategies for comprehension building that help readers read "stronger"; read *Catwings* by Ursula LeGuin to practice together: Pause at transitional moments to ask questions, reread parts that seem unclear, ask a partner for clarification.	• practice reading longer and stronger by taking a picture walk with a partner through a new text and talking about what would help them read faster together; practice reading longer with a familiar text, a familiar genre, or series; discuss with a partner how rereading helps you read longer—because we know the ideas and can smoothly go through the text and increase speed. • increasingly read for longer periods of time using egg timer to monitor. • practice strategies for comprehension building that help them read "stronger": Pause at transitional moments in the text to ask themselves questions to check comprehension; reread parts that seem unclear; check picture clues; ask a friend to clarify a part; check that the book is level or downhill to practice stamina effectively and change books in book bag if necessary.
COMMITMENT 2 days	• create an anchor chart called "How We Build Stamina" (choose level or downhill books, reread favorites, read series book, read in different genres). • sum up how the class read *Catwings* together: "What did we do when we got to the hard parts, to read stronger?"	• write a brief reflection: "How I Build Stamina"; share reflection with a partner, as well as books in bag that feel like they helped to build stamina. • discuss how choosing level or downhill books impacts stamina; add books to bag.
TOTAL: 10 DAYS		

Getting Started

Building stamina gives children the capacity to read for longer periods of time, read more pages of text, and sustain interest in the text. We know, of course, that quantity is not everything. But with the right instruction, quantity alongside quality will yield good reading and writing, and that is what this stamina unit can do. Help your students choose books wisely and return to texts to reread. Create opportunities for them to read not just at their level or above but also using what we call "downhill" books: ones that seem "easy" for them but in truth are really helping to build stamina. Rereading is key to building stamina: Parents often ask us if it is okay that their child is rereading *Magic Tree House* or *Frog and Toad* for the gazillionth time. We reassure them that children are working on all kinds of skills and building on all kinds of strengths as they read, and that stamina is one of those capacities that needs time to build. Rereading allows a reader to power through content more easily, giving him the opportunity to practice fluency, to practice speed, to practice incorporating larger chunks of words into his visual memory.

Structures and Routines

Students have a plastic bag that contains the texts they are reading independently. The bags help students and teachers organize the texts and keep them accessible at all times. Students are reading from their book bags and practicing their reading skills while paying attention to themselves as readers: Where do they read with high stamina and where do they feel their stamina flags?

Predictable Problems	Possible Solutions
The student picks up a book and can't stay with it, then tries another.	Confer with the student to help him make better choices for what goes into his "short stack." It is likely that the choices he has made for his independent reading are not at his level.
The student is not able to stay in his seat during reading time. He is wandering around the room.	He may need to practice increasing his stamina by reading for smaller increments of time. Establish reading sessions of a length that feel doable for this student, and then allow him to stand and stretch, or to begin other work. Explain to the student that you are going to help him build toward the minutes of reading the others can do with a minimum of stress for him.
	You also might want to consider the physical space and if it is just right for him. Are his materials comfortably arranged? Does he need less distraction from other people nearby? Would a quiet spot away from the action work best? Does he prefer to be in the middle of things? Ask him to take note of his own actions and what feels best for him.
The student is not able to talk easily to a partner about what he has read that day.	The student may be in the wrong book—either the book is too uphill for him or it is not of high interest. Confer with him about alternative book and genre selections.

The student does not seem deeply engaged with the book he is reading and is easily distracted.	You may want to encourage him to try a downhill book for this stamina unit, or a set of downhill books. Even if the book is at his level, it may require a bit of extra work in terms of comprehension. Since this unit is about stamina-building, it is a good idea to include some downhill books in the "short stack" so the student can read smoothly and swiftly through them.

Teaching Materials

The Classroom Library

Access is a key component for success in reading. A classroom library motivates children to read and become readers. Books in the library should represent a variety of authors, topics, themes, levels, and genres, including nonfiction, fiction, and poetry. Books should be placed in baskets in a way that encourages browsing. Be sure the covers are facing out. The baskets can be sorted by topic, genre, or author.

Leveled Books

A section of your library has baskets of leveled books. In order to level a book, we look at the amount of print on a page, the placement of the words and pictures, and the vocabulary. Irene Fountas and Gay Su Pinnell have written many books on the topic of leveling. They have created an A–Z system for leveling books.

Leveled books should make up approximately 20 to 30 percent of your library. These books are meant for children to read independently, so you will need a nice variety. Children can choose from these books once they have learned how to make wise book choices. If you choose to use the A–Z leveling system, you may want to assign colored stickers to minimize the issue of competitiveness among the children. Place a color sticker corresponding to the book's level on the outside cover of the book. The book can go in a leveled basket, or be a leveled text in another (genre, author, topic) basket in the library. Your second graders will quickly absorb your system. If you are positive and excited about their choices, they will not be competitive with one another.

Independent Book Bags

Your students will be creating bags of books for their independent books. They need a place to keep their book bags that is convenient and easy for them to access during independent reading time.

Differentiation

Reading books that are level or downhill is the best way to build stamina. But do not dissuade a student who wants to try an uphill book during this unit. The point is that whatever motivates a child to read is going to build stamina. It is really as simple as that. For your additional support, here are lists of books for vulnerable, steady, and strong readers in a reading stamina unit.

For vulnerable readers

Title of Book	Author	Fountas & Pinnell Level
Biscuit	Alyssa Satin Capucilli	Level F
More Spaghetti, Say!	Rita Gelman	Level G
Little Critters	Mercer Mayer	Level H
Danny and the Dinosaur	Syd Hoff	Level J

For steady readers

Title of Book	Author	Fountas & Pinnell Level
Poppleton	Cynthia Rylant	Level J
Mr. Putter and Tabby	Cynthia Rylant	Level J
Owl at Home/Frog and Toad	Arnold Lobel	Level J/K
Frances	Russell Hoban	Level K
Nate the Great	Marjorie Wyman Sharmat	Level K

For strong readers

Title of Book	Author	Fountas & Pinnell Level
Tales of Oliver Pig	Jean Van Leeuwen	Level K/L
Little Bill	Bill Cosby	Level L
Amelia Bedelia	Peggy Parish	Level L
Weather Fairies	Daisy Meadows	Level L
Bailey School Kids series	Marcia Thornton Jones and Debbie Dadey	Level M

Stages of the Unit

Immersion

Through modeling and conversation, work with students to define stamina and discuss how it applies to different aspects of your students' lives.

Identification

Work with students to identify and define how to increase reading stamina. Through conversations and identification of new strategies, students discover ways to read longer and stronger. These new strategies help them as they move into Guided Practice and begin reading for longer periods of time.

Guided Practice

Students work on building their reading stamina. The lessons during this stage help support the group as readers by focusing on how to read stronger for increasing increments of time.

Commitment

Students reflect on how this unit went for them and create an anchor chart that lists these new strategies and how they helped.

How to Use the Lessons in the Spotlight Units

In every Spotlight Unit, we have scripted out each lesson: the Focused Instruction, the Independent Practice, and the Wrap-Up. Where you see italics, we have provided model language: You are free to use it as is or you may prefer to adapt it to suit your needs. For example, if we mention a book we might read aloud to our class, but you have one you like better, feel free to use that one instead. Or if we use a personal anecdote as a demonstration, you should replace it with one of your own. The lesson plans also include bullet points with guidelines for what you and the students could be doing at each point in the lesson. You will notice that there is always a balance of teacher talk and suggested actions.

Day-by-Day Lessons

DAY 1 Immersion

Focused Instruction

What is something that you can do for a long period of time? Do you ride your bike, read, or play ball with your dad? Why do you think you can do this for long periods of time?

- Provide an example: I can drive for long periods of time. I am always the one who drives on long car trips...
  - Elicit student activities that demonstrate stamina.

Independent Practice

- Assign students partners. Have partners do the following:
  - Name activities they can do for long periods of time.
  - Identify what it feels like to do an activity for a long period of time.
  - Think about why they can do an activity for a long period of time.

Wrap-Up

- Create a chart with three categories:
  - Activities students can "stick with."
  - What it feels like for students to stick with their favorite activity.
  - Why students think they can stick with their favorite activity.
- Introduce students to the term "stamina" and provide a definition. Keep the definition in a central location so that students can refer back to it.

DAY 2 Immersion

Focused Instruction

Today we are going to continue to think about and identify stamina. We are going to begin to explore what it means to build stamina in reading.

- Use a video or visit a classroom where older children are reading.
- What does stamina look like? What were the students whom you watched doing? For how long did the students read?
- Model how to complete the Stamina Observation sheet (Resource 2.9).

Independent Practice

- Pass out copies of the Stamina Observation sheet.
- Have students do the following:
  - Record what they noticed about the other readers that allowed them to read for a long time.
  - Identify characteristics that they share with the readers they observed.

Wrap-Up

- Start a stamina chart that defines what building stamina looks like, sounds like, and feels like. Discuss with students what they think building stamina means.

DAY 3 Immersion

Focused Instruction

Today we are going to find out what makes us feel good as readers when we read a book. What makes a book easier to read for a long time? Is there a genre like poetry or comic books that makes it easier for you to read longer? What makes a book harder to read for a long time? If you read somewhere special, can you read for a longer time? How can we find new strategies to help us read longer and stronger?

- Describe your favorite place to read and ask students where their favorite places to read are. In bed? On the couch? On the bus? In a chair? In a hammock?
- Choose a book that is appropriately leveled and of high interest, choose a comfortable spot, and model for students how you can read longer and stronger.

Independent Practice

- Assign students a partner. Each partnership should talk about what the teacher did to read for a longer time. The partners should then think about what makes them feel good as readers.

When you read, what strategies are you going to try doing to read for a longer time?

- Begin to record information on the Student Stamina Reading Rubric (Resource 2.10).

Wrap-Up

- Regroup and, as a class, add to the stamina chart by filling in strategies the class came up with.

DAY 4 Identification

Focused Instruction

Today we are going to try to understand how we can improve our reading stamina. Let's read from our read-aloud book and spy on ourselves. We are going to talk about what strategies we use during read-aloud to inspire stamina. How can we read books for a longer time? How can we become stronger readers as we read for longer times?

- Model reading with stamina as students watch closely.

How does the topic of the book make us want to read longer? How does knowing strategies for getting through the hard parts of the book help us become stronger readers?

Independent Practice

- Students read independently, observing what helps them build stamina.

Wrap-Up

- Add to the class chart strategies for inspiring stamina for reading, including information discussed in earlier lessons about how to build stamina for other activities.

DAY 5 Identification

Focused Instruction

When I read books that are interesting to me, I can stick to my reading and read for longer periods of time. There are other things that make me feel good about reading for a longer time. The size of the book—is it thick or thin? The size of the font—is it big or small? We talked about how important it is to be thinking about choosing the books that are right for us as readers. When we're trying to build stamina, it becomes even more important.

- Model looking at the book baskets or book bags to determine whether weekly choices will help to build stamina.

Independent Practice

- Have students fill their book bags with books that will inspire stamina.

Wrap-Up

- Discuss how their independent reading went.
- Chart responses as students share their experiences of reading appropriately leveled books of high interest.

DAY 6 Guided Practice

Focused Instruction

When I read a book, I find that I can read it much longer if I love the book. Lots of times when I reread a book I love, I am amazed at how quickly I read. I also find that there are some genres, like poetry, that I can read longer and stronger. I especially like reading books that are part of a series because I already know how that kind of book will go. We are going to practice timing ourselves today with an egg timer to see how long we can read.

- Demonstrate a picture walk using *Danny and the Dinosaur* by Syd Hoff. A picture walk is a technique used by a reader to preview the book and orient himself to the structure, characters, and plot. Model this by using the pictures to tell the story.

- Set the egg timer to model timing independent reading for students. Explain to them that each day the amount of time they read will grow longer.

Independent Practice

- Have students practice reading longer and stronger by taking a picture walk with a partner through a new text. Ask them to consider what would help them read faster.
- Ask students/partners to choose a familiar book. Ask them why reading the familiar text takes less time.
- Have them select a book that is part of a series they are familiar with. Ask them why this book is easier to read.
- Finally, have students/partners find a poem that they like. Ask them whether they can read a poem faster than they can read nonfiction.
- During independent reading, practice reading a book with an egg timer.

Wrap-Up

- Discuss what helps people build stamina.

DAY 7 Guided Practice

Focused Instruction

- Brainstorm with the students a list of behaviors that might affect our stamina during reading.

Independent Practice

- Students read independently for ____ minutes (a few minutes longer than the day before), while trying to maintain their stamina and flow.

Wrap-Up

- Discuss what helped students read more, and for more minutes.

DAY 8 Guided Practice

Focused Instruction

Today we are going to talk about how to break longer texts apart into meaningful chunks so that they are easier to read. When I set stopping points, it helps me to stay with my reading for longer periods of time.

- Read *Catwings* by Ursula LeGuin to model these strategies for comprehension building:
  - Pausing at transitional moments.
  - Asking questions to check comprehension and reread parts that are unclear.
  - Clarifying a section that is confusing.

Independent Practice

- Set the egg timer and have students practice some of these reading strategies during independent reading.

Wrap-Up

Have students look through their book bags and complete the following chart:

Name _____

I have _____ books in my bag that feel level.
I have _____ books in my bag that feel uphill.
I have _____ books in my bag that feel downhill.
I can tell that most of my books are level.
YES or NO

DAY 9 Commitment

Focused Instruction

We have learned so many new strategies for how to read longer and stronger. Now I want us to create an anchor chart that will help us to remember all of the information that we learned!

- Title the chart "How We Build Stamina" and add the following strategies.

Choose level or downhill books.
Choose favorite books to reread.
Read books in lots of genres.
Read books that really interest us.
Read to a set stopping point, pause, think, and keep reading.

Independent Practice

- Have students write a brief response to the question "How do I build stamina?"

Wrap-Up

- Share students' responses.

DAY 10 Commitment

Focused Instruction

- Review with your students what they did when they got to the hard parts of *Catwings*.

Independent Practice

- Have students look through their book bags with a partner and find the books that they feel helped them build stamina.

Wrap-Up

- Discuss the books students chose and why they chose them.

Building Stamina: Writing Long and Strong

PROCESS

Why Teach This?

- To show students that writers can get through the hard parts of writing by using strategies for generating ideas.
- To help students build stamina for writing for longer periods of time.
- To teach students how to build stamina for staying with one idea over several days.

Framing Questions

- How can we increase our writing stamina?
- How do we build strategies for finding ideas and staying with them?

Unit Goals

- Students will learn how to sustain writing ideas over time.
- Students will understand that writing is possible under a variety of conditions and circumstances.
- Students will increase time spent writing.

Anchor Texts

- Meet the Authors and Illustrators series by Deborah Kovacs
- *You Have to Write* by Janet S. Wong

Resource Sheets

- Stamina Observation (Resource 2.9)
- Student Stamina Writing Rubric (Resource 2.11)
- Writing Strategies for Building Stamina: Strategies for Generating Writing (Resource 2.12)

Unit Assessment Building Stamina: Writing Long and Strong			PROCESS
Student name:	EMERGING	DEVELOPING	INDEPENDENT
Sustains writing for 20 minutes.			
Rereads writing to further stamina.			
Continues through the hard parts.			
Adds to writing over time.			

Stage of the Unit	Focused Instruction You will	Independent Practice Students will
IMMERSION 3 days	• watch older writers writing (through video or visits to another classroom); model how to complete the Stamina Observation sheet (Resource 2.9).	• use the Stamina Observation Sheet to record what they notice writers doing during writing time.

IMMERSION *(continued)*	• interview writers about how they get through the hard parts (principal, other teachers, older students). • model what you notice about yourself when writing feels strong (you are writing about a topic that matters to you, you are in a comfortable spot, you know what to do when you get stuck); model how to record information on the Student Stamina Writing Rubric (Resource 2.11).	• talk to a partner and record what they notice about writers who are engaged with their writing: What are the conditions for their writing? What kinds of ideas are they writing about? • think what they need to have in place for writing to feel successful (writing spot, writing ideas, strategies for what to do when stuck); begin to use the Student Stamina Writing Rubric (Resource 2.11).
IDENTIFICATION 2 days	• chart with students the ways writers can write "long and strong" about a topic (choosing a topic they know a lot about, telling a story aloud and adding more words, rereading their writing to get inspired); model how to tell and write a story about a familiar topic. • use an egg timer and write as a class for a set length of time, increasing it by a few minutes each day until the end of the unit.	• talk with a partner about what helps them write longer and stronger. Use I wonder, I remember, I observe, and I imagine (the Four Prompts) to generate writing topics. • practice writing for set periods of time.
GUIDED PRACTICE 4 days	• model increasing your stamina by telling your story before writing it. • chart the many different environments writers write in, the challenges, and what gets us through them (tuning out noise by becoming really invested in your idea or doing something fun with it; finding a cozy spot to write; being sure you have the right materials). • read from the Meet the Authors and Illustrators series to show all the ways authors find to get inspired and sustain themselves. • increase time on the egg timer for class independent writing sessions.	• practice writing longer and stronger by putting a mark at the end of the page to see if they can get there; rereading own text to see if they can extend an idea; talk with a partner to extend ideas. • discuss the distractions and solutions for maintaining stamina and then write. • practice using techniques learned from authors, including writing in different genres. • practice writing until the egg timer goes off, no matter what; see what strategies they used to get through.
COMMITMENT 1 day	• model choosing a piece of writing for light editing.	• edit piece and then share favorite excerpt from writing with the class; discuss the strategies learned that enable them to write with more stamina.
TOTAL: 10 DAYS		

Getting Started

Some children in your class are overflowing with writing ideas. But some of your students may get tired easily. The act of writing still feels physically stressful to them, and it is also intellectually stressful. They watch while other children speed down the page, and they feel slower and less able to speed. It is critical to build their confidence at this time of year, and also to give them strategies to build their writing stamina—ones that will allow them to put more words on a page, spend more minutes writing, and sustain one idea for a longer period of time. For some of your children, building stamina may mean increasing their writing output from one page to two; for others it may mean moving from pictures to words; for others it may mean sustaining an idea they have for more than one class writing session. Second graders love counting up words per page and even the page numbers themselves. They also love and wish to feel like the "big kids." Let this unit be about creating and environment and opportunities to build and cultivate the muscles for writing a lot.

Structures and Routines

There are some management issues that come up in a unit such as this one—and throughout the year when students are engaged in independent writing. Here are a few suggestions for how to resolve them:

Predictable Problems	Possible Solutions
The student starts on a topic and can't stay with it, then tries another.	Confer with the student to help him make wise choices by reminding him of the Four Prompts. In the ARCH unit, your students were introduced to the concept of the Four Prompts (I wonder, I remember, I observe, I imagine). Remind your student of the power of the Four Prompts as a way to keep his ideas moving forward. Also, some topics lend themselves to "quick writes." Allow your student to finish a piece quickly and then move on to a new one. Not every topic requires hours of concentration or attention.
The student is not able to stay in his seat during independent writing time. He is wandering around the room.	He may need to practice increasing his stamina by writing for smaller increments of time. Establish writing sessions of a length that feels doable for this student, and then allow him to stand and stretch or to begin other work. Explain to the student that you are going to help him build toward the minutes of writing the others can do with a minimum of stress. You might also want to consider the physical space and if it is just right for him. Are his materials comfortably arranged for him? Does he need less distraction from people around him? Would a quiet spot away from the action work best? Does he prefer to be in the middle of things? Ask him to take note of his own actions and what feels best.
The student is not able to talk easily to a partner about what he has written that day.	The student may need a different partner. Perhaps it is hard for him to share a personal topic with this particular partner. Spend a day watching them work together and see what you think.

The student struggles to get to the end of a page and expresses frustration.	Just as there are downhill books, there are also downhill topics. Make sure you are not being judgmental about topic choice; in other words, the student may really love to write about a television character and retell a show: It may not instantly strike you as a very deep topic. But in terms of building stamina, it may be really helpful and liberating for him to use this kind of comfortable, fun topic to generate lots of writing. Give the student permission to select downhill topics.

Teaching Materials

Using Writers as Mentors

The Meet the Author and Illustrator series from Scholastic and the Meet the Author series from Richard C. Owen Publishers are both valuable resources for this unit. Refer to these books as examples of writers staying with ideas and continuing to write even through the hard parts. The writers' own voices are our most powerful teachers.

Setting Up Student Writing Notebooks

You will find it useful to have your students keep a simple notebook or a folder in which they can explore being a writer. Many teachers prefer to begin the year in second grade with folders to accommodate a variety of paper choices. Students often feel more comfortable working with individual sheets of paper rather than the more daunting notebook. On the other hand, many teachers feel that their students are ready for a notebook and jump right in. By the end of second grade, all your students should be very comfortable writing in a notebook. You may want to begin the year with folders and segue to notebooks in midyear. Either way, this should be a place your students can return to throughout the year, to read and reread their writing, to collect writing ideas and look for new ones, to reflect on their growing abilities as writers. Have students set aside the back of the notebooks for lists of writing topics. As they come up with new ideas, they can add these to their lists.

Stages of the Unit

Immersion

Students identify the characteristics of writing stamina as they observe or talk to other writers.

Identification

Students devise new strategies for writing long and strong. They set goals for their time spent writing and the length of their writing.

Guided Practice

Students practice ways to generate ideas, avoid distractions, and find comfortable writing places. They are asked to focus on using the new strategies as they begin to use the egg timer and write for longer times each day.

Commitment

Students commit to recognizing how to increase their writing stamina. They create an anchor chart of the strategies they used to do so.

Day-by-Day Lessons

DAY 1 Immersion

Focused Instruction

Today we are going to watch other writers and try to learn how these writers write long and strong. What do they do that allows them to have what we call stamina, the ability to write for longer periods of time?

- Show a video or visit a classroom of older children writing.

What does writing stamina look like? What were the students that you watched doing? For how long did the students write?

- Model how to record information on the Stamina Observation Sheet (Resource 2.9).

Independent Practice

- Give students the Stamina Observation sheet. It has two columns: "What I See" and "What I Want to Try."
- Have students do the following:
  - Record what they noticed about the older writers and consider what things they did that let them write for a long time.
  - Identify characteristics that they share with the writers they observed.
  - Think about something they might try differently now that they watched these other writers.

Wrap-Up

- Start a chart that names the qualities of stamina.

DAY 2 Immersion

Focused Instruction

I know that sometimes when I am writing, I have trouble starting. I know that once I begin, I can keep writing, but I get stuck trying to figure out how to start my writing assignment. What we are going to do today is interview other writers about what part of writing they find hard and how they break through to write longer and stronger.

Independent Practice

- Assign students a partner and have the partners record their observations about the writers they interviewed. They should consider the following questions:
  - Where were the conditions for their writing?
  - Was the room quiet or loud?
  - Where were the writers sitting?
  - What tools did they have around them?
  - What kinds of ideas were they writing about?

Wrap-Up

- Have students discuss what they learned from these writers about stamina.
- Add new observations to the stamina chart.

DAY 3 Immersion

Focused Instruction

Today I want you to spy on yourselves as you write. As you watch yourselves write, you are going to learn what strategies you use to help you write longer and stronger.

- Discuss with your students what they want to focus on when they are writing in order to become writers with stamina. Have them consider the following questions:
  - Does the topic matter to you? What topics do you prefer to write about?
  - Where do you feel most comfortable when you write?
  - What strategies do you use when you get stuck?
- Model how to record information on the Student Stamina Writing Rubric (Resource 2.11).

Independent Practice

- Have students engage in independent writing, keeping these questions in mind as they work:
  - What do you need to have in place for writing to feel successful?
  - Where is your favorite writing spot?
  - What ideas are you writing about?
  - Did you get stuck? What did you do when you came to a hard part?
- Begin recording information on the Student Stamina Writing Rubric (Resource 2.11).

Wrap-Up

- Talk about how independent writing went today.

DAY 4 Identification

Focused Instruction

- Add to the stamina chart with students the ways writers can write long and strong about a topic.
- Choose a familiar and comfortable topic and model for students how to tell the story aloud. Then model how to write the story, adding more words and rereading the writing when stuck.

Independent Practice

- Have students revisit the Four Prompts: I wonder, I remember, I observe, I imagine. Choose a prompt to generate a topic for writing.

Wrap-Up

- Discuss with students their experience writing on a topic of strong interest.

DAY 5 Identification

Focused Instruction

We have been talking about strategies to help us write longer, so today I would like to talk about timing ourselves as we write. We will start by writing for ___ minutes today and then by the end of the unit we will be writing for ___ minutes. I am going to use an egg timer to help us keep track of the time.

    As a class, make a commitment about how much time you will spend writing today.

- Explain how much time will be added each day.
- Write stamina goals on a chart.

Independent Practice

- Students practice writing for a set period of time.

Wrap-Up

- Discuss with students their experiences writing for a set period of time.

DAY 6 Guided Practice

Focused Instruction

- Tell the students a story before writing it to model how doing so helps you write longer and stronger (see Writing Strategies for Building Stamina, Resource 2.12).

Independent Practice

- Before students begin to write, they should mark the end of the page to see how much they can write. Tell them that if they get stuck, they can try to extend their ideas by talking to a partner or rereading what they've written so far.

Wrap-Up

- Discuss with students how their writing went.

A student extends her thinking by writing more from one idea and by marking her goal point with an "X."

DAY 7 Guided Practice

Focused Instruction

Have you ever noticed that sometimes there are things that interfere with your writing stamina? What does that do to your concentration?

- Brainstorm factors that interfere with writing stamina (noisy places, uncomfortable writing spots, etc.).

Independent Practice

- With a partner, students discuss solutions to some of the environmental distractions that interfere with their writing stamina.

Wrap-Up

- Create a chart with two columns: "Distractions" and "Solutions."
- Have students complete the chart based on their experiences and discussions.

DAY 8 Guided Practice

Focused Instruction

Today we are going to see how famous authors find inspiration for their writing.

- Read from the Meet the Authors and Illustrators series and *You Have to Write* to show all the ways that writers find inspiration.

Independent Practice

- Students select one thing they learned from published writers and try it to help them write longer and stronger.

Wrap-Up

- Students share what they wrote.

DAY 9 Guided Practice

Focused Instruction

We have been slowly increasing time on the egg timer. Today we are going to write for the longest time we have so far.

Independent Practice

- Students practice freewriting until the egg timer goes off, no matter what.

Wrap-Up

So how did writing for a longer period of time go for you today?

DAY 10 Commitment

Focused Instruction

Today let's select one of our pieces and do some light editing, polishing it so we can share it with a friend.

- Model editing a piece of your writing.

Independent Practice

- Students polish and edit their work.

Wrap-Up

- Students share their writing with a friend. Discuss: What strategies help us to write longer and stronger?

From Early Fall to Late Fall

As late fall arrives, your year is in full swing. Students are establishing their fundamental skills with the help of synthesized word-attack strategies and spelling strategies. They are reading and writing longer and stronger as they embrace strategies for book choices and for building stamina. By the time late fall arrives, your room will be alive with these budding readers and writers ready for the newness of these next months. They have the grown-up feeling of carrying their series books around, seeing the mysteries and magic of new punctuation skills, and experiencing the joy of fairy-tale endings.

Chapter 3

LATE FALL

The Second Grader as Explorer

"Come on, sit on the balcony and look out over the sea. I have a story to tell you. It happens on an island where the waves follow each other, one after another, to the sandy shore. The waves are always beginning a story that never comes to an end. You can hear them when they touch the shore saying Once... Once... Once..."
—from *Sugar Cane: A Caribbean Rapunzel* by Patricia Storace

Join us for this series of units in late fall, which honor the second grader who is both a believer in magic and a reader and writer who is absorbing new information and able to use it in new ways. Fairy tales illuminate this season with magic, while a close look at authors raises the bar for new thinking.

SPOTLIGHT UNITS

EARLY FALL

LATE FALL

WINTER

SPRING

Really Magical and Magically Real

In late fall, our second graders step into a more complex relationship with reading and writing as they become able to read more, read longer, and read more complicated texts. A spirited look at fairy tales is timely. Fairy tales offer plenty to discuss that is as serious as all that your students are becoming, but they also have a playful side. Everything is exaggerated, dark or light, good or bad. The story elements are pronounced and very easy to see and discuss for all readers. And of course, for all of us, young and old, there is nothing so satisfying as a happy ending.

Deepening Our Understanding of Fairy Tales

GENRE

Why Teach This?

- To introduce the elements of a fairy tale.
- To enable students to deepen reading comprehension through reading, understanding, and comparing fairy tales.

Framing Questions

- What is a fairy tale?
- How can understanding the genre of fairy tales enable us to deepen our knowledge of story elements?

Unit Goals

- Students will understand that a fairy tale contains critical story elements: setting, character, and a plot with a problem and solution.
- Students will identify the standard language of a fairy tale ("once upon a time," "happily ever after").
- Students will compare fairy tales (different versions of the same story).

Anchor Texts

- *Beauty and the Beast, Goldilocks and the Three Bears* by Jan Brett
- *Goldilocks and the Three Bears*, retold by Joan Gallup
- *The Irish Cinderlad* by Shirley Climo

- *Little Red Riding Hood* by Heather Amery
- *Little Red Riding Hood* by Jerry Pinkney
- *Lon Po Po: A Red-Riding Hood Story From China* by Ed Young
- *Rainbow Crow*, retold by Nancy Van Laan
- *The Three Bears, The Little Red Hen* by Byron Barton
- *Twelve Dancing Princesses* by Jane Ray
- "White-Bear-King Valemon," from *The Starlight Princesses* collection, retold by Annie Dalton

Additional Texts

- *Cendrillon: A Caribbean Cinderella* by Robert D. San Souci
- *Cinderella* by Jane Sanderson
- *Hansel and Gretel*, retold by Gaby Goldsack
- *The Little Red Hen* by Lilian Obligado
- *My Side of the Story Cinderella, Lady Tremaine*, as told to Daphne Skinner
- *The End* by David LaRochelle
- *The True Story of the Three Little Pigs*, as told to Jon Scieszka

Unit Assessment Deepening Our Understanding of Fairy Tales			GENRE
Student name:	EMERGING	DEVELOPING	INDEPENDENT
Identifies characters and their characteristics.			
Identifies the setting and its importance.			
Identifies the symbolism of the number three in many fairy tales (in characters, objects and plot).			
Retells using story language: "once upon a time" for the beginning and "happily ever after" for the ending.			
Names similarities and differences between two fairy tales.			
Compares and contrasts two versions of the same fairy tale.			

Stage of the Unit	Focused Instruction You will	Independent Practice Students will
IMMERSION 3 days	• read *Little Red Riding Hood* by Heather Amery and discuss with students; ask them to name what kind of book this is (genre). • read *Goldilocks and the Three Bears* by Jan Brett; review the characters, setting, and plot; note that the story has a happy ending. • read *The Twelve Dancing Princesses* by Jane Ray; discuss typical plot elements and language used in a fairy tale.	• browse through familiar and unfamiliar fairy tales. • notice elements common to fairy tales (happy endings, characters with strong traits, fanciful settings). • with partner, read fairy tales together and discuss plot elements.

IDENTIFICATION 1 day	• read "White-Bear-King Valemon"; identify important parts of a fairy tale (character with a problem; setting, such as cabins, forest, castles; use of threes as a central part of the story, for example, there are three wishes in *Sleeping Beauty*, *Little Red Riding Hood* asks the wolf three questions, Goldilocks tries three things; language used in fairy tales plots in which the main character finds a happy solution to a major problem).	• work with partner to name the elements in fairy tales.
GUIDED PRACTICE 6 days	• read *Little Red Riding Hood* by Jerry Pinkney and name the traits of the characters. • reread *Lon Po Po* by Ed Young and discuss the setting; compare it to the setting in other fairy tales. • read *Sleeping Beauty*; discuss the use of the number three in many fairy tales. • read *Beauty and the Beast*; compare and contrast its characters, setting, and plot with those of *Sleeping Beauty*. • read *The Three Little Bears* by Byron Barton and compare and contrast it with the version by Jan Brett. • read *The Irish Cinderlad* by Shirley Climo; compare and contrast it to other versions of Cinderella.	• read/reread the fairy tale and identify the main character; describe traits to their partner. • with their partner, identify setting and discuss whether it is typical of fairy tales. • read fairy tale independently and then retell it to their partner, making sure to point out the three elements in the story and the use of typical fairy-tale language. • read fairy tale independently and compare it with one their partner is reading. • read a fairy tale and meet with a partner who has read a different version and discuss and compare the characters, setting, problem, and ending.
COMMITMENT 1 day	• invent a class fairy tale based on what you all now know about fairy tales.	• reflect on what they know about fairy tales; make up a fairy tale based on what they now know about the genre and tell it to a partner.
TOTAL: 11 DAYS		

Writing Fairy Tales

Why Teach This?
- To build reading/writing connections through the genre of fairy tales.
- To enable students to create an original literary text using fairy tales of their own.
- To provide an opportunity for children to write in a genre they are familiar with as readers.

Framing Question
- How can we use our imaginations as inspiration and our knowledge of story elements as a foundation to build our own stories?

Unit Goals
- Students will use their knowledge of the elements of a fairy tale to write one of their own.
- Students will use a storyboard to plan their writing and organize their ideas.
- Students will create a fairy tale that incorporates the key elements of the genre.

Anchor Texts
- *Once Upon a Cool Motorcycle Dude* by Kevin O'Malley
- *Previously* by Allan Ahlberg
- *The Rough-Face Girl* by Rafe Martin
- *Sugar Cane: A Caribbean Rapunzel* by Patricia Storace
- *Twelve Dancing Princesses* by Jane Ray

Additional Texts
- *Beauty and the Beast, Goldilocks and the Three Bears* by Jan Brett
- *Cinderella* by Jane Sanderson
- *The Egyptian Cinderella* by Shirley Climo
- *Glass Slipper, Gold Sandal* by Paul Fleischman
- *Goldilocks and the Three Bears*, retold by Joan Gallup
- *The Little Red Hen*, Golden Book Illustrated by Lilian Obligado
- *Little Red Riding Hood* by Heather Amery
- *Little Red Riding Hood* by Jerry Pinkney
- *Sleeping Beauty*, adapted by Michael Teitelbaum
- *The Starlight Princess and Other Princess Stories*, retold by Annie Dalton
- *The Three Bears, The Little Red Hen* by Byron Barton

Unit Assessment Writing Fairy Tales			GENRE
Student name:	EMERGING	DEVELOPING	INDEPENDENT
Creates multiple strong characters.			
Creates contrasting settings: dark and light.			
Creates a problem and a solution.			
Identifies symbols such as the number three as ways the storyteller conveys an important idea.			

Stage of the Unit	Focused Instruction You will	Independent Practice Students will
IMMERSION 2 days	• read *Once Upon a Cool Motorcycle Dude*, using this and texts from the reading unit to look at the perspectives, characters, and settings of fairy tales. • browse and notice texts used in the reading unit such as *The Twelve Dancing Princesses* to name the kinds of problems typically found in a fairy tale.	• look through books with a partner and put sticky notes on the different kinds of characters and setting found in fairy tales. • browse through fairy tales, noticing the problems and solutions.
IDENTIFICATION 1 day	• read *Sugar Cane* and identify and name the key elements of fairy tales: setting, character, symbols, story language, problem and solution.	• begin a list of possible characters and setting for their fairy tale.
GUIDED PRACTICE 6 days	• use *The Rough-Face Girl* to model how to come up with characters, setting, problem and solution, and three key words or phrases to be used in a fairy tale. • reread *Once Upon a Cool Motorcycle Dude* and demonstrate how to flesh out a character for a fairy tale. • model using a storyboard to plan the first, second, and third parts of the story, including the solution and happy ending. • demonstrate creating a draft of a fairy tale. • using *Previously*, demonstrate revising a draft to include a happy ending and strong engaging beginning that sound like a fairy tale. • model rereading and revising to create a fairy tale that includes typical language, phrases, and words.	• create a chart listing the story elements to help them plan and write their fairy tale. • create a character map for the protagonist of the fairy tale. • plan out the beginning, middle, and end of their fairy tale. • create a draft of their fairy tale. • revise the draft, making sure it includes all the elements of a fairy tale, especially a happy ending and an engaging beginning. • review their draft with a partner to check fairy-tale language.
COMMITMENT 2 days	• demonstrate how to publish individual books. • celebrate the students' work.	• edit and publish fairy tale. • celebrate with peers.
TOTAL: 11 DAYS		

The World of Independent Readers

Second graders are really just learning how to navigate the world of independence. We want to encourage them to visit the public library and to browse on their own in our classroom libraries. They need lots of reminders about book choice—to give them the confidence to select books that are a great match for them and help them understand why uphill or downhill books may be just right, too.

Making Wise Book Choices

PROCESS

Why Teach This?

- To help students monitor their book choices.
- To help students be more reflective about the level of the books they're reading.
- To help students understand that when they make wise choices they will be able to read for longer periods of time.

Framing Questions

- How can you tell if a book feels level, uphill, or downhill?
- What kinds of books should you read most of the time to become a stronger reader?
- How can you become the kind of reader who reads for a variety of purposes (to seek information, to question or confirm an idea you have, to learn how to do something)?

Unit Goals

- Students will learn how to make wise book choices.
- Students will learn how to manage and monitor books in their book bags.
- Students will learn how making wise book choices will help them grow stronger as readers.
- Students will learn how making wise book choices will help them build stamina as they read.

Anchor Texts

- *Arthur's Loose Tooth* by Lillian Hoban
- *Cam Jansen* by David Adler
- *The Empty Pot* by Demi
- Magic Tree House series by Mary Pope Osborne
- *Nate the Great* by Marjorie Weinman Sharmat

Unit Assessment Making Wise Book Choices			PROCESS
Student name:	EMERGING	DEVELOPING	INDEPENDENT
Identifies a book that feels downhill.			
Identifies a book that feels level.			
Identifies a book that feels uphill.			
Understands that to get stronger as a reader most of the book he reads should be level.			
Chooses a variety of books for his box or bag, making sure most are level.			
When reading a level book, knows that it is level by the amount of time he can focus on it.			

Stage of the Unit	Focused Instruction You will	Independent Practice Students will
IMMERSION 2 days	• read a part of *Arthur's Loose Tooth* and *Nate the Great*; model how to choose books from the classroom library that you find interesting. • discuss how finding a book is like finding a pair of shoes—it must be a good fit. What kind of reader would be a good fit for these books?	• choose a few books from the classroom library based on interest and browse through them to decide which will go into their "short stack." • discuss how they choose books based on interest and name some of their favorites; share titles to add to short stacks.
IDENTIFICATION 3 days	• discuss what a level book looks and feels like and compare it with something like riding a bike on flat ground versus riding a bike uphill or downhill; share how to decide which books in your short stack are level reading books. • discuss what a downhill book looks and feels like and how to decide which books in their short stack are downhill. • discuss what an uphill book looks and feels like and how to decide which books in their short stack are uphill.	• read from their short stack and find books that feel level for their book bag or box; share their thinking with a partner. • read from their short stack, find books that feel downhill, and place them back into the classroom library; share their thinking with a partner. • read from their short stack, find books that feel uphill, and place them back into the classroom library; share their thinking with a partner.

GUIDED PRACTICE 4 days	• read from *Cam Jansen* or one of the anchor texts and model how reading a level book helps readers develop stamina. • model how readers monitor the books in their book bag or box to make sure most of the books are level by reflecting on their choices and changing them on a regular basis. • discuss why readers sometimes abandon books. • read *The Empty Pot* by Demi and discuss that readers sometimes read more than one book at a time for different purposes.	• choose a level book and practice reading independently for a sustained period of time. • monitor that most of the books in their book bag or box feel level; discuss current text before reading. • reflect on different times to read level, uphill, and downhill books. • share texts in their short stack that are not as long as chapter books. What other books could go in our bags?
COMMITMENT 1 day	• reflect on making wise book choices, discussing how readers choose mostly level books and change their books on a regular basis.	• share with a partner their reading plans and their short stacks.
TOTAL: 10 DAYS		

Punctuation Power

This unit is a message to our students that punctuation is fun and purposeful. Using work they have done or new ideas, they can play with punctuation in all kinds of joyous ways, as only second graders can.

Beginning and Ending Punctuation

CONVENTIONS

Why Teach This?
- To have students add to their understanding of basic conventions.
- To have students understand when to use beginning and ending punctuation.

Framing Questions
- How does beginning and ending punctuation help us understand what we're reading?
- How can we remember to use beginning and ending punctuation in our own writing?

Unit Goals
- Students will understand the role and importance of ending sentences with an exclamation point, a period, and a question mark.
- Students will use exclamation points, periods, and question marks to punctuate sentences in their own writing.
- Students will understand the connection between ending punctuation and beginning capitalization.
- Students will understand and use the rules of beginning capitalization in their writing.

Anchor Texts
- *Don't You Feel Well, Sam?* by Amy Hest
- *A Good Day* by Kevin Henkes
- *The Moon Was the Best* by Charlotte Zolotow
- *Roller Coaster* by Marla Frazee
- *Some Dog* by Cynthia Rylant

Unit Assessment Beginning and Ending Punctuation			CONVENTIONS
Student name:	EMERGING	DEVELOPING	INDEPENDENT
Understands the role and importance of ending punctuation.			
Uses ending punctuation accurately.			
Recognizes the connection between ending punctuation and beginning capitalization.			
Uses beginning capitalization correctly.			

Stage of the Unit	Focused Instruction You will	Independent Practice Students will
IMMERSION 1 day	• read *The Moon Was the Best* by Charlotte Zolotow and ask students what types of beginning and ending punctuation they notice; focus on a few pages of the book for the class to view together.	• look through their writing folder or notebook with a partner and notice beginning and ending punctuation.
IDENTIFICATION 2 days	• read *Some Dog* by Cynthia Rylant; name ending punctuation marks and discuss the different ways they are used. • read *A Good Day* by Kevin Henkes; discuss how the first word of a sentence begins with a capital letter.	• look through their writing to find examples of complete sentences using different ending punctuation and write them on a sticky note. • look through their writing to find examples of complete sentences starting with beginning punctuation and write these on a sticky note.
GUIDED PRACTICE 2 days	• demonstrate using a period at the end of a sentence and a capital letter at the beginning of the next sentence by editing a writing entry; model how to use a period to make two sentences out of one. • using *Don't You Feel Well, Sam?* demonstrate using an exclamation point for an exclamatory statement, a question mark for a question, and a capital letter at the beginning of the next sentence.	• reread a writing entry and edit it by putting in the appropriate periods and capital letters. • reread a writing entry and edit it by putting in the appropriate exclamation points, questions marks, and capital letters.
COMMITMENT 1 day	• create a plan for remembering to automatically use end punctuation and beginning capitalization in each sentence.	• celebrate an edited piece of writing and put it on display in the classroom.
TOTAL: 6 DAYS		

SPOTLIGHT on Strategy

- Enhancing Comprehension Strategies Through Series Books
- Enhancing Craft Strategies: Authors as Guides

Strategy is thinking about what tools (physical or cognitive) we need and have available to understand and solve a problem, creating a plan, and putting the plan into action to solve the problem. The effective reader and writer and thinker asks: What are the ways of looking at this problem others have successfully employed, and what "tricks of the trade" can I use? We often spend time teaching different strategies separately (making connections or asking questions, for example) when the real challenge is how to help our children understand what type of strategy would be best used to solve a particular problem and then identifying the particular strategy to solve it. The strategies we use as readers and writers depend on our intuitive understanding of what is happening in that moment as we read and write, and how that relates to the goal we are trying to achieve. By properly identifying the problem, we can use the right strategy to fix it.

In *Strategies That Work*, Stephanie Harvey and Anne Goudvis (2000) write:

"The term strategic reading refers to thinking about reading in ways that enhance learning and understanding. Researchers who explicitly taught students strategies for determining important ideas (Gallagher, 1986), drawing inferences (Hansen 1981), and asking questions (Gavelek & Raphael, 1985) found that teaching these thinking/reading strategies improved students' overall comprehension of text. Research by Palincsar and Brown (1984), and Paris, Lipson, and Wixon (1983), however, suggests that it isn't enough for students to simply understand a given strategy. They must know when, why, and how to use it."

In second grade, our students are developing keen connections to characters and story lines, which guide them though increasingly sophisticated narratives and keep them engaged in series books as they build stamina. In these next units we will take a close look at how we can help our students become more strategic in thinking about theme, allegory, and symbolism as readers, and we will explore how we feel about these world issues as writers. For more information on strategy units for your second-grade readers and writers and how we can categorize strategies so as to teach them effectively, see pages 73–79 in *The Complete 4 for Literacy*.

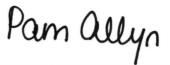

Making Meaning

Series books have been a gift to effective reading instruction and to children who adore them! For the reader in the midst of change, series books are a haven of sameness. The comfort of their sameness offers the growing reader the chance to take risks as readers—thinking about characters and story patterns, reading longer, stronger, and faster.

Enhancing Comprehension Strategies Through Series Books

STRATEGY

Why Teach This?
- To enable students to develop self-monitoring strategies.
- To provide students with tools for comprehension.
- To help students learn that reading is a meaning-making process.

Framing Questions
- How can we recognize when our comprehension is breaking down?
- How can we use fix-up strategies to aid our comprehension?

Unit Goals
- Students will identify when they don't understand a part of a text.
- Students will stop and think during reading to ensure that the text is making sense.
- Students will reread parts of a text to maintain comprehension.
- Students will decide to read ahead and think back as a strategy to maintain comprehension.
- Students will use collaboration, such as talking to a partner, to ensure that they are making meaning in a text.
- Students will use what they know about words to support meaning

Anchor Texts
- Frog and Toad series by Arnold Lobel

Resource Sheet
- Checking for Meaning Parent Letter (Resource 3.1)

Categorize series books so they are easy for your students to find.

Unit Assessment Enhancing Comprehension Strategies Through Series Books	STRATEGY		
Student name:	EMERGING	DEVELOPING	INDEPENDENT
Identifies when he or she loses meaning while reading.			
Uses "stop to think" strategy to monitor comprehension.			
Uses rereading as a tool for clarifying meaning.			
Uses the "skip and return" strategy to clarify meaning.			
Uses context clues and word parts to determine the meaning of a word and clarify a part of a text.			
Uses collaborative structures, such as talking to a partner, to make meaning in a text.			
Thinks about series characters and structures to make meaning in a series text.			

Stage of the Unit	Focused Instruction You will	Independent Practice Students will
IMMERSION 2 days	• define series books. • model browsing through a variety of series texts.	• browse through a variety of series texts. • think about what series they may want to stick with and study for the next few weeks.
IDENTIFICATION 3 days	• read aloud from the chapter "The Corner" from *Frog and Toad All Year* and model stopping at a place when the reading does not make sense; create an anchor chart naming the comprehension strategies. • read "Ice Cream" from *Frog and Toad All Year* and model "stopping and thinking" as you read. • read "The Surprise" from *Frog and Toad All Year* and model how reread tricky parts to improve comprehension.	• read independently noticing when they get stuck and what they do to get through that part. • practice "stopping and thinking" as they read their independent texts. • practice rereading as they read their independent reading.

GUIDED PRACTICE 8 days	• read *Frog and Toad Together* and model how to use the "skip and return" strategy for reading comprehension. • read from *Frog and Toad Together* and model how to figure out words you do not know by looking at the context of the sentence. • read *Days With Frog and Toad* and model how to stop and talk to improve reading comprehension. • read "Spring" from *Frog and Toad Are Friends* and model how to use the chapter title as a comprehension strategy. • identify the character or personality traits of the characters in *Frog and Toad*. • identify how the characters in *Frog and Toad* react to certain situations and how knowing their actions might help us monitor for meaning as we read. • using the *Frog and Toad* series, model how to monitor for meaning by thinking about the structure in the series. • review chart identifying the structures that support readers and identify one in Frog and Toad such as episodic chapter or strong chapter titles.	• read and use the "read ahead and think back" and the "skip and return" strategies. • put sticky notes on words they do not understand in their independent reading. • talk to a partner about their independent reading both before and after reading as a strategy to comprehend a text. • discuss with a partner the chapter title of the series book they are reading and think about how the title can help them understand their book. • talk with a partner about the character traits of one of the characters in their independent reading. • discuss with a partner how a character in their independent reading usually reacts to a situation; identify one example and mark it with a sticky note. • with a partner, discuss the structures that are consistent throughout their series. • place a sticky note on a structural element that helped them read.
COMMITMENT 2 days	• demonstrate how to create a bookmark that will remind them of strategies learned in this unit. • assess and reflect on what we've learned to do that will add to our repertoire as readers.	• create a bookmark with the comprehension strategies on it. • discuss with partner what you have learned to do in this unit.
TOTAL: 15 DAYS		

Getting Started

Share your own enthusiasm for series books and discuss how you, too, love their sameness and predictability.

Structures and Routines

With all the different books in the room, some predictable challenges may crop up. Here are some of our solutions:

Predictable Problems	Possible Solutions
My students have trouble working in a group together and staying on task.	Create groups for this series study using your knowledge of how students work together. Students should each choose three different series they are interested in studying. They will get one of their choices, but not necessarily their first choice.
We do not have enough books in our classroom to support the series study.	Series books are easy to find in your local library. In addition, using bonus points from book orders or asking students to donate books when they have moved on in their reading are two great ways to build up your supply of series books.
My students say they are finished doing the series work before the time is up.	Use an egg timer to guide students with the amount of time they should be working on a particular day. If they finish the task, students can spend time reading another book in the series.

Teaching Materials

In this unit, our lessons will center around a class anchor text or texts, so we can model for our students how we read series books. *Frog and Toad* by Arnold Lobel, *Henry and Mudge* by Cynthia Rylant, *Lionel and His Friends* by Stephen Krensky, and The Rainbow series by Daisy Meadows are all good choices for anchor texts.

Choosing Series Books

Books for vulnerable readers

Title of Series	Author	Fountas & Pinnell Level	Text Features
Biscuit	Alyssa S. Capucilli	Level F/G	• Simple sentences • Repetitive structure in each book
Danny the Dinosaur	Syd Hoff	Level J	• Simple sentences • Endearing characters • Look of chapter book, but no chapters

Henry and Mudge	Cynthia Rylant	Level J	• Dependable characters • Simple chapter book format • Table of contents • Use of dialogue • Theme that carries through each book
Littles First Readers	John Peterson	Level J	• More sophisticated text • Predictable characters • Supportive pictures • Look of chapter book, but no chapters
Poppleton	Cynthia Rylant	Level J	• Simple chapter book format • Table of contents • Supportive chapter titles • Episodic
Young Cam Jansen	David Adler	Level J/K	• Strong, predictable characters • Mystery series • Clues in story to support comprehension
Chicago and the Cat	Robin M. Koontz	Level J/K	• Beginning chapter book • Short episodic chapters • Central theme or event in each chapter • Simple humor • Dialogue

Books for steady readers

Title of Series	Author	Fountas & Pinnell Level	Text Features
Hopscotch Hill School Books	Valerie Tripp	Level K	• Simple and appealing layout • About typical school events • Introduction page with pictures of each character • Supportive pictures and chapter titles
The High-Rise Private Eyes	Cynthia Rylant	Level K/L	• Reader-friendly layout • Mystery series • Supportive table of contents and chapter titles • Introduction page introduces character and mystery • Sophisticated vocabulary
Nate the Great	Marjorie W. Sharmat	Level K/L	• Mystery series • No chapters or sections • Consistent character
Frog and Toad	Arnold Lobel	Level K	• Episodic chapters • Sophisticated humor • Strong friendship theme • Dialogue

| The Golly Sisters | Betsy Byars | Level K/L | • Historical fiction
• Detailed chapter titles
• Supportive pictures |
| Commander Toad | Jane Yolen | Level K/L | • No chapters
• Complex vocabulary and punctuation
• Word bubbles
• Sophisticated humor |

Books for strong readers

Title of Series	Author	Fountas & Pinnell Level	Text Features
Cam Jansen	David Adler	Level L	• Mystery series • Clues throughout series • Strong female character • Uses word "click" as a scaffolding device
The Rainbow Fairies	Daisy Meadow	Level L	• Seven books in series (one for every color of the rainbow) • Starts with a poem that summarizes the plot • Introduces main character in first chapter • Short, fast-moving chapters • Varied punctuation
The Littles	John Peterson	Level M	• Adventure series • Strong setting • Themes • Multiple scene changes • Strong picture support
Cobble Street Cousins	Cynthia Rylant	Level M	• Similar settings in each book • Three lead female characters • Sophisticated vocabulary • Extended dialogue • Strong plot with clear solution
Magic Tree House	Mary Pope Osborne	Level M	• Mystery series • Historical settings • Strong chapter titles • Fair amount of picture support • Groups of four titles arranged around the same mystery • Dependable characters
Animal Ark Pet	Ben Baglio	Level M	• Friendship, competition, and animal themes • Longer chapters • Strong dialogue • Complicated sentence structure

The Kids of Polk Street School	Patricia Reilly Giff	Level M	• Realistic fiction • Numbered, short chapters • Simple sentences throughout • Some picture support
Jenny Archer	Ellen Conford	Level M	• Mystery series • Strong female main character • Short chapters • Some picture support
Zack Files	Dan Greenberg	Level M	• Fast-moving plot • Short text • Strong dialogue and plot • End of each book in series contains introduction to next one
Jigsaw Jones Mystery	James Preller	Level M	• Strong main characters who are introduced in the first few texts • Detailed chapter titles and pictures • Clues given in text must be remembered through the whole book
Melvin Bederman Superhero	Gren Trine	Level M	• Sophisticated punctuation • Strong dialogue • Chapter titles • Predictable characters

Stages of the Unit

Immersion

Parents are often doubtful about series books. They look "light" and sometimes seem downright silly, so some parents worry that these books are not "pushing" their kids enough. This becomes an excellent opportunity to teach parents the value of these books and encourage them to nurture their children's interest in them. In addition to being fun, series books are also instructional.

Checking for Meaning Parent Letter

Dear Parents,

Series books provide support for readers in many ways. Their predictable and definitive structures allow readers to make meaning and think about this process.

We are going to read a lot of series books together this month. Please encourage your child to enjoy them, reread them, and notice their patterns. Even if you think they might be a bit easy, don't dissuade your child from enjoying them again. We are using these books to teach important comprehension strategies. Thank you!

Warmly,

RESOURCE 3.1

Identification

Explicitly identify, name, and define the strategies that a reader uses to monitor for meaning in a series book.

Guided Practice

Students do reading exercises that further develop their ability to recognize a breakdown in meaning and apply a strategy for correcting the situation.

Commitment

Students reflect on their learning and create a strategy bookmark that lists the specific fix-up strategies that worked best for them. This bookmark serves as a reminder of strategies to use as students read independently throughout their year.

Day-by-Day Lessons

DAY 1 Immersion

Focused Instruction

Over the next few weeks, we will be looking closely at series books. In a series of books, an author creates repeating characters who have different adventures in each of the books. As a class, we will study the Frog and Toad series. In small groups you will study your own series. In order to choose a series that will work for you, remember to think about finding books that you are interested in and that feel "level" (not too easy and not too hard).

- Show students the different series books they can choose from.

Independent Practice

- Students browse through two different sets of series books.

Wrap-Up

- Students share their thoughts.

DAY 2 Immersion

Focused Instruction

Today we are going to look through a few more series books and then decide what series we want to study. As you look through the books, think about which series you'd like to stick with for a long period of time. Consider the characters, the themes, and your interest level in the books. At the end of reading time today, we will decide on the series we are going to read.

Independent Practice

Your reading work today is to continue to browse through series books.

- Students browse through two more series books.

Wrap-Up

Each of you looked closely at four different series. We are now going to decide the series we will study for the next few weeks. Remember, your choice needs to be a series that you feel passionate about and one you can stick with over time. It also needs to feel level for you as a reader.

- Make a chart identifying the readers and series they are reading.

Series	Readers
Biscuit	Jon, Tameka, Gabe, Erin
Poppleton	Alex, Juan, Emily
Nate the Great	Sheila, Peter, Aubrey, Derek

DAY 3 Identification

Focused Instruction

We have now chosen the series we are going to study over the next few weeks. The most important part of reading a book is to understand what we're reading. When something does not make sense, we need to monitor and use strategies to make sense of our reading.

We need to be aware of those parts of books where we do not understand what is happening. So for the next few weeks, I want for us to really look at what it means to be a reader who checks for meaning and uses strategies when they get stuck.

- Read aloud *Frog and Toad All Year*. In the chapter titled "The Corner," model confusion in the tricky part where Frog is waiting for Spring "around the corner."

- Model thinking aloud what that means before reading on.

Independent Practice

Today you will be reading your series book. If you get to a part that doesn't make sense and is tricky for you, put a sticky note at the place where you got stuck. Think about what you did as a reader to help you get through that part.

- Students read in their series books and place sticky notes on places where they lost their way while reading.

Wrap-Up

Some of you came to a part in your reading today that did not make sense. Let's talk about some of these tricky places and name things we can do when this happens. We will practice using these different strategies over the next few weeks to better understand our series books.

- Chart responses of specific strategies readers are using. Sample chart:

How do readers monitor for meaning?	How does this help you as a reader?
Stop reading and think about the tricky part (stop to think).	Slowing down and stopping helped me to take time to make sense of a tricky part.
Go back and reread.	Rereading helped me get my thinking straight and reading it again gave me more information.
Read ahead and then think back about the tricky part (skip and return).	Reading ahead gave me the information I was missing and made the tricky part make sense.
Use what I do know to find the meaning of a word or part that doesn't make sense.	When I use what I know and what the book tells me, I can figure out a word or part that does not make sense.
Talk to a partner in my series group.	Talking to a partner gave me new ideas that I was not thinking about before.

As we continue in our series work, we will learn other ways to monitor for meaning in our books.

> **Other ways we can monitor for meaning in a series book:**
> Use chapter titles.
> Use what we know about the character's personality.
> Use what we know about how the series is structured.

DAY 4 Identification

Focused Instruction

Sometimes when I am reading, my mind starts to wander and I think about other things, or I am reading a part and I suddenly forget what I am reading. When that happens, I stop and ask myself, "Does that make sense?" After I stop, I think about that part before I go on. I call this strategy "stop to think." I want you to try this during a tricky part today.

- Reread the chapter "Ice Cream" from *Frog and Toad All Year* to model "stopping to think."
- Have students turn to a partner and talk about how they "stopped to think."

Independent Practice

Use your series book to practice checking in with your reading. Every few pages, stop and make sure that the part you've just read makes sense. If you get to a tricky spot, slow down and stop to think about what you just read. Put a sticky note on the place where you stopped to think.

- Students read from their series book and practice the "stopping to think" strategy.

Wrap-Up

Today many of you stopped to think as you read. Talk to a partner next to you. Show them where you put your "stop to think" sticky note.

DAY 5 Identification

Focused Instruction

Another strategy you can use when you do not understand what you are reading is to reread. You can reread the last few paragraphs of a series book to remind you of what happened the last time you put the book down, especially if you were not finished with the book. You can reread a word that does not seem to be coming out right. And most important, you can reread when you get to a really tricky part. Let me show you how I do that in Frog and Toad All Year *in the chapter called "The Surprise."*

- Think aloud and model for students how you reread to make sense of a part of the text.

Independent Practice

When you are reading today, if you get to a part that does not make sense, reread that part one or two times slowly to help you figure out what is happening.

- Using their individual series text, students reread parts where the meaning is breaking down.

Wrap-Up

Who used rereading as a strategy today and how did it help you as a reader?

- Add students thoughts to the right-hand side of the class strategies chart.

DAY 6 Guided Practice

Focused Instruction

Sometimes when we are reading, we come to a part we cannot understand. A strategy we can use when this happens is called "skip and return." If we skip over a small part of the reading and see what happens next, it sometimes helps us to think about what would have made sense in the part we skipped. Watch how I do this with this part of the book Frog and Toad Together.

- Model "skip and return" strategy in *Frog and Toad Together*.

Independent Practice

Today as you continue to read in your series books, try the "skip and return" strategy if you get to a part you do not understand.

- Students read in their series books and try "skip and return" when they get to a part they do not understand.

Wrap-Up

Today we tried the "skip and return" strategy. How did this strategy help you understand the books you were reading better?

- Add thoughts to the strategies chart.

DAY 7 Guided Practice

Focused Instruction

As readers, sometimes we come to words that we do not understand. One strategy we can try is to keep reading and try to figure out the word based on the context and what would make sense.

- Read from *Frog and Toad Together*.

Independent Practice

When you come to a word you do not know today, try skipping and returning to it or stopping to think about what the word could mean based on what you know about the series and what you are reading.

- Students read series books and put a sticky note on any word they had to think about.

Wrap-Up

What are some of the words that were tricky for you?

- Chart words and how students tried to figure out what they mean.

DAY 8 Guided Practice

Focused Instruction

One of the most important things to do to help monitor for meaning is to have conversations about books. When we talk to others about our reading, it helps clarify things we don't understand. Let's read Days with Frog and Toad. *While I read, we are going to stop and talk two times during our reading. When we stop, talk about either a part you did not understand, something you liked, or something you noticed about the characters or anything else in the book.*

- Read the book *Days With Frog and Toad*. Stop and have students turn and talk two times during the reading.

Independent Practice

Today during Independent Practice, you will stop and talk about the chapter you are reading to students in your small group. We will stop twice to talk.

- Students read and stop to talk in order to discuss a tricky part of their books and make meaning.

Wrap-Up

Turn to the group next to you and share what you talked about during your reading time today. How did this help you better understand your reading?

DAY 9 Guided Practice

Focused Instruction

Our series books help us to make sense of our reading. They do that in a few ways. One way is through chapter titles. Chapter titles help us to think about and predict what may happen in the chapter. It gives us a clue as to what the chapter may be about. Let's look at Frog and Toad Are Friends. *The first chapter is called "Spring." What does that tell us? What information does that give us about the chapter? Turn to the person next to you and think about what the chapter "Spring" may have in it.*

Independent Practice

- Students tell their partner the title of the current or next chapter they are reading. They share with their partner some thoughts about what this chapter is about and then continue to read their series books.

Wrap-Up

Turn to the person next to you and talk about how the chapter titles helped you think about your books.

DAY 10 Guided Practice

Focused Instruction

We can use the characters in series books to help with comprehension. When we read books in a series, we begin to learn characters' traits, and these can help us to better understand the book. For example, we have been reading Frog and Toad books together. What are some personality traits of Frog and Toad?

- Students turn and talk about what they now know about Frog and Toad as characters.
- Chart their responses.
- Sample chart:

Frog	Toad
organized	messy
responsible	careless
clean	sleepy
busy	lazy
a good friend	a good friend
takes care of Toad	sometimes cranky
serious	needs help

Because we know all of these things about Frog and Toad, it makes it easier for us to understand the series. We have a good idea of how both characters may act in a situation.

Independent Practice

Your reading work today is to think deeply about the characters you are studying before you read more of your series books. Spend some time talking with a partner or your group about the character in the series just like we did for Frog and Toad. This will help you to better understand character actions as you read.

Wrap-Up

What are some of the character traits that you and your partner or small group discussed? Turn to another group and discuss whether any of your traits were the same. How did this help you as readers?

DAY 11 Guided Practice

Focused Instruction

Yesterday we thought about how character traits can help us with our comprehension as we read. Today we are going to think about character actions. A character often responds to situations in a very similar way over the course of a series. For example, Frog usually helps Toad out of some situation. Think about the characters in your series books. How do they react to certain situations?

Independent Practice

Work with your series group or a partner. Take some time to talk about how the characters in your series react to certain situations. Keep this information in your head as you read today. If you get to a spot in your reading where your character either reacts in the way you thought or in a different way, put a sticky note at that spot.

- Students read from series books, looking for how characters respond to situations.

DAY 12 Guided Practice

Focused Instruction

The last strategy we are going to learn to help monitor for meaning as we read series books is to think about the structure in a series. Series books each have the same format. This is one of the things that makes them a series. In Frog and Toad we know that each chapter is really its own little story. This can help us as we read the book—we know that when we finish a chapter, the next one will be another little story.

Independent Practice

Your reading work today is to spend some time talking about some of the structures of your series books. Are there chapters? Is there strong picture support? Is there something that happens over and over again in each book? How do these structures help you better understand the series?

- Students meet with their series groups and talk about what structures are consistent throughout the series.

Wrap-Up

Let's chart some of the similarities and differences across the different series we are reading.

- Sample chart:

Name of Series	Structures That Support Reader
Frog and Toad	Episodic chapters, four chapters in most of the books, problem and solution in each of the chapters, strong chapter titles
Magic Tree House	Something gets solved in each book; every four books are solving part of the same mystery (The Mystery of the Tree House, books 1–4); strong chapter titles

DAY 13 Guided Practice

Focused Instruction

Yesterday we talked about the structures that support us in the series books. Today we are going to use our time to read through our series and see how these structures help us. As you are reading, think back to your conversations yesterday. Put a sticky note when you find a place where one of these structures helped you as a reader.

Independent Practice

- Students continue to read from their series. When they find a place where the structure of the series helped them, they mark it with a sticky note.

Wrap-Up

Let's look back at our chart from yesterday and add how some of these structures helped us as readers today.

DAY 14 Commitment

Focused Instruction

We have spent the last few weeks looking closely at different series books. For the next two days, we are going to celebrate all we have learned and create a tool that will allow us to remember strategies we can use to monitor for meaning as we read. We are going to make a bookmark to remind us of the nine strategies we use to check for meaning.

Independent Practice

- Students make a bookmark listing these strategies, using words and pictures.
- Sample bookmark:

My Checking for Meaning Strategies
• Stop to think
• Reread
• Skip and return (read ahead and then think back about the tricky part)
• Use what I know to find the meaning of a word or part
• Talk to a partner
• Use chapter titles or picture support
• Think about character personality traits
• Think about character actions
• Think about how the series is structured

Wrap-Up

- Students share their bookmarks.

DAY 15 Commitment

Focused Instruction

Let's celebrate and talk to other groups about your work.

Independent Practice

Find a classmate from another series group. Spend some time sharing whether you liked the series you studied and why you would recommend the series to others.

Wrap-Up

- Celebrate what you've learned. Create a class list of favorite series or create a recommendation board that identifies which series the class feels most strongly about.

Authors as Mentors

In a response to an author study Patty's class was doing, author Betsy Byars wrote: "When you write, you are an author. And when you are an author, you need to write in a way that makes the reader want to listen—you need to write with authority. Author and authority. The two words go together."

Second graders watch everything and everyone to emulate what they admire. They try to walk just like a big brother. They cook the pancakes just like their dad. Writing is no different. Writers need guides, mentors, heroes. That is what this unit is all about.

Enhancing Craft Strategies: Authors as Guides

STRATEGY

Why Teach This?

- To enable students to be strategic writers who understand the role of using techniques to enliven their writing.
- To understand how to craft a piece of writing.
- To help students understand that all writers use authors as mentors to increase their abilities.

Framing Question

- How can we learn from Tomie dePaola as a guide and become writers who can craft a text?

Unit Goals

- Students will identify elements of Tomie dePaola's writing.
- Students will understand how dePaola's life has influenced his writing.
- Students will use their own lives to get ideas and material for their own texts.
- Students will incorporate craft elements into their own writing.

Anchor Texts

The following books by Tomie dePaola:
- *The Art Lesson*
- *The Baby Sister*
- *The Legend of the Indian Paintbrush*
- *Nana Upstairs and Nana Downstairs*
- *The Popcorn Book*
- *Strega Nona*

Resource Sheets

- Author Study Parent Letter (Resource 3.2)
- Author Information (Resource 3.3)
- Author Comparison: How Am I Like Tomie? (Resource 3.4)
- Author-Inspired Writing (Resource 3.5)
- Author-Inspired Writing Ideas Paper (Resource 3.6)
- Student Editing Checklist (Resource 3.7)

Unit Assessment Enhancing Craft Strategies: Authors as Guides			STRATEGY
Student name:	EMERGING	DEVELOPING	INDEPENDENT
Identifies at least three strategies found in Tomie dePaola's writing.			
Names topics that the author writes about in his texts.			
Makes connections from the author to his life and experiences, identifying at least one way he gets ideas.			
Writes using one line of dialogue.			
Uses at least one other technique learned in this unit in his or her writing.			

Stage of the Unit	Focused Instruction You will	Independent Practice Students will
IMMERSION 5 days	• read *The Art Lesson* and discuss it, asking, "What does Tomie dePaola write about? What do we notice about the writing?" • read *Strega Nona* or *The Legend of the Indian Paintbrush* and discuss how his writing of a tale differs from that of his memoir texts. • read excerpts from the author's website, www.tomie.com; discuss dePaola's life and how it relates to you and your students. • read and discuss *The Baby Sister*; notice his techniques: his word choice and use of color words (snow-white diapers), dialogue, gathering ideas from his life, reflective ending, and so on. • read *The Popcorn Book* and name features of the book and techniques dePaola uses in his writing.	• browse and read a variety of Tomie dePaola texts to notice and discover techniques dePaola uses in his writing. • read a dePaola text with a small group and look for techniques we are noticing he uses. • discuss information about Tomie dePaola's life and how it might relate to his writing; make connections to dePaola's texts and discuss how they represent different aspects of his life. • read a dePaolo text with partner and put a sticky note on the techniques that they admire. • read a dePaola book and put a sticky note on one to three techniques that he used.
IDENTIFICATION 2 days	• model how to imagine our own writing in relation to a mentor author, asking students, "How are we like Tomie? How do we want to be like Tomie? What strategies are our favorites? What do we want to try?" • recap learning and categorize texts by technique.	• compare themselves with dePaola, identifying their favorite strategies and setting goals for using those strategies in their own own writing. • in small groups, categorize texts by theme, idea, technique, genre, and so on.

GUIDED PRACTICE 7 days	• demonstrate how to use the words and language of dePaola as a model. • model how to use your own life for your writing. • using a student or yourself, model how to write about a new idea from your ideas list. • model how to incorporate one line of dialogue into a piece. • revisit *The Baby Sister*, and demonstrate how to use description such as color words in your writing. • notice how dePaola uses different types of print for emphasis; model writing like dePaola by adding or changing text. • demonstrate choosing a strategy learned from your mentor authors such as creating a reflective ending.	• find a part of a dePaola text and try using his words and language to inspire and guide their own writing. • create a chart of new and fresh ideas, that they can write about. • choose one new idea to write about. • incorporate one line of dialogue into their piece. • incorporate description through the use of color words in their writing. • try italicizing or using bold print to emphasize a point they have made in their writing. • choose a strategy they would like to try and incorporate it into their writing, such as a reflective ending.
COMMITMENT 4 days	• model choosing one piece of writing to publish. • demonstrate revision by reexamining dePaola's beginnings and working on your own beginning. • model editing using editing checklist. • publish writing; model reflection of the process and discuss what students have learned from studying the work of dePaola.	• choose a piece to publish. • revise the piece by using words from another language, adding a new beginning or ending, in order to engage a reader. • edit the piece using an editing checklist. • publish the piece by making a cover and title for it; reflect on and celebrate what they have learned from reading the books of Tomie dePaola that they can use all the time in their writing.
TOTAL: 18 DAYS		

Getting Started

There are so many ways to learn about authors: via the Internet, books about authors, or author's notes on the backs and inside flaps of books. Include your students in the inquiry into authors' lives/work so you do not feel you have to start this unit with everything "done."

Structures and Routines

Students learn the different craft strategies their mentor author uses. They work in partnerships or with two partnerships coming together to make a small group, noticing the techniques of the author.

Teaching Materials

Choosing an Author

There are many authors to choose as mentors for an author study. The most important part of choosing an author is to make sure it is an author you love, and who has a large enough body of work for you all to study deeply.

Here are are some of our favorite authors for a second-grade author study:

Name of Author	Possible Writing Strategies to Study
Angela Johnson	descriptive language, use of punctuation, strong images
Eloise Greenfield	sound, rhythm, writing across genres
Charlotte Zolotow	repetition, writing across genre, memoir, sensory images
Mem Fox	repetition, rhyming, varied punctuation, creative stories
Cynthia Rylant	memoir, poetry, fiction, short stories, literary language, repetition
Steve Jenkins	nonfiction, comparisons, creating images, varied ways to give information
Donald Crews	print arrangement, detailed pictures, sound words, descriptive language
Amy Hest	varied narrative structures, bold print, varied punctuation
Ezra Jack Keats	use of dialogue, internal thinking, same characters used in multiple texts
Tomie dePaola	descriptive language, dialogue, characters develop over time

For this unit you will need at least five texts that you feel embody the characteristics of the author.

In this unit, we have chosen Tomie dePaola. He is a strong mentor author who uses his imagination, his own life story, and his ideas about the world. Also, he writes about genuine things that children can relate to easily.

Tomie dePaola Texts

Memoir	Fiction, Legends, and Tales	Nonfiction
The Baby Sister	*Strega Nona*	*The Cloud Book*
Nana Upstairs and Nana Downstairs	*The Legend of the Indian Paintbrush*	*The Popcorn Book*
26 Fairmont Avenue	*Big Anthony: His Story*	
The Art Lesson	*Bill and Pete*	
Tom	*The Legend of Bluebonnet*	
Stagestruck	*The Mysterious Giant of Barletta*	
Now One Foot, Now the Other	*Watch Out for the Chicken Feet in Your Soup*	

To learn about Tomie dePaola, you can read books about him, visit his website, research him on the Internet, and read his book blurbs:

- *Tomie dePaola: His Art and His Stories* by Barbara Elman
- Tomie dePaola's website is www.tomie.com
- Meet the Authors and Illustrators series from Scholastic
- Meet the Author series from Richard C. Owen Publishers

Choosing Craft Strategies to Study

Name of Craft Technique	How It Helps Our Writers
One line of dialogue	Teaches students how to use a line of dialogue instead of narration to convey what a character said.
Words from another language	Illuminates the essence and traits of a character, appealing to second-language learners.
Using your life to fuel your writing	Writers' best work comes when they use memories, favorite people, wonderings, observations, and experiences.
Changing print	Creates emphasis and excitement in a text.
Interesting punctuation	Use of ellipses, commas, question marks, and exclamation marks makes writing more interesting and emphasizes certain parts of a book.
Reflective endings	Emphasizes ending by separating it onto its own page.
Strong beginnings	Emphasizes beginning by separating it onto its own page.

Stages of the Unit

Immersion

Students browse books, internalizing the sound and rhythm of this author, getting to know the texts well, and finding favorites.

Identification

The students list their favorite craft techniques in Tomie dePaola books, the most interesting piece of information they've learned about the author, and then choose a technique of dePaola's they'd like to try in their own writing.

Guided Practice

Students integrate the strategies identified in Tomie dePaola texts into pieces they've written and new writing.

Commitment

Students demonstrate what they've learned from this mentor author. They publish, reflect, assess, and celebrate their learning.

Day-by-Day Lessons

DAY 1 Immersion

Focused Instruction

Today we will begin to study one of our favorite authors—Tomie dePaola. We are going to spend the next few days looking closely at some of his books and asking ourselves what we can learn from him in order to become better writers.

Students explore and identify the craft elements in Tomie dePaola's books.

- Read aloud *The Art Lesson*.
- Point out that the main character, Tom, appears in many of dePaola's books; note that he represents the author.
- Begin a chart titled "What Do We Notice About Books by Tomie dePaola?"

Independent Practice

Today you are going to receive a Tomie dePaola text to look at with a small group. Your work is to read or reread the book with a partner. Think about what you notice as you read.

- Students read and browse through the books.

Wrap-Up

What did you notice about your texts?

- Students share their thinking.
- Add these ideas to the class chart.

DAY 2 Immersion

Focused Instruction

Today we are going to read another book by Tomie dePaola. Yesterday we read a memoir and today we are going to read one of his fiction stories. While I am reading, think about some of the things you notice about the book. How is it the same and how is it different from yesterday's?

- Read one of his fiction/legend books such as *Strega Nona* or *The Legend of the Indian Paintbrush*.
- Continue to add to the chart documenting things the class notices about Tomie dePaola's writing.

Independent Practice

Today you are going look at another Tomie dePaola book with a small group. Read or reread the book and see what you notice about the style, photos, characters, or anything else. See if what we noticed yesterday occurs in the book: his consistent illustrating style and use of "Tom" as the main character.

- Students sit in small groups browsing through books and putting sticky notes on what they notice.

Wrap-Up

What did you notice about your text?

- Students share their thinking.
- Add these ideas to the class chart.

DAY 3 Immersion

Focused Instruction

Today I am going to share with you some information about Tomie dePaola. We learn from writers not only by looking at their writing style, but also by looking at who they are as people. Who we are, where we live, and what we do each day are things that influence what we do as writers. Let's learn about Tomie.

- Visit www.tomie.com or print out some information from the site to share with students. Note especially the fact that dePaola tells both classic tales and stories from his own life.

Students record information about Tomie dePaola.

Independent Practice

During our writing time today, I am going to ask that you continue to learn about Tomie dePaola. I am going to give you a page from his website. You and your partner will read what he says about his life and his writing and put a sticky note on something that is interesting or surprising to you.

- Students talk more about the author and put a sticky note on one piece of information they learned about Tomie.

Wrap-Up

Let's talk about some of the things we learned about Tomie dePaola.

- Sample chart:

What do we know about Tomie dePaola?	How do we think this effects his writing?
Tomie dePaola loved to draw as a child.	Tomie writes about art in some of his stories.

What are we learning about this author? Tonight you will continue to find out about Tomie dePaola. You can continue looking at his website, you can look at some of his books, read books about him, and so on. Add at least three pieces of information to the biographical information on the Tomie dePaola sheet (Resource 3.3).

DAY 4 Immersion

Focused Instruction

- Read aloud *The Baby Sister*. While reading, think aloud, making observations on the techniques that Tomie dePaola uses.

I love how he uses such exact, precise words to give us, the readers, a really clear picture of what he is talking about. For example, here in The Baby Sister, *he uses those vivid color words ("snow-white diapers and red ribbon in her hair") over and over again.*

- As you continue to read, ask students to put their thumb up if they notice another place in the text where this was used.
- Illuminate other techniques, such as use of dialogue, print changes (large print or italics), strong beginnings that get the reader's attention, and clear endings that make the books sound like they are over.

Independent Practice

We just learned some of the things Tomie does as a writer. He uses vivid color words, dialogue, different types of print, including bold and italics, and strong beginnings. Your work today is to look through one of Tomie's books that I will give to you and your partner and find where you see writing techniques you admire.

- Students browse the books, placing sticky notes on the spots where they notice techniques.

Wrap-Up

We have noticed four techniques that Tomie dePaola uses. In what books are we finding these strategies?

- Begin a new chart with four columns: the title, technique(s) used, genre of text, and connection to his life.
- Sample chart:

Title	Techniques	Genre	Life Connection
The Baby Sister	Dialogue Italics Color words	Memoir	About his life
Strega Nona	Dialogue Bold print	Tale	Fictional but uses his heritage/culture to generate ideas and words used
Now One Foot, Now the Other	Dialogue Strong beginning Print changes (Italics)	Realistic fiction	Fictional but uses childhood memories to generate story

DAY 5 Immersion

Focused Instruction

- Read aloud *The Popcorn Book*, one of Tomie's nonfiction works.

Today I am going to read one of my favorite Tomie dePaola books, The Popcorn Book. *This book is different than the other dePaola books that we have been reading. It is a different genre, nonfiction. As I read, listen for places where you hear something that Tomie dePaola is doing as a writer. We will add these findings to our chart.*

Independent Practice

I would like for you and your partner to continue to investigate this Tomie dePaola book. I am going to give you one page of the book. Look closely and put a sticky note in one to three places—where you see Tomie doing something we have noticed him doing as a writer. Also be on the lookout for any new techniques you find.

- Give partners a copy of one page of this text. Students record one to three noticings and spend the rest of Independent Practice rereading their favorite Tomie dePaola text.

Wrap-Up

What did we notice today? Is this something you have noticed before? Did anyone find something that we have not seen in any of our other books yet?

- Add to the technique chart.

DAY 6 Identification

Focused Instruction

We have been learning so much about what Tomie dePaola does as a writer. As writers, we do some of the things that he does in his books. Let's think about that. How are we like Tomie dePaola? How are we different? In what ways as writers do we want to be like Tomie dePaola?

- Create a Venn diagram, noting dePaola's strategies on the left, our strategies on the right, and common strategies in the middle (see Author Comparisons: How Am I Like Tomie dePaola?, Resource 3.4).

Independent Practice

- Students share information from dePaola's life and complete the Venn diagram.
- Students reread favorite Tomie dePaola texts, putting a sticky note on a technique they love and want to try.

Wrap-Up

In what ways would we like to be like Tomie dePaola as writers?

- Create a chart listing students' names and what strategy they want to try.

- Sample chart:

Name	Strategy I Want to Try
James	"Tomie writes about special people (like his two grandmothers) and writes about memories from his life. I want to try writing about those things, connecting them to my life."
Ian	"Tomie's books have great endings. They leave you with his final thoughts and make you remember his books. I want to work on my endings."
Megan	"Tomie changes the print in his books to show the words that are really important to him. I want to try that in my books."

DAY 7 Identification

Focused Instruction

Today I want us to think about putting all of our learning and smart thinking into categories. We are beginning to write using some of Tomie dePaola techniques, so I think it is important to review what we have noticed about him. Let's categorize our books.

- Model for students how to categorize texts by theme, genre, structure, crafting technique (use of page, placement of words, dialogue, use of italics and use of large print to emphasize words), structure, and so on.

Independent Practice

- Students put texts in piles by category. Discuss why you might think to put that text in that particular category. Discuss what to do if a text belongs in more than one category.

Wrap-Up

What have we learned about Tomie dePaola and his texts?

- Recap and review with students.

DAY 8 Guided Practice

Focused Instruction

We have learned so much about Tomie dePaola and good writing that now I want to put our ideas into action. We have talked about how one author can inspire another. So, I want to show you how I am going to find my favorite line or part from a Tomie dePaola text and use that line to inspire my own writing. I have so many choices of lines I could pick. Maybe I'll use, "'Now you are both upstairs,' he thought," from Nana Upstairs and Nana Downstairs. *Or, I can use. . .*

- Find a favorite line to write off of. Model for students how you can choose interesting, intriguing, or beautiful words to inspire your own writing.
- Students brainstorm and talk to their partners about what book they want to choose a line from.

Independent Practice

- Students find a part from their favorite text and find a line to use for inspiration. Then they "write in the air," saying out loud what they will be writing (see Resource 3.5).

Wrap-Up

Let's talk about how some of Tomie's words inspired our own writing.

- Have small-group discussions about the writing from today. Share one or two examples.

DAY 9 Guided Practice

Focused Instruction

We are learning so much from Tomie dePaola, and one important way I want him to teach us, or mentor us, is for us to think about where he gets his ideas. Today, we are going to go back to our information about his life to add to the list of ways we can get ideas. Let's think about how Tomie uses his life to generate ideas and fuel his writing. What can we learn from this as writers?

- Refer to the autobiographical information from dePaola's website.
- Model creating a writing ideas list inspired by dePaola's ideas.

Independent Practice

- Students create a writing ideas list inspired by dePaola and how he gets ideas (see Resource 3.6).

Wrap-Up

What ideas did you put on your writing ideas list?

DAY 10 Guided Practice

Focused Instruction

We now have so many more ideas for writing. Today we are going to take an idea from the chart we created yesterday, one that we have never written about before, and write about that idea.

- Use student (or yourself) to model how to use your list to choose an idea for writing.

Look at your list and choose an idea. Talk it out, or "write it in the air," first with your partner.

- Students find an idea, rehearse, and then go write.

Independent Practice

- Students write using their idea and help from their partner.

Wrap-Up

Check in with your partners, telling them how writing from this new idea went for you today.

DAY 11 Guided Practice

Focused Instruction

One technique that we noticed that Tomie dePaola uses is "one line of dialogue" in writing. My favorite example is from The Art Lesson. *Instead of saying that Tomie's parents told him not to write on the walls, he writes one line of dialogue: "No more drawing on the sheets, Tomie." Today let's try to add one line of dialogue to our writing.*

Independent Practice

- Students find a place in their writing where they can add one line of dialogue to what was said, rather than through narration.
- Students continue to generate new writing from their revised writing ideas lists.

Wrap-Up

- Feature one student's line of dialogue and ask the student to describe why he chose to use dialogue there.

DAY 12 Guided Practice

Focused Instruction

We noticed another technique that Tomie dePaola uses in his writing is to make his descriptions more effective by choosing his words with care, like the color words he uses. This gives the reader a clear picture of what he is describing in his stories. We saw this in The Baby Sister—*"snow-white diapers," "red ribbon in her hair," "yellow walls."*

Independent Practice

- Students find a part of their writing where they want to use color words to describe an object, place, or person. Students try this technique in different places and, if time permits, generate new writing.

Wrap-Up

Turn to the person next to you and share where you added color words to describe an object, person, or place.

DAY 13 Guided Practice

Focused Instruction

Yesterday we tried using vivid language to make our writing more descriptive. Today let's try another strategy that Tomie uses—adding different types of print. We noticed that Tomie uses italics and bold print to emphasize something. Remember in Strega Nona *when Strega Nona says the magic words over the pasta pot? Those words are in italics to emphasize them.*

Independent Practice

Today look for a place in your own writing to add different types of print to emphasize something. You can try italics or bold print.

Wrap-Up

Turn to the person next to you and share with them the place in your writing where you tried different types of print. How did this change the emphasis in your writing?

DAY 14 Guided Practice

Focused Instruction

Over the last few weeks we have noticed that Tomie does many things as a writer that makes his writing strong. He uses vivid color words, dialogue, different types of print, beginnings that get the reader's attention, and endings that are clear and concise. You may have noticed some other strategies as well. Today look back at your writing and try writing a reflective, strong ending. You can do this by separating out the ending and putting it on its own page.

Independent Practice

- Students try using a favorite technique, including writing a reflective ending, in their writing.

Wrap-Up

Let's share some of the strategies we tried today. How do you think trying this made your writing better?

DAY 15 Commitment

Focused Instruction

We are coming to the end of our unit, so we want to put this learning out into the world. One way we can do that is by publishing. We will decide which piece we'd like to polish up and share with others.

- Using a student to model this process, sift through the pieces the student has been working on during this unit and find one to polish, celebrate, and reflect on.

Independent Practice

- Students work alongside a partner to find a piece to polish and celebrate.

Wrap-Up

- Create a chart of students' names and the pieces they've each chosen, along with the techniques demonstrated in the piece. This class chart will identify what students are experimenting with in their writing, and allow you to plan small-group instruction and conferences.

DAY 16 Commitment

Focused Instruction

Yesterday we chose a piece to publish. One thing that writers do often is go back and revise. When we revise, we read through our writing and see if there are any changes we can make to make the writing better. It may be that you need to add more words or create a stronger beginning. You may try any of the Tomie dePaola writing strategies we have learned over the last few weeks.

Independent Practice

- Students read through the piece they chose and work on revising their writing.

Wrap-Up

Share with a partner some of the revisions you made.

DAY 17 Commitment

Focused Instruction

Each time we publish, one of the last things that we do is edit the piece. For us, editing has meant going through the piece and rereading what we have written. Let's look at our editing checklist and look at what we need to do to edit this piece.

- Model editing a piece, correcting and conventionally spelling words that are expected to be correct in students' writing.

Independent Practice

- Students use the Student Editing Checklist (see Resource 3.7) to edit and polish their work.

Wrap-Up

Turn to the person next to you and show them a place where you worked on fixing some "no excuse" spelling words.

DAY 18 Commitment

Focused Instruction

We have spent a lot of time working on our writing and learning how to use strategies like Tomie dePaola! Today we are going to finish up our pieces of writing by adding a cover, and then we are going to celebrate our writing.

Independent Practice

- Students work on finishing up their writing and adding a cover to their writing pieces.
- Students celebrate their writing in a small group.

Wrap-Up

We have learned so many strategies that Tomie uses as he writes, and we have tried them in our own writing. Remember, you can now use these strategies to make your writing stronger anytime that you write!

From Late Fall to Winter

As fall turns to winter, your second graders have developed their understanding of fairy tales and they have written beautiful fairy tales of their own. They are gaining confidence in their book choices and finding new role models as writers. Now, as winter approaches, they will be ready to explore nonfiction. Their awareness of the world continues to deepen and grow, and this reading and writing year deepens and grows along with them.

Chapter 4

WINTER

The Second Grader as Researcher

"Slow was careful and deliberate in everything he did. It might take him a while to decide, but once he put his head down and went forward, he would not turn back."

—from *A Boy Called Slow* by Joseph Bruchac

The winter brings us units of study in two major genre areas: fiction and nonfiction. We "punctuate" the season with a great unit on dialogue. Come with us as we journey through new learning landscapes together.

Characters Come to Life

Our second graders are busy in the hum of the life of the classroom. They have incorporated the routines of classroom life and they are eager to see what your next steps will bring to them. These units extend their thinking, their talk, and their investigations through an inquiry into story elements in reading and writing. As a bonus, students delight in the study of dialogue immediately following these two units. They see how dialogue helps them understand characters and their behaviors and bring them to life.

Investigating Characters in Reading   STRATEGY

Why Teach This?
- To show students that the traits of a character help bring that character to life.
- To teach students that sometimes authors tell a character's traits and other times authors show a character's traits through the character's behavior.
- To show students that interesting characters often have conflicting traits.

Framing Questions
- How can I learn about a character through the author's descriptions?
- How can I learn about a character through the character's behavior?
- Why do authors often endow a character with conflicting qualities?

Unit Goals
- Students will learn how to identify traits that bring storybook characters to life.
- Students will learn how to identify character traits told by the author ("overt") and those that are shown through a character's behavior ("covert").
- Students will learn that interesting characters often have traits that conflict.

Anchor Texts
- *Chinese New Year's Dragon* by Rachel Sing
- *Jessica* by Kevin Henkes
- *Shortcut* by Donald Crews
- *Skippyjon Jones* by Judy Schachner
- *Stand Tall, Molly Lou Melon* by Patty Lovell
- *Tough Boris* by Mem Fox

Unit Assessment Investigating Characters in Reading			STRATEGY
Student name:	EMERGING	DEVELOPING	INDEPENDENT
Identifies "overt" character traits told by the author.			
Identifies "covert" character traits revealed by the author through the character's behavior.			
Identifies conflicting traits in a character.			
Articulates why conflicting traits make a character interesting.			

Stage of the Unit	Focused Instruction You will	Independent Practice Students will
IMMERSION 2 days	• model (by thinking aloud) how a reader considers character traits explicitly described by the author as you read aloud *Stand Tall, Molly Lou Melon*. • as you read aloud *Skippyjon Jones*, model (by thinking aloud) the process by which a reader infers a character's traits from his actions, using the language, "If he did…that must mean that he is…"	• choose a book from the strong characters box and think about the character traits the author depicted in the story. • choose a book from the "strong characters" box and think about the character using this model sentence: "If he did…that means that he is…"
IDENTIFICATION 4 days	• name and define the term "character traits." • read *Shortcut* and create a chart of the characters and their traits and model adding information to the chart. • read *Jessica* and explain that authors don't always tell the traits of their characters, but at times show them through the actions of the characters. • explain that sometimes characters have traits that seem to conflict with each other, and that this can make a character interesting (as in *Tough Boris*); introduce conflict chart.	• read from familiar books and identify overt character traits for main characters. • read from independent book bag and, with a partner, reflect on traits of characters. • read from familiar books or book bag; with a partner discuss the actions of the characters and what the actions tell us about those characters. • begin to think about conflicting traits within a known character.

GUIDED PRACTICE 3 days	• guide students in identifying "overt" (told) character traits and "covert" (shown) character traits in familiar characters such as the characters in *Chinese New Year's Dragon*. • help students identify characters who may have contradictory traits. • confer with students about character traits in the books they are reading independently.	• identify overt (told) traits in familiar books and record them on a character card. • identify covert (shown) traits and record them on index cards. • identify conflicting traits within a character and record them on a character card.
COMMITMENT 1 day	• reflect on character traits both told and shown and how some characters may have traits that conflict.	• add new information from the character card to one of the two class charts.
TOTAL: 10 DAYS		

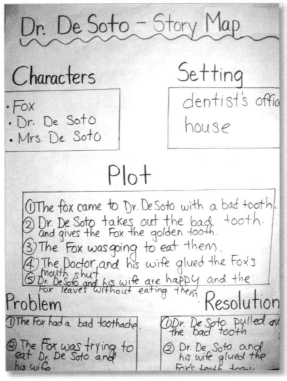

Charting the work helps create a record of student learning.

Investigating Story Elements: Writing Fiction

GENRE

Why Teach This?

- To teach students to identify the important elements of a story.
- To show students that planning the story elements improves a story.
- To help students plan story elements prior to writing stories.
- To guide students in creating a well-developed story that includes all story elements.

Framing Questions

- What are the important elements of a story?
- How can I plan story elements before I write?

Unit Goals

- Students will identify the important elements of familiar stories.
- Students will understand the need for planning story elements prior to drafting a story.
- Students will use graphic organizers to plan elements for a story.
- Students will write a story that includes strong story elements.

Anchor Texts

- *Doctor De Soto* by William Steig
- *Enemy Pie* by Derek Munson
- *A Million Fish…More or Less* by Patricia McKissack
- *My Name Is Yoon* by Helen Recorvits
- *A Perfect Snowman* by Preston McDaniels
- *Pet Show* by Ezra Jack Keats
- *Spoken Memories* by Aliki
- *Three Snow Bears* by Jan Brett

Unit Assessment Investigating Story Elements: Writing Fiction			GENRE
Student name:	EMERGING	DEVELOPING	INDEPENDENT
Identifies characters, setting, main problem, solution, and theme in familiar stories.			
Develops characters in own writing.			
Describes setting in own writing.			
Plans three sequenced events in own writing.			
Develops a clear main problem in own writing.			
Writes a logical solution to main problem.			
Plans a theme or "life lesson" in own writing.			

Stage of the Unit	Focused Instruction You will	Independent Practice Students will
IMMERSION 3 days	• look back at favorite read-alouds with strong story elements such as *A Perfect Snowman*; model identification of story elements by thinking aloud about characters and setting. • look back at favorite read-alouds such as *Pet Show*, thinking aloud about their problems and solutions. • continue to reread and revisit familiar books such as *The Three Snow Bears* while modeling retelling of the main events in the story; retell the kickoff event, three sequenced events, and the tie-up event.	• choose a familiar read-aloud and reread/revisit the book, thinking about the characters and setting. • choose a familiar read-aloud and reread/revisit the book, thinking about the problem and solution. • choose a familiar read-aloud and reread/revisit the book, thinking about the main events in the story.
IDENTIFICATION 4 days	• use *My Name Is Yoon* to discuss character and setting; define the terms "character" and "setting"; explain that great story authors (like Jan Brett and Helen Recorvits) use vivid details to describe the characters and the setting; chart definitions. • read *A Million Fish... More or Less*; name and define "main problem" and "solution"; explain that the main problem is the "big deal" problem the main character has in the story, and the solution is how that "big deal" problem gets fixed (second graders often need help differentiating the main problem from all the other minor problems in the story); chart definitions. • read *Spoken Memories* and define the term "theme"; explain that the theme of a story is the author's "life lesson" and that story writers leave them like secret messages; explain that readers must be clever enough to discover the "secret life lesson" in stories they read so they don't miss the best part; chart definitions.	• find a book from their independent book bags in which the author includes vivid details about the characters and setting. • find a book from their independent book bags in which the main character has a problem and thinks about how that problem gets solved. • find a book that has a life lesson in it; think about the life lesson the author is trying to teach through the story.

IDENTIFICATION (continued)	• explain that authors think about and plan their story elements before they begin writing their stories; use *Doctor De Soto* to illustrate this thinking.	• discuss with a partner story elements (including character, setting, problem, solution, and theme) for their own stories.
GUIDED PRACTICE 5 days	• model thinking through and articulating your ideas for story elements you will include: "I think I'll write a story about a coyote who lives in the desert. My coyote can't howl like the other coyotes. This is a problem because he feels left out. My coyote decides that he can dance when the moon is full instead of singing. My theme is that you can think of ways to overcome obstacles." • model planning character and setting for your own story. • model planning the problem and solution for your own story. • read *Enemy Pie*; model planning the theme or "life lesson" you hope to teach with your story. • model writing the sequenced events of the story.	• work with a partner and tell their ideas for story elements they are thinking about including in their stories. • write details for describing characters and setting for their own stories. • write the main problem and the solution for their own stories. • write the theme for their stories; tell how readers will know that this is the life lesson to be learned. • write the sequenced events for their stories.
COMMITMENT 2 days	• model writing a final story using the information from your planning. • model sharing a final story with a partner.	• write final stories including all story element details. • share their final stories with a partner.
TOTAL: 14 DAYS		

Characters Talk!

This unit complements the prior units so that your students can apply the impact of conventions to an understanding of characters and enhance the complexity and pleasure of story.

Using Dialogue and Punctuation to Bring Characters to Life

CONVENTIONS

Why Teach This?

- To teach students how to accurately read dialogue.
- To teach students how to identify dialogue through punctuation marks.
- To show students that dialogue is a powerful tool for bringing characters to life.

Framing Questions

- How are quotation marks used in print?
- Why is dialogue important in stories?
- In what ways does dialogue help develop the characters in a story?

Unit Goals

- Students will learn that quotation marks and commas are used to indicate dialogue.
- Students will understand that dialogue helps build strong stories.
- Students will learn that dialogue helps develop interesting characters in stories.

Anchor Texts

- *Chrysanthemum* by Kevin Henkes
- *The Gift of the Sun: A Tale From South Africa* by Dianne Stewart
- *Kiss Good Night* by Amy Hest
- *Tales of Oliver Pig* by Jean Van Leeuwen

Unit Assessment Using Dialogue and Punctuation to Bring Characters to Life			CONVENTIONS
Student name:	EMERGING	DEVELOPING	INDEPENDENT
Recognizes dialogue in print.			
Understands the role of dialogue in a story.			
Understands that written dialogue gives the audience some sense of a character's personality.			
Correctly reads dialogue in stories.			

Stage of the Unit	Focused Instruction You will	Independent Practice Students will
IMMERSION 2 days	• explain that in most of the story-books we read, the characters talk; thumb through a few familiar texts and give examples of famil-iar characters talking. • think aloud about how "talking sentences" look different from other text in the story; use *Kiss Good Night* to demonstrate this.	• search for examples of characters talking in familiar storybooks; think about why the characters are talking in these stories. • notice the ways in which "talking sentences" look different from the other sentences in the story.
IDENTIFICATION 3 days	• explain that authors use dialogue to bring their characters to life; play Guess the Character; say something a familiar character might say and have students guess the character ("I must visit 1,567 children tonight and leave money under all of their pillows!" —The Tooth Fairy). • introduce quotation marks; display pages of *The Gift of the Sun: A Tale From South Africa* on a pro-jection device; discuss placement of quotation marks and commas in the dialogue and explain that quotation marks "open" and "close" what is being said. • revisit the idea that dialogue in stories helps develop character; read dialogue from *Chrysanthe-mum* and discuss what it says about those characters.	• play Guess the Character with a partner. • while rereading a familiar storybook, notice the placement of quotation marks when a character is talking. • browse a familiar storybook with dialogue; read the dialogue out loud and think about what it says about the characters.
GUIDED PRACTICE 3 days	• read the chapter "A Bad Day" from *Tales of Oliver Pig*; show a page with the dialogue and then show it without (covering dialogue with sticky notes). How is the story different without the dialogue? • demonstrate reading dialogue in *Chrysanthemum* by changing your voice; discuss how characters bring a story to life. • choose a student or two to demonstrate reading dialogue aloud, each playing one of the characters in the story.	• look at chapters from Oliver and Amanda Pig stories with a partner and discuss what the dialogue does for the story and characters; practice reading the dialogue with a partner. • work with a small group and choose different characters to portray from *Chrysanthemum*; read and act out a part of the story with dialogue written on sentence strips or index cards. • practice reading dialogue with a partner, each playing one of the characters.
COMMITMENT 1 day	• model performing the rehearsed dialogue for the class.	• perform the rehearsed dialogue for the class.
TOTAL: 9 DAYS		

Admiring an Author

A wonderful interlude: take a text by any author you love (we use the author Charlotte Zolotow here), and do a one-week investigation of the text with your students. This intense focus is terrific for two reasons: One, your students will have a week to home in on specific craft elements in the text, and two, your students will take a piece through to the end of the writing process rapidly. The evidence of their learning will be very apparent in the work they do. They will be very proud to see craft elements emerge in their writing, and you will be too.

Growing a Sense of Language and Craft Through Text Study

STRATEGY

Why Teach This?

- To teach students how to use a text to guide their use of language and craft in writing.
- To enable students to use repetition and sensory details in their writing.

Framing Question

- How can we notice and admire the specifics of craft in a text?

Unit Goals

- Students will understand that writers can organize and structure their writing in a variety of ways.
- Students will identify how authors use techniques such as repetition, lively dialogue, precise words, and sensory images.
- Students will create an original literary text that uses repetition.
- Students will recognize sensory imagery in text and begin to apply it to their writing.

Anchor Text

- *The Moon Was the Best* by Charlotte Zolotow

Unit Assessment Growing a Sense of Language and Craft
Through Text Study

STRATEGY

Student name:	EMERGING	DEVELOPING	INDEPENDENT
Identifies the two external structures used in the text: listing memories and circularity.			
Chooses a vivid and engaging memory to write about.			
Identifies examples of dialogue, repetition, precise word choice, and sensory images.			
Uses purposeful repetition in a piece of writing.			
Uses at least one sensory image in a piece of writing.			

Stage of the Unit	Focused Instruction You will	Independent Practice Students will
IMMERSION 1 day	• read *The Moon Was the Best*, paying attention to the external structures and internal devices author Charlotte Zolotow uses to engage readers (repetition, dialogue, word choice, and sensory images).	• examine parts of the text on sentence strips with partners and discuss Zolotow's craft techniques.
IDENTIFICATION 1 day	• name the craft elements used in the text (repetition, dialogue, word choice, and sensory images); chart an example from the text for each; model for students choosing a memory from your life to write about.	• choose a memory from their lives and write a short entry about this memory.
GUIDED PRACTICE 4 days	• demonstrate using repetition of a carefully chosen word, phrase, or sentence in your writing. • demonstrate the use of visualizing and sketching to create a sensory image in a piece of writing. • model rereading the piece you wrote about your memory, noticing word choice; revise words to make them more engaging and vivid.	• work on writing incorporating the use of repetition. • add a sensory image to their writing. • attend to word choice in their writing by circling words in the piece to replace with more engaging and vivid words.

GUIDED PRACTICE *(continued)*	• revisit the end of the text and discuss the reflective, engaging ending; note that it uses dialogue and that it is circular; model creating an engaging and reflective ending.	• create a reflective ending for their writing.
COMMITMENT 1 day	• ask students what looking at one text has taught you to do in your own writing.	• publish their writing and celebrate with peers.
TOTAL: 7 DAYS		

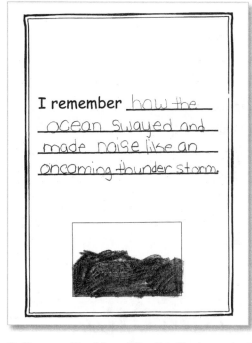

Callie uses *The Moon Was the Best* as a text to inspire her own writing.

SPOTLIGHT on Genre

- Exploring Learning Through Reading Nonfiction Texts
- Sharing Learning Through Writing Nonfiction Texts

There are a few great writers who have been able to write across several genres. E. B. White comes to mind. He wrote the classic children's books *Charlotte's Web*, *Trumpet of the Swan*, and *Stuart Little*. He wrote small humorous snippets for the *New Yorker* in the Talk of the Town column. And as if all that were not enough, he cowrote the seminal how-to guide to grammar: *The Elements of Style*. White was the rare genius who could accommodate all genres, fitting his observations, his wonderings, his memories, and his imagination into a wide variety of "containers." Great ideas are like water, flowing clear: a stream. Genre is a container we use to hold those ideas. The ideas are the same, but they look different depending on the container that holds them. Loneliness inside a poem, for example, looks different from loneliness inside a science-fiction novel. Courage inside a biography looks different from courage inside a letter. A clear idea, held inside the right container, can change someone's mind, even someone's life. See pages 47–61 in my book *The Complete 4 for Literacy* for a more detailed description of the elements and categories of genre and the importance of these units to the lives of our students, who are seeking to clarify, extend, and share from their own stream of ideas.

Pam Allyn

Nonfiction: Essential Readings, Joyous Writing

By reading nonfiction, we can access parts of life that otherwise might not be within our direct grasp. We can connect to the past. We can connect to nature. We can connect to other people's passions. Second graders are open to and endlessly questioning of the world. We are constantly trying to figure out how to respond to their questions, which are generally a combination of fact-seeking missiles and existential meditations on the nature of the universe. These units in nonfiction will provide our students with ways to learn about how this genre functions and how they can use it to answer some of their most urgent questions. The structure of a question-and-answer book provides them with nourishment for the open-ended "Why?" they are roaming around with this year.

Research has shown that 85 percent of the texts read by adults are nonfiction, and yet in school our children are being exposed to nonfiction only 30 to 40 percent of the time. In *Nonfiction in Focus* by Janice V. Kristo and Rosemary A. Bamford (2004), we learn that "even very young children can read and write nonfiction (Caswell & Duke, 1998) and that those early experiences establish a strong base for reading more sophisticated nonfiction in later grades (Newkirk, 1989; Pappas, 1991)." Kristo and Bamford note that "perhaps the most compelling reason for the rising tide of nonfiction is the possible impact it has on students. When you incorporate high-quality nonfiction into your program, you help students in many ways. Specifically, you:

- meet the needs of students with a range of reading levels and interests.
- provide examples of writing in various content areas.
- open the door to classroom research and inquiry.
- develop and expand vocabulary.
- influence growth and development of primary-grade readers and writers."

The icing on the cake is that your students will love studying nonfiction! Their curious minds are seeking and seeking, and their bountiful hearts are giving and giving. These units are a perfect match for those inclinations.

Exploring Learning Through Reading Nonfiction Texts

GENRE

Why Teach This?
- To engage students in deepening their understanding of nonfiction.
- To provide students with opportunities to learn through reading nonfiction texts.
- To enable students to understand how structure and features assist a reader.

Framing Question
- How can we use nonfiction's structure, purpose, and features to help us understand it?

Unit Goals
- Students will deepen their understanding of the difference between fiction and nonfiction.
- Students will learn how to use the nonfiction features of bold print, pictures, and captions to aid their reading.
- Students will understand how to use a glossary, introduction page, and table of contents .

Anchor Texts

- *Almost Gone: The World's Rarest Animals* by Steve Jenkins
- *Calling All Doves/El Canto de las Plaomas* by Juan Felipe Herrera
- *Duke Ellington: The Piano Prince and His Orchestra* by Andrea Pinkney
- *Explore and Discover Sharks* by Steven Savage
- *Freedom River* by Doreen Rappaport
- *Frog and Toad Are Friends* by Arnold Lobel
- *Knut: How One Little Polar Bear Captivated the World* by Juliana Hatkoff, Isabella Hatkoff, and Craig Hatkoff, and Gerald R. Uhlich
- *Look to the North: A Wolf Pup Diary* by Jean Craighead George
- *Rain* by Honor Hear
- *Rosa* by Nikki Giovanni
- *Watch Me Grow: Frog* by Lisa Magloff
- *What Do You Do With a Tail Like This?* by Steve Jenkins

Resource Sheets

- Nonfiction Reading Parent Letter (Resource 4.1)
- Nonfiction Reading Graphic Organizer (Resource 4.2)

Unit Assessment Exploring Learning Through Reading Nonfiction Texts			GENRE
Student name:	EMERGING	DEVELOPING	INDEPENDENT
Can name the difference between a fiction and nonfiction text.			
Understands that the purpose of nonfiction is to engage, inform, instruct, and answer.			
Identifies the use of bold print, pictures/photos, and captions in nonfiction texts and can explain their purpose.			
Uses the introduction page and letter to the reader in a nonfiction book and understands their purposes.			
Chooses a nonfiction text to read according to purpose.			

Stage of the Unit	Focused Instruction You will	Independent Practice Students will
IMMERSION 4 days	• use *What Do You Do With a Tail Like This?* by Steve Jenkins and *Scholastic News* or other classroom magazines to introduce the genre of nonfiction. • read from *Frog and Toad Are Friends* as an example of a book that is not nonfiction, and explain why; read a part of *Watch Me Grow: Frog* from the Dorling Kindersley series and compare it with a fiction book. • read *Explore and Discover Sharks* and discuss question-and-answer texts; introduce the "About the Book" page, the glossary, and features such as bold print, text placement, pictures and captions, headings, and sidebars; discuss why readers read nonfiction (because of an interest, to become informed). • read *Knut: How One Little Polar Bear Captivated the World*, and *Look to the North: A Wolf Pup Diary* to further identify features of nonfiction; discuss their use of comparisons and how these books interest and engage the reader.	• find a nonfiction text in the classroom library and browse through it. • notice features of nonfiction such as photos, captions, labels, fact boxes, glossary, table of contents, using a page from *Watch Me Grow: Frog*. • notice and name nonfiction features, using a page from *Explore and Discover Sharks* (or another text from this series). • read nonfiction texts and mark three features of this genre with sticky notes.
IDENTIFICATION 1 day	• recap discoveries by rereading class-generated nonfiction chart; discuss what kinds of topics readers might be interested in reading.	• choose nonfiction texts to read independently.
GUIDED PRACTICE 6 days	• use *Duke Ellington: The Piano Prince and His Orchestra* to model how to preview a nonfiction book in order to identify the subject and format and whether the book fits your interests and purpose. • read *Almost Gone: The World's Rarest Animals* to model how to use an introduction page and how it assists the reader. • continue reading *Almost Gone: The World's Rarest Animals* and demonstrate how to identify the big ideas in a topic and read to find out more about these ideas.	• preview the nonfiction book you chose and share findings with a partner; begin reading text. • read a nonfiction book that contains an introduction page; preview the introduction page and share findings with a partner. • share with a partner a big idea they have about their topic; read to find out more information on their topic.

GUIDED PRACTICE (continued)	• demonstrate how to use questioning to guide your reading of nonfiction; using *Rain*, think aloud, ask questions and find answers to your questions in the text. • use *Rosa* to demonstrate how a reader learns about a topic of interest; model for students how to use the Nonfiction Reading Graphic Organizer (Resource 4.2) to record what you've learned. • continue reading *Rosa* to model reading a nonfiction book of interest; demonstrate how to write thoughts and ideas (the my thinking box) responding to new factual information learned.	• share with a partner questions they have about their topic. • read a nonfiction text and fill out the Nonfiction Reading Graphic Organizer. • continue reading a nonfiction text and record thoughts in their thinking box.
COMMITMENT 3 days	• model how to create a split-page poster that demonstrates the learning about nonfiction and about your topic; include fact box, diagram, or other features to show information learned from nonfiction reading. • model for students using the right side of the poster thinking that illustrates what kind of nonfiction reader you are; share titles, topics, series, and so on that you like to read. • celebrate and share your learning about nonfiction!	• begin individual poster to demonstrate information learned from reading nonfiction. • continue creating nonfiction learning poster; use the right of the poster to reflect and share thinking about what topics/titles they find appealing. • share nonfiction posters and reflect on the kind of nonfiction reader they are.
TOTAL: 14 DAYS		

Getting Started

In *Is That a Fact?* Tony Stead emphasizes that there are "a number of purposes for writing nonfiction that we need to be aware of and certainly need to introduce to children in the primary grades."

There are many different forms of nonfiction that help readers explore and discover. However, the following are especially applicable to second graders:

What This Writing Does	Sample Forms
Writing that describes	• Feature article • Picture book • All-about text • Author profile • Brochure

Writing that explains	• Question-and-answer book • All-about text • Recipe • Letter
Writing that teaches	• How-to • Directions • Recipe • Manual • Question-and-answer book
Writing that persuades	• Book review • Poster • Letter • Picture book

Structures and Routines

Collaboration is essential. Students need frequent and varied opportunities to talk with peers about what they are reading and what they are writing, especially with nonfiction, where the conversations will be lively and informative.

Heterogeneous but like-minded partnerships work well. The compelling content provides an opportunity for students reading at different levels to have great conversations together.

Teaching Materials

Magazines

Carus Publishing features a continuum of leveled literature-based and nonfiction-based magazines that "grow" with the child. For example, if a child is just learning to navigate nonfiction, he might find some good material in *Click* magazine. As he progresses as a reader, he will be ready to look for articles in the sister publication, *Spider*. And if he is rocketing ahead of the class, he can turn to *Ask*. Carus also publishes the nonfiction magazines, *Appleseeds* and *Ladybug* (information on all these titles can be found at www.cobblestonepub.com/magazines.html).

Click This magazine is perfect for the second grader. Both nonfiction and fiction are featured in this magazine, as Click the mouse and his friends take readers on a journey into science, nature, art, games, and other activities.

Ask Published with the *Smithsonian* magazine, *Ask* invites young readers to explore the world through various topics, themes, disciplines, and ideas. Each issue is dedicated to a single theme or topic.

Appleseeds Another themed magazine, *Appleseeds* exposes readers to nonfiction writing about history, and culture. Each issue's articles, activities, and photos are written on one theme, allowing readers to fill their minds and imaginations with the new topics. Great for a strong reader.

Spider This is another example of an engaging multigenre magazine filled to the brim with articles, stories, "fabulous facts," and other engaging sections sure to keep steady and strong readers going for a while.

Ladybug Perfect for vulnerable and steady readers, *Ladybug* is a multigenre monthly magazine with interesting stories, activities, poems, articles, and directions for projects.

National Geographic Kids A lively, engaging, and fun-to-read magazine that explores our world. Each issue contains multiple articles and favorite sections such as Pet Vet, Weird But True, and What in the World? (Go to www.nationalgeo graphickids.com for more information.)

Your Big Backyard Published by the National Wildlife Federation, this magazine is a great way to bring second graders into the world of nonfiction through their curiosity about the natural world. Favorite sections include What's the Difference? which compares creatures, Ask Ranger Rick, recipes, posters, and excellent articles with engaging and informative photos. (Go to www.nwf.org for more information.)

Kids Discover Excellent nonfiction magazine on various topics in history and science for students in grades 2 and above. Each issue is devoted to a topic (e.g., pioneers, weather) with articles, photos, maps, recipes, and projects. Also, the website has a resource for teachers that allows you to enter your grade level, state, and the topic you are studying and will give you titles that will help you to meet state standards. (Go to www.kidsdiscover.com for more information.)

Classroom Libraries

In addition to newspapers and magazines, your classroom libraries should contain the following.

Nonfiction Texts

- Literary nonfiction/picture books
- Historical nonfiction
- Nonfiction with varying structures—how-to, all-about, question-and-answer
- Biography
- Science
- Narrative nonfiction

Nonfiction Texts in Baskets

You should have nonfiction genre baskets in your room, but nonfiction should also be part of other baskets in your classroom library. If you have baskets or sections for interesting and inspiring books that are must-reads, be sure to include nonfiction texts in addition to fiction. Baskets that should have a nonfiction component include:

- Recommendations
- Anchor texts
- New arrivals
- Topic baskets
  - Friendship

- Family
- Animals
- School

With the array of nonfiction books available to our readers, we have found it useful to look for texts according to structure. These are some of our favorite nonfiction texts structured as picture books, all-about books, question-and-answer books, and how-to books.

Reading nonfiction inspires collaborative conversations.

Nonfiction Picture Books

- *Actual Size*, Steve Jenkins
- *Animal Dads*, Sneed B. Collard III
- *Animals in Flight: What Would You Do*, Steve Jenkins
- *Big Blue Whale, One Tiny Turtle*, Nicola Davies
- *Caves and Caverns: Apples*, Gail Gibbons
- *The Cloud Book*, Tomie dePaola
- *Coral Reef, The City That Never Sleeps*, Mary M. Cerullo
- *Dogs, Cats*, Seymour Simon
- *The Librarian of Basra*, Jeanette Winter
- *Reptiles*, Steve Parker
- *The Shell Book*, Barbara Hirsch Lember
- *Somewhere Today*, Bert Kitchen
- *The Tortilla Factory*, Gary Paulsen
- *Urban Roosts*, Barbara Bash
- *Welcome to the Greenhouse*, Jane Yolen
- *Wild and Woolly Mammoths*, Aliki

All-About Books

- *Dinosaur Reports* (Little Red Readers), Peter Sloan and Sheryl Sloan
- *The Dolphin*, Animal Close-ups series
- Eye Know series, Dorling Kindersley
- *From Frog to Tadpole, A Safe Home For Manatees* (Let's Read and Find Out Science)
- *Let's Look at Animals*, Nicola Tuxworth
- *Living in a Rainforest, Living in Mountains*, Rookie Read-About Geography
- Look Closer series (*Reptiles, Sea Creatures*, etc.), Dorling Kindersley
- Touch and Feel series, Dorling Kindersley
- *Trees*, Joy Richardson
- Watch Me Grow series (*Bear, Butterfly, Frog*, etc.), Dorling Kindersley
- *Wild Baby Animals, A Day at Greenhill Farm*, Karen Wallace (Dorling Kindersley Readers)

How-To Books

- *Chop, Simmer, Season*, Alexa Brandenberg
- *Growing Radishes and Carrots*, Mondo Publishing
- *How to Make Salsa*, Mondo Publishing
- *How to Talk to Your Cat*, Jean Craighead George
- *Planning a Birthday Party*, Mondo Publishing
- *Six Things to Make*, Mondo Publishing

Question-and-Answer Books

- *All About Rattlesnakes*, Jim Arnosky
- *Are You a Butterfly?*, Judy Allen and Tudor Humphries
- *Dinosaurs and Other Prehistoric Reptiles*, Denny Robson
- *Explore and Discover Reptiles*, Claire Llewellyn
- *How Come? In the Neighborhood*, Kathy Wollard
- *How Do Flies Walk Upside Down?*, Melvin Berger and Gilda Berger
- *How to Be a Baby by Me, the Big Sister*, Sally Lloyd Jones and Sue Heap
- *I Face the Wind* (Science Play series), Vicki Cobb
- *I Wonder Why the Telephone Rings? and Other Questions About Communication*, Richard Mead
- *It Could Still Be a Fish* (Rookie Read-About Science series), Allan Fowler
- *What Lives in a Shell?* (Let's Read series), Kathleen Weidner Zoehfeld
- *Who Hoots?* Katie Davis
- *Why Do Cats Meow?*, Joan Holub
- *Why? The Best Ever Question and Answer Book About Nature, Science and the World Around You*, Catherine Ripley

Differentiation

It is important to consider the challenges nonfiction texts present so that readers can choose books that are level and not too uphill for them. However, one of the wonderful aspects of nonfiction reading is that children can step a bit outside their comfort zones because there is so much picture support for them, and they are compelled by topics of interest that push them forward in their reading. A combination of uphill, downhill, and level books for their book bags is key. The following is a list of what to consider when matching readers to nonfiction books:

External Organizing Structure Is this text a question-and-answer, all-about, or how-to book, and can the structure assist the reader as he navigates the text?

Internal Features Are there sidebars, zoom boxes, or charts in the text? Do these features of nonfiction explain the content or make the book more challenging to read and understand?

Vocabulary Does the book contain content-specific or challenging words?

Length What is the length of the text? Does it have particularly long sections?

Visual Presentation Do the illustrations, photos, and diagrams help the reader learn new information? Is there a lot of text on the page, making it harder to understand?

Independent Nonfiction Reading/Chapter Books

The following is a list of books that are perfect for independent nonfiction reading. These books are series books; some are structured into chapters. Because each series contains two to four reading levels, there are plenty of titles for vulnerable, steady, and strong readers.

Series	Sample Text	Author
Rookie Read-About Science	*Really Big Cats*	Allan Fowler
Step Into Reading	*Vanished! The Mysterious Disappearance of Amelia Earhart*	Monica Kulling
Hello Reader!	*Tornadoes!*	Lorraine Jean
Eyewitness Readers	*Titanic: The Disaster That Shocked the World!*	Mark Dubowski
Time for Kids Science Scoops*	*Butterflies!*	*Time for Kids* editors with David Bjerklie
Scholastic Science Readers	*Penguins*	Kathleen Weidner Zoehfeld
All Aboard Reading/ Science Reader	*Gorillas*	Patricia Demuth
Dorling Kindersley Readers	*Wild Baby Animals*	Karen Wallace
Puffin Easy-to-Read	*Why Do Rabbits Hop?*	Joan Holub

*These texts use the Fountas and Pinnell leveling system.

Stages of the Unit

Immersion
Engross your students in the breadth and depth of this genre through read-alouds and browsing.

Identification
Name features of nonfiction texts. Students recognize their interests in topics and that reading about those interests is something strong readers do.

Guided Practice
As your students begin to read nonfiction, steer them toward texts that will engage them and help them explore diverse topics. Demonstrate how to use the structure and features commonly found in nonfiction texts to make meaning and learn about the various topics.

Commitment

Students name what worked well for them as readers of nonfiction and reflect upon the topics and structures they enjoyed reading. They commit to reading nonfiction as the year continues to unfold and share their recommendations with one another.

Day-by-Day Lessons

DAY 1 Immersion

Focused Instruction

In this unit we will study nonfiction together. Let's look at What Do You Do With a Tail Like This? *by Steve Jenkins and our classroom news magazine,* Scholastic News. *What do you notice that is similar about them?*

- Note that both texts give information. Also note where the pictures and words are on the page and any features of nonfiction such as sidebars and captions.

Independent Practice

Find a text that you think is nonfiction. Spend some time with that text today, browsing, reading, rereading, and looking at the parts and pages.

Wrap-Up

Let's begin to share what you have noticed about these texts.

- Begin class chart. Name the text, reasons why the student thinks it is nonfiction, any features or genre elements noticed, and why a reader may choose to read this nonfiction text.

DAY 2 Immersion

Focused Instruction

Today let's continue to investigate nonfiction books, thinking about how they are different from fiction books. I have paired two books up together on the topic of frogs. The first is one of our favorite books from this year, Frog and Toad Are Friends. *Let us now look at another book about frogs,* Watch Me Grow: Frog *from the Dorling Kindersley series.*

- Read part of both books to students.

Stop every few pages and ask them how they think the books are the same or different.

Independent Practice

Look at the copy of the page I am giving you from Watch Me Grow: Frog *and talk to your partner about why this is nonfiction and how it is different from fiction.*

- Students read, notice, mark text, and gather evidence that the text is nonfiction.

Wrap-Up

What did you discover about this nonfiction book, and how it different from fiction?

- Continue to chart what students notice on this page, such as that is had a heading, photographs, captions, fact box sidebar, labels, and factual text.

DAY 3 Immersion

Focused Instruction

Let's continue to look at nonfiction today by exploring more of the ways that nonfiction books give us information. Look at a book today called Explore and Discover: Sharks. *It is from Kingfisher's Question Time series. On the first page, it has a section called "About This Book."*

- Read the first few pages of this book. Notice the question-and-answer structure, bold print, text placement, pictures and captions. Use the glossary to find meanings of the words in bold.

Independent Practice

Find examples of the features that we are noticing, but also be on the lookout for interesting sidebars and other ways that this nonfiction book is giving you, the readers, factual information.

Wrap-Up

As we can see, nonfiction books use the page in different and interesting ways to give the reader information and enjoyment. Let's make a chart of what we have noticed and how this helps us as readers of nonfiction.

- Using a split-page format, make a chart of the structures and features you've found.

Table of contents	Helps the reader locate information and answers to particular questions.
Bold print	Helps the reader to see important teaching words.
Headings	Helps the reader know what kind of information is on the page (a heading can also be a question).
Pictures with captions	Gives the reader information and helps the reader see what the writer is teaching or talking about.
Sidebars	Special boxes or parts of a page that explain ideas and facts to a reader. Some of our favorites are: fact boxes, "Now I Know" boxes, and "That's Amazing!" boxes.
Glossary	A page in a nonfiction book that gives a reader the meaning, explanation, or definition of a word or important idea.

DAY 4 Immersion

Focused Instruction

Let us look at two books that both have an interesting feature. One is called, Knut: How One Little Polar Bear Captivated the World. *The other is* Look to the North: A Wolf Pup Diary. *When we open up and look at the first pages, I see letters to the reader.*

- Read aloud the letter to the reader.

How does this letter help us get ready to read the book? How does it interest us in the book?

Independent Practice

- Distribute copies of letters to the reader to the class. Have the students read them and discuss them with one another.

Wrap-Up

What does an author's letter do to set up the reader and bring the reader into the topic of the book?

DAY 5 Identification

Focused Instruction

- Review charts. Recap findings and learnings.
- Discuss kinds of topics the students are interested in reading about.

One thing that we have noticed is that people read nonfiction to be engaged, to follow an interest, and to investigate what they wonder and think about. What are the topics that you love or are curious about?

Independent Practice

Take a few books from the pile that you think might interest you as a nonfiction reader. Look closely at these books in order to decide what books you want to be reading in this unit.

- Students fill their book bags with nonfiction texts.

Wrap-Up

What books have you chosen? What topics are they about? What do you like about these books? What features do they have in them that will help you as a nonfiction reader?

- Create a chart identifying the topics students are interested in and the books they will be reading. For example:

Name	Topic of Interest	Books to Be Read
Peter	Reptiles, especially snakes	All About Rattlesnakes Explore and Discover: Reptiles
Alana	Planets	Planets! 1,000 Facts About the Earth

DAY 6 Guided Practice

Focused Instruction

Today we are going to look at how to find the right nonfiction texts to read based on both interest and features of the book that draw us in.

- Use *Duke Ellington: The Piano Prince and His Orchestra* in order to model previewing a nonfiction text in order to determine if the book is a good fit.

Independent Practice

Before you begin your book today, preview it by looking at the cover, title, and nonfiction features. Share your findings with your partner.

Wrap-Up

Did you like your book? What features helped you to read?

- Reflect on the reading of the day and ask for students to share how previewing the book helped them.

DAY 7 Guided Practice

Focused Instruction

One of the features we have seen in a few books is a special page called an "introduction" or "about this book" page. It tells you about the book, the kind of information in the book, and it is a clue to the big ideas that you can learn by reading this book. Today I am going to share with you a book called Almost Gone: The World's Rarest Animals *by Steve Jenkins and its introduction.*

Let's think about what this introduction is telling us and how an introduction can help a reader.

- Read the text once to glean information as a reader. Discuss your findings.
- Reread all or part of the text to discuss how this introduction helped prepare you to read this book.

Independent Practice

Read a book from your selection that has some kind of introduction, even if it's something short, like a guide to reading hard words or a letter to the reader. After you read it, share with your partner what this page told you about your book and how this is going to help you read this book.

- Students read and discuss with partner.

Wrap-Up

What kind of introduction did your book have? What did you learn about the book by reading the introduction?

DAY 8 Guided Practice

Focused Instruction

Yesterday we learned how to preview a book to find out what big ideas it contains. Today I want us to continue reading for big ideas. What big ideas do you know about your book? Knowing those big ideas helps you to read and learn more. Let's use yesterday's book, Almost Gone. *What big ideas do we know? (For example every living thing is connected to every other living thing; human kind has done many things to contribute to animal extinction.) Let's take our second big idea about man's causing extinction and read to find out more about that.*

- State the big idea and read the text.
- After each section, discuss information that was learned about the big idea.

Independent Practice

Today you will name a big idea you know about the book you're reading to your partner. Then continue to read on your topic. During Wrap-Up we will share what you are learning.

Wrap-Up

What did you learn today about your big ideas?

DAY 9 Guided Practice

Focused Instruction

As a reader of nonfiction, I often have questions before I begin reading my book. Let's think about the questions that we have and how they help us to read and explore our topics. Let's read one of the books from the QEB Weather Watch Series. I am going to read the book Rain *by Honor Head. Before I read, let's think about how we enter our reading experience; what questions do we have?*

- Record questions from students.

Now I am going to use those questions to guide my reading. I can read this whole book— it is not too long and I am really interested in this topic—but I can also look for answers to my questions. I can look here in the table of contents and find pages that might contain the answers.

Independent Practice

Talk to your partner and share with him the question or two that you have about the topic and the book you are reading. Jot those questions down on the sticky notes I am giving you. When you go off to read, try to find the answer to your questions. Remember to use your headings to help you.

Wrap-Up

How did having a question help you read nonfiction?

DAY 10 Guided Practice

Focused Instruction

Let's go back to Almost Gone *by Steve Jenkins. We can record information about the topics we are reading about. Let's practice with this book first.*

- Reread a few pages of the text.
- Discuss findings and how and where to put the information into the Nonfiction Reading Graphic Organizer (Resource 4.2).

Independent Practice

- Students read or reread a nonfiction text on their topic of interest. They jot down information into the graphic organizer.

Wrap-Up

What new and interesting information did you learn today? Share your organizer with the readers at your table.

- Students share in small groups.

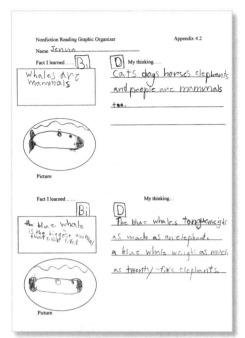

Graphic organizers help students learn to record research.

DAY 11 Commitment

Focused Instruction

Today we are going to continue to read Rosa *and practice recording ideas about what we are learning. However, today we are also going to look at recording ideas in the "My Thinking" box.*

- Continue (from yesterday) to model using the graphic organizer to write about a nonfiction topic of interest. Today, model writing thinking in response to factual information.
- Model how to respond to a fact with ideas, thoughts, wonderings, and comments. Record that thinking in the "My Thinking" box.

Independent Practice

- Students read or reread a nonfiction text on their topic of interest. They jot down thinking in the "My Thinking" box on the graphic organizer.

Wrap-Up

What information have you learned? What ideas and thoughts have you put down in the "My Thinking" box?

DAY 12 Commitment

Focused Instruction

Today we will create a poster that shares all of the interesting information we have learned by reading nonfiction.

- By using features of nonfiction, demonstrate how to share information on your topic of interest.

Independent Practice

- Students each create a poster sharing all of the information they learned in this unit about their topic of interest.

Wrap-Up

- Students show a partner the left side of their poster containing information they learned.

DAY 13 Commitment

Focused Instruction

Let us use the right side of the poster you started yesterday to share what we have learned about nonfiction books and the kinds of nonfiction readers we are. At the bottom, be sure to include what new books, authors, series, or topics you will read in the future.

Independent Practice

- Students create their posters, sharing the topics, titles, and authors they love to read.

Wrap-Up

Let's share and celebrate all of the work that we did!

- In small groups or in a class museum, share the work you did during this unit and celebrate your learning.

DAY 14 Commitment

Focused Instruction

What a great job you all did on your posters! I want for us to share the posters today by having a museum share. We will take turns being the presenters, or being the admirers listening to and learning from our nonfiction posters.

- Demonstrate how to present a piece of information from a poster. Then model how to be a listener and learner during a museum share.

Independent Practice

- Students share the work they did in this unit celebrating what they have learned and the nonfiction reader they are becoming.

Wrap-Up

We have really become such great nonfiction readers. Let's reflect on what kind of nonfiction readers we are now!

Sharing Learning Through Writing Nonfiction Texts

Why Teach This?

- To engage students in sharing information they know and new information they learn.
- To enable students to understand the genre of nonfiction as writers.
- To provide students with an opportunity to learn about structure and organization as writers.

Framing Question

- How can we use the question-and-answer structure and features of nonfiction writing to share information with others?

Unit Goals

- Students will understand that nonfiction writers create texts with factual information that informs and engages readers.
- Students will understand various structures of nonfiction texts, including those of all-about, how-to, question-and-answer, and narrative picture books.
- Students will understand features of nonfiction texts, including use of print, headings in the form of a question, sidebars for information, and captions for graphics, and use in their writing.
- Students will create an original piece of nonfiction text structured as a question-and-answer book.

Anchor Texts

- *All About Rattlesnakes* by Jim Arnosky
- *Did Dinosaurs Live in Your Backyard?* by Melvin Berger and Gilda Berger
- *Father Knows Less, or "Can I Cook My Sister?" One Dad's Quest to Answer His Son's Most Baffling Questions* by Wendell Jamieson
- *It Could Still Be a Fish* by Allan Fowler
- *One Tiny Turtle* by Nicola Davies
- *Why Do Cats Meow?* by Joan Holub
- *Wilma Unlimited: How Wilma Rudolph Became the Fastest Woman* by Kathleen Krull

Resource Sheets

- Nonfiction Writing Parent Letter (Resource 4.3)
- Nonfiction Expert Ideas Paper (Resource 4.4)
- Nonfiction Question-and-Answer Paper (Resource 4.5)
- Nonfiction Split-Page Paper (Resource 4.6)
- Nonfiction Research Question Homework (Resource 4.7)
- Nonfiction Glossary Paper (Resource 4.8)
- Nonfiction Editing Checklist (Resource 4.9)

Unit Assessment Sharing Learning Through Writing Nonfiction Texts			GENRE
Student name:	EMERGING	DEVELOPING	INDEPENDENT
Connects nonfiction writing to passions and interests in own life.			
Uses features in own writing (bold print, captions, zoom-in boxes, and sidebar).			
Writes a three- to five-page question-and-answer book using own ideas and interests.			
Incorporates research into a question-and-answer book.			

Stage of the Unit	Focused Instruction You will	Independent Practice Students will
IMMERSION 4 days	• read *Father Knows Less, or "Can I Cook My Sister?" One Dad's Quest to Answer His Son's Most Baffling Questions* by Wendell Jamieson and talk about how writers are compelled to do research to get their questions answered. • use *One Tiny Turtle* by Nicola Davies to demonstrate the different voices a nonfiction text can contain (narrative and expository). • read *All About Rattlesnakes* by Jim Arnosky to model how a nonfiction writer writes from experience and expertise. • read *It Could Still Be a Fish* and other question-and-answer texts to demonstrate the structure.	• read a book of their choice and notice what they admire about the author's choice of features. • examine texts to determine the voice used by the writer. • discuss possible "expert ideas" and create an expert ideas list on paper. • work with a partner to discover and examine ways to organize questions and answers within a text.
IDENTIFICATION 2 days	• model with a student how to discuss possible publishing ideas; name this structure an "expert circle." • model how to create a nonfiction notebook to house all of the students' nonfiction materials and demonstrate how to ask questions on a topic.	• discuss possible topics in groups of three or four and identify a topic on which they would like to publish a nonfiction question-and-answer book. • create a nonfiction notebook and use a question-and-answer format to begin asking questions.

GUIDED PRACTICE 10 days	• model using free-writing to generate answers for questions from what you already know. • use *Watch Me Grow: Frog* to model a research strategy called "read, think, talk, write"; create a split page with fact and reflections from your reading, thinking, and talking. • demonstrate the use of a primary source for researching writing (an interview). • demonstrate how to incorporate a sidebar as a feature of nonfiction text. • model how to incorporate bold print to emphasize important words. • model writing a table of contents as an organizational/planning tool. • model how to create a heading for each page to further define and organize writing. • model using a partner to revise text; model such revisions as adding features, taking out parts, clarifying words. • model using editing checklist to review the editing stage of publishing a piece. • model using a nonfiction question-and-answer checklist to publish text, including an introductory page.	• free-write the information they already know about their topic to generate answers to their questions. • read, think, talk, and write with a partner to create a split-page chart on their topic, listing factual information and reflective thinking. • create two to three questions for an interview with an "expert" to answer questions on their topic. • create two sidebars for their piece. • use bold print for at least three important words in their piece and define those words in a glossary. • organize writing into a draft by creating a table of contents page. • create a heading for each page of questions and answers; continue to draft and organize writing. • reread their piece with a partner and clarify it by adding or deleting information; create introductory page. • edit their piece of writing. • use editing checklist to complete publishing of book.
COMMITMENT 1 day	• demonstrate reflection, asking students what nonfiction writers do.	• celebrate and reflect on the strategies they've learned.
TOTAL: 17 DAYS		

Getting Started

In Wendell Jamieson's book *Father Knows Less, or "Can I Cook My Sister?" One Dad's Quest to Answer His Son's Most Baffling Questions*, a father sets out to answer questions his young son has, ranging from "Why do policeman like donuts?" to "What happens if your plane flies over a volcano?" The father interviews experts in the fields relating to the questions: the former mayor of New York for a question on New York City history, along with scientists, historians, educators, and other politicians. He goes right to the "horse's mouth." The key to this unit is inquiry: allowing your students the opportunity to browse, wonder, explore, notice, observe, and question.

Structures and Routines

Students talk to one another in expert circles (small groups of students sharing what they know about various topics they are interested in).

You might want to consider having students use a folder for this unit or create a notebook just for nonfiction.

Partnerships

Students help one another choose topics they are passionate about and serve as sounding boards as they create the text for their nonfiction books. Partners also help each other use the "read, think, talk, write" research strategy as the "talk" part is done with a partner. Partnerships can be heterogeneous as students can assist each other in a variety of ways.

Teaching Materials

The following is a list of texts that will work well with this unit.

All About Rattlesnakes, Jim Arnosky	Nonfiction writers are experts at writing from passion and research.
One Tiny Turtle, Nicola Davies	The voice of nonfiction can be expository or narrative but should always engage the reader.
Dogs, Seymour Simon	Nonfiction writers give information and support their big ideas.
What Do You Do With a Tail Like This? Steve Jenkins *It Could Still Be a Fish*, Allan Fowler *Explore and Discover: Sharks*, Stephen Savage *Did Dinosaurs Live in Your Backyard?* Melvin Berger and Gilda Berger *Rain*, Honor Head *Why Do Cats Meow?* Joan Holub	Nonfiction texts can be structured as question-and-answer texts, which ask questions in different ways and give readers information by answering them.
Penguins, Gail Gibbons *Zoo Animals*, Dorling Kindersley *How to Be a Baby, by Me the Big Sister*, Sally Lloyd-Jones	Nonfiction writers use features such as pictures, labels, captions, zoom-in boxes, maps, and charts. Nonfiction writers use content-specific words to teach the reader about their topic.
Sea Creatures, Sue Malyan	Nonfiction writers use a table of contents, glossary, and special sidebars (such as fact boxes, size circles, "did you know" sections) to give readers information.

How Do Flies Walk Upside Down? Melvin Berger and Gilda Berger *Explore and Discover: Sharks*, Stephen Savage *One Tiny Turtle*, Nicola Davies *Almost Gone*, Steve Jenkins *Knut: How One Little Polar Bear Captivated the World*, Juliana Hatkoff, Isabella Hatkoff, Craig Hatkoff, and Gerald Uhlich	Nonfiction writers use special pages (introduction or "about this book") to begin a nonfiction text.
Butterflies! Editors of *Time for Kids* with David Bjerklie	Nonfiction writers think about clear, interesting, and engaging ways to put print, pictures, and supporting graphics together in their books.

Stages of the Unit

Immersion
Read aloud to your students so they can capture the flavor of great nonfiction writing. Call their attention to the strength of writers' voices when they are writing about topics they love. Send home the Nonfiction Writing Parent Letter (Resource 4.3).

Identification
Look carefully at structure, features, and voice in this stage. Help your students find topics that matter to them.

Guided Practice
Teach students to plan their books. They need to generate information from their own thinking, research the topic to add factual information and thinking, and craft a text in a question-and-answer format, using bold print and pictures or photos with captions. They need to write an introductory page, include an engaging and informative sidebar of information, and use headings in the form of a question to guide the reader. Model for them how writers love their topics and become invested in them.

Commitment
Students polish and publish a nonfiction question-and-answer text. Students reflect on the learning in this unit and commit to their learning by identifying qualities of nonfiction writing that cross all topics.

Day-by-Day Lessons

DAY 1 Immersion

Focused Instruction

During the next few weeks, we are going to create a piece of nonfiction writing. Let's begin by looking at a nonfiction book to see what the author did that might guide us in our own writing.

- Read excerpts from *Father Knows Less, or "Can I Cook My Sister?" One Dad's Quest to Answer His Son's Most Baffling Questions* by Wendell Jamieson and talk about how writers are compelled to do research to get their questions answered.

Independent Practice

- Students read nonfiction books of their choice, noticing what they admire about the author's choice of features.

Wrap-Up

What did you notice about your book?

- Students name the topic, features used, and what the author may have done to find the information for his book.

DAY 2 Immersion

Focused Instruction

- Read *One Tiny Turtle* by Nicola Davies to notice the purpose and sound of nonfiction writing.
- Begin by reading the introductory page, titled "About Turtles," and describe this as a special page that introduces the topic and book to the reader.
- Read text and think aloud about both the purpose of the text to engage, inform, and explain as well as the different authors' voices in narrative nonfiction ("Let me tell you a story") and expository text ("I am an expert").

Independent Practice

- Students read some nonfiction books of their choice, noticing what they admire about the features the author chooses to use as well as the sound of the author's voice.

Wrap-Up

- Students share what they admire in the books they are reading.
- Record students' ideas on a class chart, identifying the title of the text and a line from the book that demonstrates the sound of the writing.

Planets! Editors of Time for Kids with Brenda Iasevoli	Expert sound
Watch Me Grow: Puppy, Lisa Magloff	"Come learn with me" sound

DAY 3 Immersion

Focused Instruction

Authors are experts on their topic. Let's look at Jim Arnofsky. He wrote a book about snakes. He observed snakes, he asked questions about snakes, and he read about snakes. That is what writers do when they are going to write about a topic.

Let me read to you the "about the author" blurb at the back of the book to see how he is such an expert on this topic. It says here that he observes snakes in the wild and that he has videotaped them.

Let us be like Jim Arnosky: finding our passions for things and building an expertise. What do you love or feel passionate about? These can all be ideas that lead you to your nonfiction topic.

Independent Practice

Today I am going to give you an "ideas paper." You will notice that there are two columns: "Ideas" and "My Expertise" so that you can think about what will be the best topic for you (Resource 4.4).

- Students generate a list of possible ideas for writing. These can come from their lives at home (siblings, friendships) or from things they do outside of the home (sports, after-school activities, or passions/interests relating to science or history).

- Students fill out expertise column, stating how and why they are an expert in this topic.

Wrap-Up

- Read (appropriate!) portions of *Father Knows Less* by Wendell Jamieson to your students; the author asks all kinds of experts questions his son has asked him ("Are rainbows hot or cold?").

DAY 4 Immersion

Focused Instruction

When we write our nonfiction books, we are going to organize them using a question-and-answer format. Some books are like It Could Still Be a Fish *by Allan Fowler. They consist of a series of questions and answers—one page has a question and then the next page has the answer. Other question-and-answer books have two to five questions and answers on each page. The Scholastic Question and Answer Series books and the Kingfisher Question Time books are all organized this way. The third way to organize a nonfiction question-and-answer book is for each page to have a heading that is a question, and the whole page (pictures, words, supporting boxes) answer that question. The book* Rain *from the QEB Weather Watch series by Honor Head has pages like that.*

- Partnerships look at a question-and-answer text and identify which structure it uses.

Wrap-Up

What have you noticed about your nonfiction question-and-answer books? Are they a series of questions and answers, a one-question-per-page book, or a many-questions-and-answers-per-page book?

- Create a class chart of what students notice. Here is an example of such a chart:

Way the Q/A Organized	Title/Author	Other Nonfiction Features
Series of questions and answers	*It Could Still Be a Fish*, Allan Fowler	Photographs, labels, diagrams, index
One question per page	*Rain*, Honor Head	Table of contents, photos, captions, bold print, glossary, index, parents- and teachers-page, how-to page
Many questions and answers per page	*How Do Flies Walk Upside Down?* Melvin Berger and Gilda Berger	Table of contents, intro page, photos and drawings, labels, index, sections for questions, key

DAY 5 Identification

Focused Instruction

Let's have expert circles for the first part of our writing time. An expert circle is when you discuss a topic you think you are an expert at in order to determine if this is a good topic for you to write nonfiction on. After about 15 minutes, I am going to ask you to take a piece of paper and free-write about the topic you think you will write about.

- Model three students having a conversation with you; each takes a turn talking for a few minutes about a possible topic from their writing ideas page to a partner. They will talk about the topic ("write in the air") for a few minutes.
- The class names what you and the three students did and gets ready for their own expert circles.

Independent Practice

- After 15 minutes, students write on the topics they feel that they will use to write a nonfiction book about. This writing will be part of their draft but is not expected to contain any particular features of nonfiction at this point. The student uses this free-write to determine whether the topic will work for him or her.

Wrap-Up

Who thinks they have found their topic? We will each have a topic and we will also have a class topic. The class topic is going to be "tadpoles" because we are learning about tadpoles in science and we have all become experts in this topic.

- Begin chart listing the class topic first and then each student's name and topic.
- The class topic can be an idea from students' everyday lives (for example going to second grade), or it can be a great opportunity to make connections to a content area.

DAY 6 Identification

Focused Instruction

- Model creating a nonfiction notebook to organize all of your thinking.

All writers, especially nonfiction writers, have a container for their ideas and writing. Today we are going to set up that container so that all of our work— organizers, free-writes, question-and-answer pages—are in one location. I am going to give you an 11-by-17-inch piece of construction paper and ask that you fold it in half, decorate it, and write your name and "Nonfiction Notebook" on it. One of the pages will be our free-writes from yesterday. Another one of the pages is your planning page. On it, you are going to write down all of the questions you have about your topic. I will show you how to do that with our class topic of tadpoles.

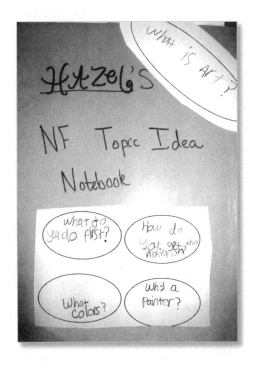

- Demonstrate writing questions about the class topic, eliciting content from students as well (e.g., What is a tadpole? What are the stages of tadpole development? What does it mean to be a froglet?).
- Model using nonfiction question-and-answer paper (Resource 4.4) to generate thinking.

Independent Practice

- Students create covers for their nonfiction notebooks.
- Students generate questions they would like to include in their books.

Wrap-Up

Share your topic questions with your partner.

DAY 7 Guided Practice

Focused Instruction

We have questions for our topics, and today we are going to look at writing answers. On the answer part of the question-and-answer page, we are going to put information down for our readers. The information is going to come from the expert information we already have, but we will remember that we want to use our nonfiction voice and sound like an expert nonfiction writer. Let me show you what I mean by writing answers to the questions on our class topic, tadpoles. Watch what I am doing first, then I am going to ask all of you to help me write the answer to other questions. The first question is "What is a tadpole?" Let me think of all that we have learned about tadpoles.

- Using free-writing, model using information that the class learned in the tadpole unit to answer the question.
- Model alongside students as together you develop an answer to one of the questions for the class topic (e.g., What are the stages of tadpole development?). Read the question, ask students to brainstorm answers with their partners, then share out possibilities. Choose a combination of thinking to create an answer (e.g., "A frog begins as an egg, then hatches into a tadpole...").

Independent Practice

Now it is your turn. Today you will write answers to your questions. If you don't feel you have enough information, then put an asterisk or a star next to that question. Later this week, we will be doing research to add information to our writing.

- Students begin planning and talking and if ready, start their writing.

Wrap-Up

- Share a student's work that demonstrates a strong answer for a question-and-answer book.

DAY 8 Guided Practice

Focused Instruction

We are putting down all of our information from our observations, research, and reading, and beginning to add this information to our nonfiction books. I am going to show you how to use split-page paper to take notes on our class topic. When I use the split page, I'll use a research strategy for gathering more information called "read, think, talk, and write." I am going to use a book we know well, Watch Me Grow: Frogs *from the DK Watch Me Grow series. We used this book to launch our nonfiction reading, and we have used it during our science time to learn more about our tadpoles. Today I am going to reread pages 16 to 18 to add information to my nonfiction book.*

- Read a page of the book. Read aloud and think aloud with a student partner to demonstrate what is going on inside the mind of the researcher during read, think, talk, and write. Use a tab to mark a spot where information is gleaned.

Then demonstrate what you would write. Sample split page using read, think, talk, and write:

Facts	Thoughts/Questions
Tadpoles hatch in spring and many new frogs appear by summer.	
Frogs use hopping, not walking or running, to get from one place to another.	

Independent Practice

Read and think for about five minutes side by side until you and your partner both feel ready to share. When you are ready to write, make sure you have three to five facts to put down on the left side of the split page (Resource 4.6).

- Students work beside partner and read, think, talk, and then write three to five facts about their topic on the left-hand side of the page.

- Students then talk about each other's topic for five minutes so that they can put thinking and reflection on the right-hand side of the page.

Wrap-Up

- Students reflect on writing and share responses.

- Point out a student's reflective thinking that demonstrates ideas and/or thoughts that would be instrumental to a nonfiction text. For example, "Many people don't like spiders because they are afraid of them" or "Spiders can be interesting to watch," from *Spiders* by Gail Gibbons are two examples of reflective statements that support facts.

DAY 9 Guided Practice

Focused Instruction

Nonfiction writers include information they know about their topic; now we will look at how to observe, talk about, and interview others to research our topic. Tom from our nature center is coming so that we can interview him about our class topic, tadpoles. What questions will we ask him to find out more about our topic?

- Generate list of questions (e.g., Why do tadpoles rest after they hatch? What are gills and what are they used for?).

- Record questions on question-and-answer paper (Resource 4.5).

Independent Practice

Today you will be writing interview questions. Also, decide on whom you will interview about your topic.

- Students create interview questions and share them with a partner.

- Students choose an expert to interview.

Wrap-Up

Great questions! Let's talk about whom you will interview. Who might be an expert on your topic? Who knows someone who can be used as an expert for another writers' topic? Continue this work for homework tonight (see Resource 4.7).

• Discuss people to interview. Utilize class/school community to generate possible interviewees. Tap into school/local community by posting requests on outside bulletin board, in a school letter, or through the local paper.

DAY 10 Guided Practice

Focused Instruction

Today we are going to think about using the nonfiction features that we have learned all about to put interesting information into our books.

One feature we have noticed and used as readers is the use of sidebars. Sidebars are boxes and sections with information that teach a reader. Let's go back to our noticing chart to rename our possible sidebars from our anchor texts. Here are some sidebar examples that we found in the Question Time, DK, and Time for Kids series that you can use with your students.

Now I Know Box: A place to summarize the new information learned.	Question Time series, *Explore and Discover Reptiles*, Claire Llewellyn
That's Amazing! Fact Box: A place to put important, amazing facts that don't match any questions in your book.	Question Time series, *Explore and Discover Reptiles*, Claire Llewellyn
Look and Find Circle: Something to look for on the page and find information about.	Question Time series, *Explore and Discover Reptiles*, Claire Llewellyn
Size Circle: A sidebar to put information about the size of something you are writing about.	DK Look Closer Series, *Sea Creatures*, Sue Malyan
Did You Know? Box: A place to put an interesting fact you think readers would be curious about.	DK Look Closer Series, *Sea Creatures*, Sue Malyan
Fact Box: A box of facts about your topic that related to the question but not essential for the answer.	DK Watch Me Grow Series, *Watch Me Grow: Frog*, Lisa Magloff
Zoom Box: A close-up picture of something you are trying to teach a reader.	*Butterflies!* The Editors of *Time for Kids* with David Bjerklie

Let's put sidebars in our class question-and-answer book about tadpoles. One sidebar could be a zoom-in box with a close-up of the tadpole's legs developing. A fact box would be another great sidebar, since we have so many amazing facts about tadpoles and no place to put this information.

• Model generating two sidebars, demonstrating why these would match the text.

• Students participate by planning, imagining, and adding content as you model.

Independent Practice

Turn and talk to your partner, telling him or her what kinds of sidebars you could imagine in your book.

- Students work on creating two sidebars to add research and information to their books.

Wrap-Up

- Students share their sidebar ideas.

DAY 11 Guided Practice

Focused Instruction

Many nonfiction books use bold, italicized, or large print. The nonfiction writer uses these type features to make something stand out to the reader. They help isolate important words. Many of the words in bold are in the glossary or are important content words a reader learning about the topic should know. Today let's put at least two words in bold in our nonfiction books. You also have to write their meaning. Let's do this with our class topic of tadpoles.

- Brainstorm a list of possible important content words that should appear in bold (e.g., webbing, hatch, spawn, gills).
- Create a definition for these words in a glossary. The first word in the glossary should be the topic. For example, "tadpoles" would be the first word in the glossary of the class book.

Independent Practice

Find two to four words in your writing that you think should be in bold. We will put those words in a glossary at the back of our question-and-answer books (Resource 4.8).

Wrap-Up

- Feature one student's selection of important content words to bold and ask that student to describe why he chose them.

DAY 12 Guided Practice

Let's take all of the information we have and put this work together in a draft. To do this in an organized way, let's use one of the features in a nonfiction book to help organize our writing. We can write a table of contents for our book and then use it to put our pages in order. Our books are going to be question-and-answer books that have at least two questions and answers on each page, with sidebars, pictures, captions, and bold print. Let's do this together with our class topic so that you can do it with your own topic afterward.

- Take paper and create a table of contents.

Independent Practice

- Students work on table of contents page to plan book.

Wrap-Up

- Share the work of a student whose table of contents page demonstrates how to organize a nonfiction text.

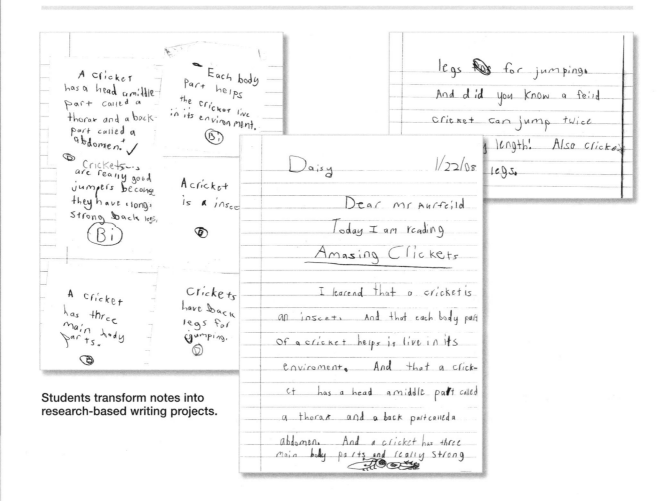

Students transform notes into research-based writing projects.

DAY 13 Guided Practice

Focused Instruction

Today we are going to continue to work on our drafts. We are going to write a heading for each part, as well as decide where our pictures, captions, sidebars, and bold print will go. Watch as I try this with our class book on tadpoles.

- Using class topic, demonstrate organizing previous writing into the book.

We have three questions about frog eggs: What is a tadpole before it is born? What is life like inside the egg? How many eggs does a frog lay? These questions will go on the "What is a tadpole before it is born?" page.

- Attach prior writing to each page by writing and pasting parts into each page.

Independent Practice

- Students continue to draft and organize writing.

Wrap-Up

- Students share the process of drafting.

DAY 14 Guided Practice

Today we are going to revise. Revising is reseeing. We will revise by looking at our drafts of our question-and-answer books and checking to see that they are clear and give enough information to the reader. We will do this by doing a "partnership test." Each partner will listen carefully and respectfully and stop his partner if he does not understand something. Also, you should share two things that you liked about your partner's book, and give one suggestion of something that could be improved. Let's listen in on this partnership so that we can all do this today.

- Two students model the partnership test.
- Debrief with students as they discuss how to do the partnership test.

Independent Practice

Now you and your partner will use the partnership test for each of your books. Remember to name what you love about your partner's book, as well as make suggestions. After you meet you can go off to work on your book—change a part, add to your answers, add a sidebar or picture.

- Students revise their books.

Wrap-Up

- Students share suggestions and compliments from their partner conference.

DAY 15 Guided Practice

Focused Instruction

We are going to edit our writing today. Let's review our Editing Checklist (Resource 4.9).

- Use one student to model using editing checklist.
- Students plan their writing time for the day (revision, editing, etc.).

Independent Practice

Remember to use your editing pens to revise and edit. Our editing pens are colored pens and pencils that we use so that we can clearly see our changes and corrections.

- Students work on revising and editing.

Wrap-Up

- Share some editing checklists.

DAY 16 Guided Practice

- Review checklist.

Let's go over what we need to do to complete our books:

Question-and-Answer Book Checklist
1. I have a table of contents identifying the parts of my book.
2. I have questions about my topic and answers to those questions. There are two to four questions and answers on a page.
3. I have at least three important words in bold.
4. I have my topic word and the three important content words in my glossary.
5. I have at least one sidebar in my book that provides the reader with information about my topic.

Note: It may take one to three days to finalize the text and publish the books.

Independent Practice

- Students work on publishing their question-and-answer books.

Wrap-Up

- Have students share their work.

DAY 17 Commitment

Focused Instruction

What have you learned to do as a writer? What was the best part of this study?

Independent Practice

- Students share and celebrate their books and learning!

Wrap-Up

- Students discuss what they learned during this unit and how it helped them write their nonfiction books.
- Students share their favorite parts of their books.

Deep Thinking in Familiar Texts

The second grader is deeply invested in thinking about things she loves. Her old stuffed animal, her favorite read-aloud, her first bicycle, her sparkly shoes. All the "firsts" in her life are still very recent for her, and they all hold an important place in her heart. We have stressed throughout this book that second grade is a year in which building stamina is crucial. To do this, our students must feel that it is not only okay to revisit books and ideas we love, but really important for their development.

Rereading Books We Love   PROCESS

Why Teach This?
- To demonstrate that favorite books make readers feel strong emotions.
- To instill a sense of the value of favorite books.
- To show students that favorite books can be revisited over and over again.

Framing Questions
- How do readers decide which books are their favorites?
- How can rereading favorite books help readers enjoy them even more?
- What kinds of things do readers say about their favorite books?

Unit Goals
- Students will equate favorite books with other favorite things in their lives.
- Students will identify favorite books that make them feel strong emotions.
- Students will learn that rereading their favorite books will enhance their enjoyment of them.

Anchor Texts
- *Calling the Doves/El Canto de las Palomas* by Juan Felipe Herrera
- *Father Knows Less, or "Can I Cook My Sister?" One Dad's Quest to Answer His Son's Most Baffling Questions* by Wendell Jamieson
- *My Name is Yoon* by Helen Recorvits
- *Over and Over* by Charlotte Zolotow
- *The End* by David LaRochelle

Unit Assessment Rereading Books We Love			PROCESS
Student name:	EMERGING	DEVELOPING	INDEPENDENT
Names a favorite book.			
Expresses emotions and/or opinions about the book.			
Rereads favorite books.			
Writes a blurb clearly stating the strengths of a book.			

Stage of the Unit	Focused Instruction You will	Independent Practice Students will
IMMERSION 1 day	• share a "treasure" of your own with the class; stress with flair how you feel about this treasure—hug it, ooh and aah over it, and explain why it is so special; explain that because it is so cherished, you go back to look at it over and over again; read *Over and Over* to convey the importance of things that happen again and again.	• share a treasured item of their own.
IDENTIFICATION 2 days	• read *The End* and explain that once in a while, a reader finds a book that makes him feel very strong emotions; explain that these books become favorites or treasures to us because they make us feel powerful feelings—they make us laugh out loud, cry, ooh, and aah. • read *Calling the Doves/El Canto de las Palomas* and explain that just as we do with our other special treasures, we can keep going back to our favorite books because they will keep causing us to feel those same strong feelings and powerful experiences.	• explore the classroom library and find a book that made them feel very strong emotions. • reread a book they love and think about the reasons they feel so strongly about it.
GUIDED PRACTICE 2 days	• read *Father Knows Less, or "Can I Cook My Sister?"* and model how you would talk about your favorite book and how you would recommend it to others. • read *My Name Is Yoon* and explain that when readers share their feelings about certain books, they often influence others to read or reread the books; read *My Name is Yoon* and model recommending a book to another reader.	• enjoy the special opportunity to recommend a treasured book. • discuss with a partner how strongly they feel about certain books.
COMMITMENT 1 day	• explain that readers write/share recommendations as a way to write about our most treasured books to suggest them to others; model writing a book blurb you might read on the back of a book; include why this is a book you will want to "keep going back to."	• write a recommendation about some of their most treasured books on an index card; add recommendation to a class bulletin board called "Our Most Treasured Books."
TOTAL: 6 DAYS		

Response to Texts

Second graders see reading and writing connections everywhere. This is a great time of year for them to practice writing responses to texts. Book blurbs are fun, fast, and creative.

Writing About Reading: Book Blurbs   STRATEGY

Why Teach This?
- To teach the purpose of book blurbs.
- To encourage students to respond to reading in creative ways.
- To give students an opportunity to write authentic, persuasive texts.

Framing Questions
- What is a book blurb?
- How do writers write exciting book blurbs?

Unit Goals
- Students will identify the purpose and features of a book blurb.
- Students will include these features in a book blurb of their own.
- Students will use exciting words in their book blurbs to draw readers in.
- Students will share their book blurbs in a class "bookstore."

Anchor Texts
- *A Boy Called Slow* by Joseph Bruchac
- *Henry and Mudge and the Snowman Plan* by Cynthia Rylant
- *Magic Treehouse: Day of the Dragon King* by Mary Pope Osborne

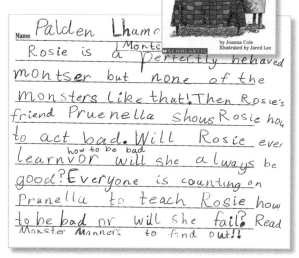

Palden writes a book blurb for *Monster Manners*.

Unit Assessment Writing About Reading: Book Blurbs			STRATEGY
Student name:	EMERGING	DEVELOPING	INDEPENDENT
Identifies the purpose of a book blurb.			
Chooses a favorite book to write a blurb for.			
Includes features of a book blurb in his or her writing.			
Chooses words that make the book blurb exciting to read.			
Edits book blurb to make it more readable.			
Shares book blurb with classmates and participates in class "bookstore."			

Stage of the Unit	Focused Instruction You will	Independent Practice Students will
IMMERSION 1 day	• read the book blurbs from *Henry and Mudge and the Snowman Plan* and *The Magic Treehouse: Day of the Dragon King*; discuss what the blurbs tell readers about the book and how it hooks them.	• read a variety of book blurbs and jot one thing down that they notice in a great blurb.
IDENTIFICATION 2 days	• read the blurb from *A Boy Called Slow* and discuss why books have blurbs; identify them as a way for authors to persuade a reader to choose a book. • create a class chart of what belongs in a book blurb (e.g., main characters, clues about what will happen in the book, questions that the reader will want to answer).	• browse a variety of book blurbs and choose one that makes them want to read the book; share it with a partner. • read a variety of book blurbs, looking for additional features to add to the book blurb class chart.
GUIDED PRACTICE 5 days	• select *A Boy Called Slow* and model choosing a book to write a blurb about, emphasizing that the book you choose should be meaningful or important to you. • using *A Boy Called Slow* model writing a book blurb, using the class chart to guide what you include. • model rereading your book blurb, noticing word choice; revise the blurb to make it more exciting. • revisit some favorite book blurbs that have hanging questions that the reader will want to answer; model adding a question to your book blurb. • reread your book blurb to make sure the punctuation, capitalization, and sentences make sense.	• choose a book they want to write a blurb for and share their choice with a partner. • write their book blurbs, using the class chart to guide them. • notice the words they used in their book blurbs, revising them to make them more exciting. • reread their book blurbs and add a hanging question (if they choose). • reread their book blurbs, editing them so they are easy to read; add illustrations, if desired.
COMMITMENT 1 day	• model how writers will visit each other's "bookstore" to learn about the book they recommended in their blurbs.	• visit "bookstores," reading blurbs to find a book they want to read; share with partners which book they chose and how the blurb persuaded them to read it.
TOTAL: 9 DAYS		

Grammar Rules

These units are designed to illuminate the often ignored workhorses of the English language: nouns and verbs. By reading wonderful picture books that teach grammar, we can inspire our students to understand and identify nouns and verbs when they are reading, and to write with a new thoughtfulness about their word choice.

Learning About Nouns and Verbs in Reading

CONVENTIONS

Why Teach This?
- To review the definitions of nouns and verbs.
- To enable students to identify nouns and verbs in print.

Framing Questions
- What is a noun?
- What is a verb?
- How can identifying nouns and verbs help me to read well?

Unit Goals
- Students will practice how to identify nouns and verbs in print.
- Students will understand how nouns and verbs enable us to read sentences.

Anchor Texts
- *Heat Wave* by Eileen Spinelli
- *Merry-Go-Round* and *Kites Sail High* by Ruth Heller

Unit Assessment Learning About Nouns and Verbs in Reading			CONVENTIONS
Student name:	EMERGING	DEVELOPING	INDEPENDENT
Identifies nouns in print.			
Identifies verbs in print.			
Highlights nouns that impact reading.			
Highlights verbs that impact reading.			

Stage of the Unit	Focused Instruction You will	Independent Practice Students will
IMMERSION 2 days	• read *Merry Go Round: A Book About Nouns*; discuss nouns and the role they play in a sentence. • read *Kites Sail High: A Book About Verbs*; discuss verbs and the role they play in a sentence.	• write nouns they find in their independent reading on sticky notes. • write verbs they find in their independent reading on sticky notes.
IDENTIFICATION 1 day	• review definition of nouns and verbs using *Merry Go Round and Kites Sail High*; ask how nouns and verbs help us as readers.	• be on the lookout for nouns and verbs in their independent reading.
GUIDED PRACTICE 1 day	• read *Heat Wave* by Eileen Spinelli; identify the many nouns and powerful verbs in the text; ask how they help us as reader to understand the text; discuss the impact of crisp and vivid noun and verb choices on a reader, as they enable the reader to make mind-pictures and to comprehend the text.	• using a page from *Heat Wave*, work with a partner to identify nouns and verbs; categorize these nouns and verbs as ordinary or powerful (that helped you to make mind-pictures and understand the text).
COMMITMENT 1 day	• reflect on the role of nouns and verbs in texts; discuss what role they play and how they help you as a reader.	• create a list of nouns and verbs that impacted them as readers; add to a class chart of crisp, powerful nouns and verbs.
TOTAL: 5 DAYS		

Learning About Nouns and Verbs in Writing

Why Teach This?

- To enable students to identify nouns and verbs in print.
- To help students become thoughtful about word choice.

Framing Questions

- What is a noun?
- What is a verb?
- How can my choice of nouns and verbs make my writing sound better?

Unit Goals

- Students will learn that their choice of nouns and verbs has a strong impact on sentences.
- Students will understand that wisely chosen nouns and verbs can strengthen their writing by painting a clearer picture in the reader's mind.

Anchor Texts

- *A Mink, a Fink, a Skating Rink: What Is a Noun?* by Brian P. Cleary
- *Nouns and Verbs Have a Field Day* by Robin Pulver
- *To Root, to Toot, to Parachute: What Is a Verb?* by Brian P. Cleary

Unit Assessment Learning About Nouns and Verbs in Writing			CONVENTIONS
Student name:	EMERGING	DEVELOPING	INDEPENDENT
Understands that nouns have a strong impact on a sentence.			
Understands that verbs have a strong impact on sentences.			
Makes thoughtful choices for nouns in own writing.			
Makes thoughtful choices for verbs in own writing.			

Stage of the Unit	Focused Instruction You will	Independent Practice Students will
IMMERSION 3 days	• review definition of nouns and verbs, using *Merry Go Round* and *Kites Sail High*. • read *A Mink, a Fink, a Skating Rink: What Is a Noun?* • read *To Root, To Toot, To Parachute: What Is a Verb?* by Brian P. Cleary	• read from familiar picture books and independent reading and watch for nouns and verbs that affect sentences. • read from familiar picture books and independent reading and watch for verbs that affect sentences. • write nouns and verbs they find in independent reading on sticky notes.
IDENTIFICATION 2 days	• read *Nouns and Verbs Have a Field Day* by Robin Pulver and name and define nouns and verbs; discuss "student" as a noun and "writes" as a verb. • begin to chart nouns and verbs, starting a class collection.	• practice writing sentences with strong nouns and verbs. • add nouns and verbs to the class charts.
GUIDED PRACTICE 2 days	• help students identify interesting nouns and verbs in their writing. • use a few pages from *Nouns and Verbs Have a Field Day* and discuss how well-chosen words paint "mind pictures" for the reader.	• write a new piece or take a part of an old piece and rewrite it, paying attention to nouns and verbs of interest. • underline words that paint "mind pictures" for the reader in their writing; find places where new nouns and verbs can be used to create these "mind pictures."
COMMITMENT 1 day	• reflect on thoughtful choices of nouns and verbs as a way to create clearer images for readers.	• edit for thoughtful nouns and verbs and share a piece with a partner.
TOTAL: 8 DAYS		

Writing Inspiration

At this time of the year, our students often come to a moment when they are feeling stymied by the blank page. It's a great time to do a mini-unit on revisiting writing ideas. Use the Four Prompts (I wonder, I remember, I observe, I imagine) to spark new ideas, and revisit ideas to assure your students that sometimes our most treasured ideas are our very best.

Revisiting the Writing Ideas We Love   PROCESS

Why Teach This?
- To provide students with an opportunity to revisit writing topics and get ideas for their writing.
- To support students as writers, helping them to use prompts to write strong.

Framing Questions
- How do writers get ideas for writing?
- What are ideas we love to write about that help us to "write strong"?

Unit Goals
- Students will revisit favorite read-alouds and think about how the writers got their ideas.
- Students will practice generating writing ideas from the Four Prompts: I wonder, I remember, I observe, I imagine.
- Students will revisit favorite ideas and generate writing on those topics.

Anchor Texts
- *If...* by Sarah Perry
- *In the Land of Words* by Eloise Greenfield
- *Miss Rumphius* by Barbara Cooney
- *My Dream of Martin Luther King* by Faith Ringgold
- *The Three Snow Bears* by Jan Brett

Unit Assessment Revisiting the Writing Ideas We Love			PROCESS
Student name:	EMERGING	DEVELOPING	INDEPENDENT
Looks at read-alouds and own writing to decide where ideas may have come from.			
Recaps the Four Prompts for writing (I wonder, I remember, I observe, I imagine).			
Names ideas that he or she loves and can write well on.			
Revisits a favorite idea and creates a piece of writing.			

Stage of the Unit	Focused Instruction You will	Independent Practice Students will
IMMERSION 1 day	• read aloud *In the Land of Words* by Eloise Greenfield, discussing how she used the Four Prompts to generate individual poems.	• skim and scan familiar read-alouds and discuss how the writers may have gotten their ideas.
IDENTIFICATION 2 days	• read *If. . .* by Sarah Perry and identify the Four Prompts (I wonder, I remember, I observe, I imagine); discuss how they help writers generate ideas. • model how to look back at writing and think about which prompt a writing idea could have come from and whether it is a favorite idea.	• read through published and unpublished student writing, reflecting on and recording which prompt the writing idea could have come from and whether it is a favorite idea. • continue reading through published and unpublished work and mark three favorite ideas with sticky notes.
GUIDED PRACTICE 3 days	• use *Miss Rumphius* to discuss how author Amy Hest may have gotten her idea by both remembering and imagining. • use *The Three Snow Bears* to discuss how Jan Brett may have gotten her ideas by both wondering and observing. • read *My Dream of Martin Luther King* and model returning to ideas from one or more of the four prompts and writing again on this idea.	• reflect on whether they use remembering and imagining to generate writing, and which favorite ideas they have that come from these prompts; mark such writing with a sticky note. • reflect if they use wondering and observing to generate writing and what favorite ideas they have that come from these prompts; mark such writing with a sticky note. • choose some ideas from one or more of the Four Prompts and try writing off of the ideas.
COMMITMENT 1 day	• choose one of the ideas you began and continue of the idea.	• reflect on your writing and choose one favorite idea to continue writing about; turn this into a published piece of writing.
TOTAL: 7 DAYS		

From Winter to Spring

Winter comes to a close. Our students have learned so much during this season. Their expanding knowledge of fiction and nonfiction is thrilling and brings a new life to their writing. They are learning through reading nonfiction texts and sharing all of their newly learned information with others. As spring arrives, we welcome our students into the world of poetry and help them strengthen their collaborative skills through writing clubs.

Chapter 5

SPRING

The Second Grader as Decision Maker

"Now I have claimed it. All I had to do was fly over it for it to be mine forever. I can wear it like a giant diamond necklace, or just fly above it and marvel at its sparkling beauty. I can fly—yes, fly."

—from *Tar Beach* by Faith Ringgold

The next units of study will help your students fly! Studies of fluency and genres, collaboration and reflection all help us mark the last season of the year. These second graders end their year soaring.

SPRING UNITS

SPOTLIGHT UNITS

Spring Awakens and Poetry Blooms

Your second graders are hopping, skipping, jumping, and leaping into spring. Their language, written and oral, should be exploding. They have a lot on their minds, both fanciful and real. The magic of poetry is a match for the magic of their minds, and a welcome reminder that these growing, leaping minds still love a small gem. They have worked hard this year in their longer texts, and now they can dig into the variety of poetry to practice their newfound language skills.

The poet and editor Paul Janeczko (1999) wrote, "Sometimes when you write a poem, you may think you know what that poem is going to be. But as you write and tinker your way through several drafts, you find that the poem wants to be something else. Maybe you thought you wanted to write a poem about a party, but the poem wound up being about friendship. As a writer, you must learn to trust your intuition. When a poem wants to go its own way, let it. See where it takes you."

Learning the Language of Poetry

GENRE

Why Teach This?

- To teach students that there are different kinds of poems.
- To teach students how visualizing the author's words in their minds can deepen their understanding of a poem.
- To teach students that the language in poetry is deliberate and should be read in a certain way.

Framing Question

- How does the author's use of language help a reader to create sensory images in order to more deeply understand a poem?

Unit Goals

- Students will learn that some poems rhyme and some do not.
- Students will learn that poems look different from each other.
- Students will learn that visualizing the author's words can help them understand a poem more deeply.
- Students will make connections to a poem to deepen their understanding.
- Students will read poetry with fluency and the correct phrasing.

Anchor Texts

- *All the Small Poems and Fourteen More* by Valerie Worth
- "Grounded" from *My Man Blue* by Nikki Grimes
- "How?" from *Spectacular Science*, edited by Lee Bennett Hopkins
- *Laughing Tomatoes/Jitomates Risueños* by Francisco X. Alarcon
- *Sing a Song of Popcorn*, edited by Beatrice Schenk de Regniers, Eva Moore, Mary Michaels White, and Jan Carr
- *Sing to the Sun* by Ashley Bryan

Unit Assessment Learning the Language of Poetry			GENRE
Student name:	EMERGING	DEVELOPING	INDEPENDENT
Recognizes poems that rhyme and poems that do not rhyme.			
Makes connection to poetry in order to help create sensory images and understand the poem more deeply.			
Reads poetry with fluency and the correct phrasing.			

Stage of the Unit	Focused Instruction You will	Independent Practice Students will
IMMERSION 3 days	• read aloud poetry across a wide range of topics, authors, and techniques, such as "Grounded" by Nikki Grimes. • read aloud "Flamingo" from All *the Small Poems and Fourteen More*, emphasizing phrasing and fluency based on line breaks and white space. • invite students to share what they know about poetry; begin class poetry chart.	• read and begin noticing elements of poetry. • begin collecting favorite poems to include in a poetry folder. • add to the poetry chart.
IDENTIFICATION 2 days	• read "How?" from *Spectacular Science* and model how to use a poem's various structures (line breaks, white space, punctuation) to read it more fluently. • read from *Sing a Song of Popcorn* as an example of a poems that use powerful language.	• read poems aloud with a partner, adjusting their voices according to various structures. • read poems with a partner, identifying poems that use strong language.

GUIDED PRACTICE 7 days	• read from *Laughing Tomatoes/Jitomates Risueños* by Francisco X. Alarcon and model how some words the poet has chosen give you a strong sensory image that helps you understand the poem better (highlight the words and phrases and share your image). • read aloud a poem with beautiful language, such as "Sun" from *All the Small Poems and Fourteen More*, stopping and sharing your thinking about the words that trigger the image, then sketching it. • share your thinking on a sticky note about how your image helped you understand the poem more deeply. • read a poem and model making a connection to the poem (having had the same experience, emotion); chart class connections. • make a connection to another poem, such as "Song" from *Sing to the Sun*, thinking aloud about those connections that deepened your understanding of the poem and those that did not (may include images, memories, feelings and experiences it evoked). • reread a few poems used throughout the unit, modeling how to answer what the poem is really about. • reread a few poems used throughout the unit, focusing on phrasing and fluency.	• highlight words or phrases within poems that give them a strong sensory image. • choose a poem that gives them a clear sensory image and sketch that part. • continue reading poems and thinking about sensory images; jot down a note about how those images deepened their understanding. • think about personal connections made while reading; share connections with partner. • think about a connection that they have made to another poem; discuss how that affected their understanding of the poem with a partner. • reread favorite poems, talking with a partner to discuss what they think the poem is really about. • choose a favorite poem to practice reading to a partner with the correct phrasing and fluency.
COMMITMENT 2–3 days	• reflect on how paying attention to the author's language gave you clear images that helped you understand a poem more deeply; model how to reflect on a poem's meaning in writing. • choose a favorite poem to read aloud.	• choose a poem with a strong sensory image and jot down how the image helped them understand the meaning of the poem; share their thoughts with partner. • choose a favorite poem to practice and read with fluency.
TOTAL: 14–15 DAYS		

Becoming Poets: Cherishing Words

Why Teach This?

- To teach students how to use language that creates a strong sensory image for the reader.
- To teach students how to use white space, line breaks, and repetition to convey meaning.

Framing Question

- How does studying author's craft and word choice help us to create poems that convey clear sensory images?

Unit Goals

- Students will learn where authors get their ideas for writing poetry.
- Students will learn how to include beautiful and interesting language in their poems to create sensory images.
- Students will learn to use the techniques of white space, line breaks, and repetition in their poetry.
- Students will collect their poetry in an anthology.

Anchor Texts

- *All the Small Poems and Fourteen More* by Valerie Worth
- *Angels Ride Bikes/Los Angeles Andan en Bicicleta* by Francisco X. Alarcon
- *Ashley Bryan's ABC of African American Poems* by Ashley Bryan
- *Before It Wriggles Away* by Janet S. Wong
- *Eats* by Arnold Adoff
- *Finding a Way* by Myra Cohn Livingston
- *Inner Chimes Poems on Poetry*, edited by Bobbye Goldstein
- *My Man Blue* by Nikki Grimes
- *Seasons* by Charlotte Zolotow
- *Sing a Song of Popcorn*, edited by Beatrice Schenk de Regniers, Eva Moore, Mary Michaels White, and Jan Carr
- *Sol a Sol* by Lori Marie Carlson
- *Spectacular Science*, selected by Lee Bennett Hopkins
- *Very Best (Almost) Friends*, edited by Paul B. Janeczko
- *Where the Sidewalk Ends* by Shel Siverstein

Unit Assessment Becoming Poets: Cherishing Words			GENRE
Student name:	EMERGING	DEVELOPING	INDEPENDENT
Chooses a mentor author to guide his or her writing.			
Generates ideas for topics in poetry writing.			
Includes beautiful and/or interesting language in his or her poems.			
Uses various techniques including white space, line breaks, and repetition.			

Stage of the Unit	Focused Instruction You will	Independent Practice Students will
IMMERSION 4 days	• read aloud from various poetry collections across a wide range of topics, authors, and styles, such as *Eats*, *Seasons*, *Where the Sidewalk Ends,* and *Inner Chimes,* commenting on where authors get their ideas. • read aloud from a variety of poetry collections, such as *All the Small Poems and Fourteen More*, *Finding a Way*, and *Carnival of Animals*, commenting on what you notice about the structure (white space, repetition, line breaks). • read aloud from a variety of poems, such as "Kitten" from *All the Small Poems and Fourteen More* or "I Am Kojo" from *Ashley Bryan's ABC of African American Poems*, commenting on language that gives you a strong sensory image. • model how to create a list of possible topics on which you could write a poem.	• browse through poetry, familiar or new, jotting down where the authors might have gotten their ideas; share a poem with a partner. • read through poems with a partner, noticing different structures. • read through poems, marking places where they get a clear picture of what the poet is describing; share with a partner and add to their poetry folders. • create a list of topics that are important to them that they might like to write about.
IDENTIFICATION 3 days	• read aloud *Before It Wriggles Away* and identify poems based on memories, feelings, imagination, observation, or special people. • read aloud and discuss the structure of poems that contain a list or repetition such as "Earthly Paradise" from *Angels Ride Bikes/Los Angeles Andan en Bicicleta* by Francisco X. Alarcon. • read aloud anchor text poems with white space and line breaks; identify and discuss the purpose of these structures.	• read poems with partners, collecting poems and discussing where they think poets got their ideas. • read poems with partners, collecting poems written as a list or that contain repetition. • read poems with partners, identifying poems that contain white space and line breaks.
GUIDED PRACTICE 9 days	• read aloud "My Grandmother" by Lori Marie Carlson from *Sol a Sol*, highlighting how the author is writing about a special person. • read aloud from an anchor poem that focuses on a memory (such as "The Swing" by Robert Louis Stevenson from *Sing a Song of Popcorn*).	• write poems about some special people in their lives. • write poems about a memory they have.

GUIDED PRACTICE *(continued)*	• read aloud anchor poems that highlight observation from the anthology *Seasons* and discuss and highlight how poets use observation to create poetry. • read aloud an anchor poem that highlights the use of line breaks such as "Teased" from *Very Best (Almost) Friends*. • read a poem aloud that is written in the form of a list, showing students how poems can be spaced on a page (such as "Knoxville Tennessee" by Nikki Giovanni from *Sing a Song of Popcorn* or "Crickets" by Valerie Worth from *All the Small Poems and Fourteen More*). • read aloud and show students the poem "My Mouth" by Arnold Adoff from *Eats*, highlighting its use of white space. • read "Quiet" by Myra Cohn Livingston from *Finding a Way* and think aloud about the power of the words "quiet" and "shouting" and the way they are written. • read "Little Snail" by Hilda Conkling from *Sing a Song of Popcorn*, noting how clearly she describes the way the snail is wagging its head. • read aloud an anchor poem that shows students how poets choose words to express sounds (such as "Birds" by Philip de Vos and Piet Grobler).	• choose a topic from their list of writing ideas to write a poem. • write a poem in the form of a list or choose a poem to revise, focusing on line breaks. • write a new poem or choose one they've already written that uses white space to convey meaning. • choose a poem that they have already written and experiment with the line breaks; cut the poem into parts and create new lines and white space. • write a new poem or choose one they've already written and add language that creates strong sensory images. • add a simile to a poem. • add description to a poem in the form of sound words or the use of the sense of sound to create images.
COMMITMENT 3 days	• model putting together your own poetry anthology, describing the significance of a few of the poems you chose. • read aloud one of your favorite poems.	• read through or add to the class poetry anthology, reflecting on why certain poems were included; share their reflections with a partner. • choose a favorite poem or two that they have written and read it aloud in small groups. • celebrate student poetry by reading aloud, choral reading, or displaying on bulletin board.
TOTAL: 19 DAYS		

SPOTLIGHT on Conventions

- Building Fluency Through Phrasing
- Building Fluency Through Punctuation and Paragraphing

As second-grade teachers, we often either dread teaching conventions because they feel so detached from the liveliness of our students' literacy experiences or cram in lots of instruction on conventions in concentrated periods of time, worried that we are not covering it all before they move on through the grades. The Complete 4 approach advocates finding a middle ground. We are not going to teach conventions in isolation (although we do advocate regular word-work time for practice with patterns and strategies), nor are we going to ignore them. Instead, we are going to carefully place conventions instruction where it belongs: alongside students' authentic work. We celebrate language, punctuation, and grammar in ways that respect and give dignity to the way second graders are coming to print. The writer Eudora Welty recalled her first glimpse as a child of the alphabet inside her storybooks and how magical the swirls and curves of each letter seemed. Let us capture that magic in units on conventions. See page 62–72 in *The Complete 4 for Literacy* for more guidelines for this component.

Pam Allyn

Building Fluency

These next units will address the topic of conventions with a close look at fluency and how conventions work together to provide students with the foundations for smooth reading and clear writing.

In *Teaching for Comprehending and Fluency,* Fountas and Pinnell (2006) define fluent reading as "using smoothly integrated operations to process the meaning, language, and print." Second graders are working to increase both their understanding of fluency and the role it plays in reading, as well as their ability to continue to read fluently even as text difficulty increases.

As second graders transition to more challenging texts, fluency not only becomes more important, it becomes more challenging. Using the Fountas and Pinnell leveling system, there is a huge jump in the complexity from level K books to level L, and from level L books to level M. This increase in complexity can be seen in the use of more dialogue with less direct indication of who is talking and the use of more complex sentence structure and punctuation—dashes, semicolons, and commas to indicate pauses.

These two units on fluency address these challenges with a focus on the lively sound of language, the attention to white space that effective reading calls for, and the markers of punctuation that propel a reader along—or get in his way. In these units we are going to try to break down some of the barriers so that our second graders, so prone to skipping hand in hand with a friend, can also skip lightly across the playing fields of text.

Building Fluency Through Phrasing

CONVENTIONS

Why Teach This?
- To enable students to be fluent, effective readers.
- To develop better fluency so that readers can attend to making meaning of text.
- To develop oral reading skills.

Framing Question
- How can readers attend to punctuation in order to build fluency?

Unit Goals
- Students will identify what fluent reading sound like and looks like.
- Students will understand that pacing, accuracy, expression, and phrasing are all key to fluent reading.

- Students will develop oral reading through appropriate pacing.
- Students will use punctuation and print to read with expression.
- Students will use pausing and ending punctuation to read fluently.
- Students will use punctuation and characters' word choice to read dialogue fluently.
- Students will attend to the white space on the page (paragraphs and transitions) to read fluently.

Anchor Texts

- "Honey I Love" from *Honey I Love and Other Poems* by Eloise Greenfield
- *Lionel and His Friends* by Stephen Krensky
- *Little Bear's Friend* (CD) by Else Holmelund Minarik
- *My Father's Dragon* by Ruth Stiles Gannett
- "Nathaniel Talking" from *In the Land of Words* by Eloise Greenfield
- *Vacation Under the Volcano* (Magic Tree House) by Mary Pope Osborne
- *Young Cam Jansen and the Library Mystery* by David Adler

Resource Sheet

- Fluency Reading Parent Letter (Resource 5.1)

Unit Assessment Building Fluency Through Phrasing			CONVENTIONS
Student name:	EMERGING	DEVELOPING	INDEPENDENT
Identifies what fluent reading sounds and feels like.			
Understands that pacing, accuracy, expression, and phrasing are all components of fluency.			
Paces reading appropriately to text and purpose.			
Uses end punctuation (.?!) and pausing punctuation (,) to read fluently.			
Reads dialogue fluently by attending to characters' words and dialogue punctuation.			
Attends to white space—paragraphs and transitions (such as chapter breaks or pauses within a chapter)—to read fluently.			

Stage of the Unit	Focused Instruction You will	Independent Practice Students will
IMMERSION 3 days	• explain that effective reading is smooth reading; share experiences of smooth reading versus bumpy reading. • read an excerpt from *My Father's Dragon* and define fluent reading as smooth reading; begin to further define fluency as reading accurately with good pacing, expression, and phrasing. • play the *Little Bear's Friend* CD for the class as an example of fluent reading; name the qualities of fluency (expression, phrasing, pacing, and accuracy).	• find a part in their texts that felt smooth when they read it; discuss with partner. • find texts (new or familiar) that they can read smoothly. • practice reading fluently with a partner.
IDENTIFICATION 1 day	• review terms used to define "fluency"; use shared reading texts or a chapter from *My Father's Dragon* to read with expression and good pacing.	• read and examine themselves as readers; listen for places where their voices change for punctuation or other print clues.
GUIDED PRACTICE 4 days	• use *Young Cam Jansen and the Library Mystery* to demonstrate reading with expression, paying attention to word choice and punctuation (!?). • use the chapter "Sandwich" from *Lionel and His Friends* to demonstrate using ending and pausing punctuation as traffic signals that help us read fluently. • read from the first three pages of *Vacation Under the Volcano* to model reading dialogue; use the dialogue punctuation and the sound of characters' voices to read fluently. • use "Nathaniel Talking" to demonstrate the use of white space on a page (the space between paragraphs, a new chapter, or a break in the chapter) and how a reader uses this white space to read fluently.	• practice reading texts with expression. • read aloud using punctuation as traffic signals that aid their fluency. • practice reading dialogue fluently by using the punctuation and changing their voices to reflect the different characters. • read aloud, making sure to pause where indicated by white space.
COMMITMENT 2 days	• introduce Readers Theater as a way to build fluency; give small groups scripts and assign the parts. • reflect on how reading now sounds different and more fluent.	• practice reading Readers Theater scripts fluently. • perform Readers Theater.
TOTAL: 10 DAYS		

Getting Started

The room should be full of the sound of reading in this unit. Or if you are working with any deaf students, as we often do, the room is full of hands and signs, as children orally or visually play with words.

Structures and Routines

Rehearsing Readers Theater scripts gives students a great opportunity to practice with oral accuracy, pacing, smoothness, expression, and phrasing. Because they are working with the same script over many days, they can move beyond comprehension work and focus the oral aspect of reading. In addition, Readers Theater scripts give students an opportunity to read dialogue, thus providing them with an opportunity to practice reading punctuation and reading with phrasing and expression.

Teaching Materials

Matching the reader to the text is always the secret ingredient for success in building capacity for reading.

We recommend offering your students texts with short stories or episodic chapters so that they can dip in and out of the text while they practice building fluency. The following is a list of early series and chapter books that lend themselves well to a fluency unit.

For Vulnerable Readers
• Frog and Toad series, Arnold Lobel
• Little Bill series, Bill Cosby
• Oliver and Amanda Pig series, Jean Van Leeuwen
• Poppleton series, Cynthia Rylant

For Steady Readers
• Amelia Bedelia series, Peggy Parish
• The High-Rise Private Eyes series, Cynthia Rylant
• Hopscotch School series (American Girl), Valerie Tripp
• Lionel series, Stephen Krensky

For Strong Readers
• The Cobble Street Cousins series, Cynthia Rylant
• Horrible Harry and Song Lee series, Suzy Kline
• The Stories Julian Tells and other books by the author Ann Cameron
• Weird Planet series, Dan Greenburg

In addition, several websites contain scripts for Readers Theater and oral reading practice. One of our favorites is www.aaronshep.com. Also, you can download decodable text from www.readinga-z.com.

Books on CD and tape are excellent resources for this unit. The Scholastic Cassettes series includes *Dear Mrs. LaRue* by Mark Teague, *The Runaway Pumpkin* by Kevin Lewis, and *The Kissing Hand* by Audrey Penn.

Use poetry to practice phrasing, expression, pacing, and fluency. Here are some of our favorites for this unit:

- *Hailstones and Halibut Bones*, Mary O'Neill
- *Honey, I Love*, Eloise Greenfield
- *Poetry for Young People*, Robert Frost
- *Sweet Corn*, James Stevenson
- *Ten-Second Rain Showers*, edited by Sandford Lyne
- *You Read to Me I'll Read to You*, Mary Ann Hoberman

Stages of the Unit

Immersion

During the Immersion stage, it is important to provide examples and help children recognize what fluent reading feels and looks like. Fluency can be demonstrated through reading buddies' reading aloud, your reading aloud, and listening to audiobooks. Fluency can also be practiced at home. Send home the Fluency Parent Letter (Resource 5.1).

Identification

Identify the qualities of a fluent reader. Explain that reading can be bumpy or smooth and that fluent readers read smoothly.

Guided Practice

Focus on specific strategies for reading with accurate pacing and expression, and according to punctuation. Create opportunities for oral reading. The read-aloud, shared reading, and Readers Theater are key elements.

Commitment

The unit ends with a Readers Theater performance, giving students an opportunity to demonstrate the fluency strategies they've learned.

Assessment

The best way to assess reading fluency is to be sure you hear each reader read aloud one-on-one with you several times throughout the unit. This can be done during conferences with a benchmark text or inside each reader's independent reading book.

Day-by-Day Lessons

DAY 1 Immersion

Focused Instruction

Reading is like lots of other things we do in our lives: sometimes it feels smooth and steady and sometimes it feels rough and bumpy. This unit is about how we can always make our reading feel as smooth as possible. What kinds of things do you do in your life that sometimes feel smooth and sometimes feel bumpy?

- Students share own experiences, reflecting on what made something feel smooth rather than bumpy (they felt confident, they felt comfortable with their skills).

Independent Practice

- Students read independently, noting where reading felt smooth and where it felt bumpy.

Wrap-Up

- Students read out a portion of their independent texts that they can read smoothly.

DAY 2 Immersion

Focused Instruction

I am going to read aloud a chapter of My Father's Dragon *by Ruth Stiles Gannett. As I read, I will use expression and try to pace myself so you can really enjoy the story. During Independent Practice, I will ask you to put books together for this unit that you think you can read smoothly.*

Independent Practice

- Students read and collect books that feel like they could be smooth reads.

Wrap-Up

- Students share their "short stacks" with one another.

DAY 3 Immersion

Focused Instruction

Let's continue to think about and notice exactly what fluent reading looks like, sounds like, and feels like. Today I am going to play aloud a portion of one of our favorite books on CD, Little Bear's Friend.

- After two to three minutes, discuss what this reading sounded like and why it seemed so smooth.

Independent Practice

- Students read independently and practice reading aloud a section of their book to a partner.

Wrap-Up

- Name with students the characteristics of fluent reading (smooth instead of bumpy, reading with phrasing instead of word-by-word, using punctuation to create expression, and reading at a comfortable pace).

DAY 4 Identification

Focused Instruction

When we read, we want to read with expression, making our voices go up and down and matching the words, the size and kind of print, and the punctuation. We also want to use smooth phrasing, paying attention to the traffic signals on the page and letting them tell us how to read. Listen to how my voice sounds as I read another chapter from My Father's Dragon. *If I do not use expression or punctuation my voice sounds like a robot and it is harder to understand what I am reading.*

Independent Practice

Today as you read with a partner, spy on yourself as a reader. Listen to the places where your voice changes as you read due to size of print and punctuation. Notice if there are places where your voice sounds smooth as a reader. Stop and talk to your partner about these noticings as you read.

Wrap-Up

What were some of the things you noticed when you were listening to each other read? What happened to your voice when you saw varied print type and punctuation?

DAY 5 Guided Practice

Focused Instruction

Fluent readers read with expression. They make their voice match the words and the punctuation. I am going to read aloud a page from a text we read earlier in the year, Young Cam Jansen and the Library Mystery. *Here are pages 22 and 23. Follow along silently while I read aloud.*

- Read pages from the text, reading with expression for the "click" that Cam says, and emphasizing the sentences with exclamation marks.
- Demonstrate and discuss how to read with expression. Ask the class what an expressive reader does.
- Invite readers to join in and read using appropriate expression.

Independent Practice

When you read today, notice a place where your expression changed based on the punctuation. Put a sticky note in this place.

- Students read their independent texts and reread parts to their partners, practicing reading with expression.

Wrap-Up

Let's share the places where the punctuation changed how your voice sounded when you read. Turn to the person next to you, someone other than your reading partner, and share these spots.

DAY 6 Guided Practice

Focused Instruction

We are really improving the sound of our reading! Smooth readers pay attention to the punctuation on the page. Punctuation marks are like traffic signals—they signal to the reader what she needs to do and how to do it. We have noticed that when you read punctuation fluently you:

Stop (like at a red light)	for a period
Raise your voice up and then stop	for a question mark
Read with emphasis and then stop	for an exclamation mark
Pause—slow down (like at a yellow light)	for a comma

Follow along as I read pages 26 and 27 in Lionel and His Friends *by Stephen Krensky. This is the chapter called "The Sandwich," and I am reading the last two pages.*

- Read the text appropriately, pausing and stopping at punctuation.
- Name with students what punctuation was there and how you phrased your reading according to these marks on the page.
- Ask students to join in and read again with you.

Independent Practice

- Students read independent texts and spend the last few minutes of this time reading with their partners and practicing reading with good phrasing.

Wrap-Up

- Put student texts on document camera or overhead if possible.
- Allow students to read aloud and name the punctuation. Compliment them on their fluency.

DAY 7 Guided Practice

Focused Instruction

Today we are going to continue to learn how to read fluently, using expression and good phrasing, by looking at dialogue. Reading the dialogue, or when the characters are talking, requires you to read smoothly, with good phrasing and with expression in your voice that feels like that character. The tone of voice can also change to represent the different characters who are speaking.

- Read aloud the first three pages of *Vacation Under the Volcano* by Mary Pope Osborne.

Independent Practice

- Give students practice rereading the excerpt.

Wrap-Up

- Students share lines of dialogue.

DAY 8 Guided Practice

Focused Instruction

Smooth readers read with attention to white space on the page. Let's practice that with the poem "Nathaniel Talking" by Eloise Greenfield.

- Read poem aloud, pausing where you see white space.

You see that we really paid attention to the white space on the page and paused and read according to the breaks in the page. Let's try this with a fiction book now. We are going to go back to the first chapter of Vacation Under the Volcano *and look this time at the white space in those first few pages as well as two other pages I want to show you, pages 10 and 11.*

- Look closely at the pages to identify and discuss the white space around the paragraphs. Discuss that each new idea or each new person talking is indicated by a new paragraph.
- Illuminate as well the large chunks of space on pages 10 and 11 where there is a typed or handwritten note with a lot of white space above and below it. Demonstrate how to read these parts fluently with proper pausing and phrasing.

Independent Practice

Today when you are reading in your independent books, pay attention as you move from each chunk or paragraph on the page and the white space. At the end of the paragraph, always take a bigger breath and pause.

Wrap-Up

- Students share passages and read them aloud.

DAY 9 Commitment

Focused Instruction

Another way to practice reading smoothly is to read a play. When there are different parts, your voice has to change so others can understand the play and the parts of the play. Today we will practice reading smoothly with scripts so that we can perform the play at the end of the week.

- Find a script (or scripts) you feel would match your students and would provide them with opportunities to practice reading fluently.
- Give scripts to students, identifying each student's part.
- The emphasis is on the oral reading—reading smoothly and with awareness of punctuation and character change.

Independent Practice

- Practice reading from scripts.

Wrap-Up

- Have students share thoughts on how reading from a script today allowed them to read smoothly.

DAY 10 Commitment

Focused Instruction

We have spent the last two weeks working on reading fluently and smoothly. We have learned that reading this way makes our reading sound more interesting and helps us to better understand what we are reading. Punctuation, dialogue, and white space all help us to read smoothly. Today we are going to get to perform our scripts for others. Use your voices to convey smoothness in your readings—watch for punctuation, dialogue, and white space.

Independent Practice

Today you are going to perform the scripts for a small group. If you are the performer, practice using all of the things we have learned to read smoothly. If you are the listener, notice the way the performers are reading. Reflect on how this makes the listening more interesting and how it helps you to better understand what you are listening to.

- Students perform the scripts for one another.

Wrap-Up

- Reflect on how their reading became smooth by noticing punctuation, dialogue, and white space.

The Architecture of Language

How inquisitive our second graders are! They are constantly peering ahead, peeking in, wondering about what's in mysterious boxes, holiday gifts, the oven. This unit should be like opening little gift packages of ideas: the paragraph. This is a study of the architecture of language. Paragraphs change when there is a change in time, in place, when a new person speaks, when something new happens, when the author wants to emphasize something. It is a signal to us as readers—something is about to happen.

Building Fluency Through Punctuation and Paragraphing

CONVENTIONS

Why Teach This?
- To enable writers to build fluency.
- To make students aware that writing is organized into clusters of related sentences.
- To teach students to organize chunks of writing into paragraphs.

Framing Question
- How can we build fluency as writers by paying attention to paragraphs and punctuation on the page?

Unit Goals
- Students will understand that a paragraph represents change in the who, what, where, or when.
- Students will recognize and identify a paragraph of writing.
- Students will learn to organize and cluster their thoughts together on the page into a paragraph.
- Students will build fluency by writing sentences that use correct end punctuation and can be organized into paragraphs.

Anchor Texts
- "The Cyprus Tree" from *A Forest of Stones: Magical Tree Tales From Around the World* by Rina Singh
- *Family Pictures/Cuadros de familia* by Carmen Lomas Garza
- *A Little Shopping* by Cynthia Rylant

Resource Sheets
- Paragraph Noticing Paper (Resource 5.2)
- Paragraph Graphic Organizer (Resource 5.3)

Unit Assessment Building Fluency Through Punctuation and Paragraphing			**CONVENTIONS**
Student name:	**EMERGING**	**DEVELOPING**	**INDEPENDENT**
Writes a complete piece with at least three paragraphs.			
Clusters ideas into paragraphs.			
Uses correct end punctuation to transition to different thoughts in each paragraph.			
Recognizes why a writer transitions to a new paragraph (who, what, where, or when).			

Stage of the Unit	Focused Instruction You will	Independent Practice Students will
IMMERSION 2 days	• read "The Cyprus Tree" from *A Forest of Stones: Magical Tree Tales From Around the World* and observe how writers use paragraphs to help readers navigate their pages. • use "The Cyprus Tree" to identify the characteristics of a paragraph and the use of conventions in the paragraph; model how to complete Paragraph Noticing Paper (Resource 5.2).	• read or browse through a text and place sticky notes to identify examples of when writers used punctuation, capitalization, or paragraph breaks to make the text more readable. • work with a partner to name the qualities of a paragraph in "The Cypress Tree" or in their independent reading and find evidence to support the the class definition of a paragraph.
IDENTIFICATION 1 day	• create an anchor chart for paragraphs titled "Characteristics of a Paragraph"; model for students that paragraphs are a cluster of sentences that belong together.	• identify why sentences in their independent reading books are grouped together into paragraphs; discuss with a partner how paragraphing makes a text readable.
GUIDED PRACTICE 4 days	• model choosing a comfortable topic to write about and using the Paragraph Graphic Organizer (Resource 5.3). • model using graphic organizers to help create paragraphs. • show how periods and exclamation points act as traffic signals to help the reader navigate the text. • identify other punctuation that helps readers read paragraphs.	• use the Paragraph Graphic Organizer (Resource 5.3) as a guide to create a paragraph; choose a comfortable topic to write a paragraph about. • write paragraphs from the graphic organizer. • revise paragraphs, paying close attention to periods and exclamation points. • add additional punctuation (commas, ellipses, and question marks).
COMMITMENT 2 days	• review what students learned about the characteristics and purpose of paragraphs; demonstrate choosing a piece to polish with punctuation and paragraphs.	• revise a piece from their writers' notebooks, paying close attention to the format of the paragraphs and the use of punctuation. • share a revised writing sample with the class.
TOTAL: 9 DAYS		

Getting Started

Your students should be familiar with all the writing in their folders or notebooks, so in this unit they can use writing from previous units if they prefer. They can also brainstorm new ideas and generate new writing if that feels more interesting and feels easier for them.

Structures and Routines

Students should be placed in homogenous partnerships in this unit, so that more fluent writers can move more quickly through the stages of the process together, and you can spend more time conferring with struggling writers.

Teaching Materials

Books in the level range of L–N would be the most appropriate—they show the purpose and structure of paragraphs but are not too complex for second graders. Texts that are levels K and below do not provide good examples of paragraphing. These texts have fewer words on the page. Books above level N are full of dialogue and more complex sentence structure and would be challenging for students just being introduced to paragraphing. If you have students in your class reading comfortably at that level, then by all means allow them to browse those for examples of paragraphing. But generally speaking, chapter books from the following series would work well:

- Cam Jansen series, David Adler
- The Cobble Street Cousins series, Cynthia Rylant
- Magic Tree House series, Mary Pope Osborne
- Rainbow Magic series, Daisy Meadows
- Zac Power series, H. I. Larry

Also, these narrative picture books would work well:
- *Koala Lou*, Mem Fox
- *Let's Go Home*, Cynthia Rylant
- *Over and Over*, Charlotte Zolotow
- *Peter's Chair*, Ezra Jack Keats

These collections would also work well:
- *Childtimes: A Three-Generation Memoir*, Eloise Greenfield
- *Family Pictures*, Carmen Lomas Garza
- *Home: A Collaboration of Thirty Distinguished Authors and Illustrators of Children's Books to Aid the Homeless*, edited by Michael J. Rosen

Stages of the Unit

Immersion

Investigate familiar texts to determine the purposes for paragraphs and to take note of ending punctuation.

Identification

It is essential to name the characteristics of a paragraph, showing students how paragraphs help us navigate a text.

Guided Practice

Students practice writing paragraphs and using punctuation in paragraphs to make their writing sound more interesting and to make it easier for the reader to navigate. Show how punctuation and paragraphing provide traffic signals for the reader.

Commitment

Commitment will be an opportunity for students to celebrate this new knowledge together and share their paragraphing skills with each other.

Day-by-Day Lessons

DAY 1 Immersion

Focused Instruction

We have spent the last two weeks working on using punctuation to make our reading smooth. Now we are going to use what we have learned to create interesting paragraphs with punctuation when we write. Let's look closely at what a writer does to guide readers. Look again at one of our favorite pieces from the collection A Forest of Stories: Magical Tree Tales From Around the World. *Let's look at "The Cyprus Tree" by Cynthia Rylant and discuss how she uses paragraphs to make her writing more readable.*

- As you read, notice the conventions in the piece—correct spelling, punctuation, capitalization—while emphasizing the paragraphs.
- Inform students that this piece has four parts and that each part contains some sentences. These parts are called paragraphs.

Independent Practice

Today I want you to look at one of the texts from my pile of books and work with your partner to notice and mark examples of what a writer did to make the writing more readable. We don't want to sticky-note the whole book, so find just one or two good examples of what we noticed in our lesson.

- Partners work to mark examples of spelling, punctuation, capitalization, and paragraphs.

Wrap-Up

Turn to another partnership on the rug. Show them where you put a sticky note on a paragraph and share what you notice about this paragraph. How are your paragraphs similar and different?

DAY 2 Immersion

Focused Instruction

Let's look again at "A Cyprus Tree." Today we will closely examine the paragraphs. Let's investigate these four chunks of writing on the page. What does a paragraph look like? What does each paragraph contain? What do we notice about the white space and the length of paragraphs? What kinds of punctuation do you see being used in the paragraphs?

- Look closely at the paragraphs with students.
- Model how to complete the Paragraph Noticing Paper (Resource 5.2).

Independent Practice

I want for you to look at the paragraphs in another text today. How many are there on the page? What do you notice about each paragraph? Are they different lengths? What punctuation do you notice? Discuss and share these thoughts with your partner.

- Students examine a text to investigate paragraphs and begin to fill in their Paragraph Noticing Papers (Resource 5.2).
- Partners jot down two to three observations about their paragraphs on a sticky note.

Wrap-Up

I have heard you say so many interesting thoughts about your paragraphs. Let's share them.

- Students share their observations.
- Begin a class chart recording their ideas about paragraphs.

DAY 3 Identification

Focused Instruction

Today we are going to name what we have noticed about paragraphs over the last two days.

Characteristics of a Paragraph				
Check off the characteristics you notice in your books:	Book Titles			
A cluster of sentences with end punctuation				
Format of either indenting or skipping a line				
White space on the page				
Can be different sizes (two sentences or many sentences)				
Is about a particular thing				
Separates ideas in a piece of writing				

Now let's look at our last read-aloud chapter book to find the paragraphs in there. Let's go back to page 8 and page 16 from the first book in the Cynthia Rylant Cobble Street Cousins series, A Little Shopping. *On these two pages there are four paragraphs. Just looking at the pages, you can see the paragraphs are different. Let's look closely and see if what we are saying about paragraphs rings true here and add it to our chart. One important question I have is why the sentences in each paragraph are grouped together. What do you think?*

- Facilitate a conversation with students about why the sentences are separated into paragraphs and why each group of sentences belongs together.

Independent Practice

Today I want you to look for a paragraph in your independent reading book. Look at one page in the book and notice the length of the paragraphs. Look closely at one of the paragraphs. Can you tell why those sentences were grouped together into one paragraph?

- Students read their independent texts, noticing the format, looking at the number of sentences, and hypothesizing on why the author put those sentences together.
- Students jot down ideas about one paragraph on the Paragraph Noticing Paper (Resource 5.2).
- Confer with students on their findings and copy a few paragraphs on chart paper to look at together.

Wrap-Up

- Add book titles and observations to class chart.

DAY 4 Guided Practice

Focused Instruction

We have spent the last few days exploring paragraphs, and today we are going to write paragraphs. We are going to use our Paragraph Graphic Organizer (Resource 5.3) to help us write a few paragraphs. Last time we used a sheet like this one, we talked about how you put your big idea in the rectangle on the top of the page, and how you then put thoughts, details, or smaller ideas in the circles that we called the "bubbles." We talked about how you can write a sentence about each bubble. Well, today I am going to show you that each bubble can really be one whole idea that you write a paragraph about.

- Model choosing a topic you are comfortable with.
- Fill in the graphic organizer and demonstrate specifically the kind of detail that would go in a bubble on the organizer.
- Model talking aloud ("writing in the air") about each bubble, or part of the big idea.

Independent Practice

Today I am going to ask that you use the Paragraph Graphic Organizer (Resource 5.3) to record ideas and plan for your writing. After you have filled in the graphic organizer, meet with your partner and really discuss each bubble so that you fill up your mind with possible ideas for each part.

- Students choose a comfortable topic to write about.

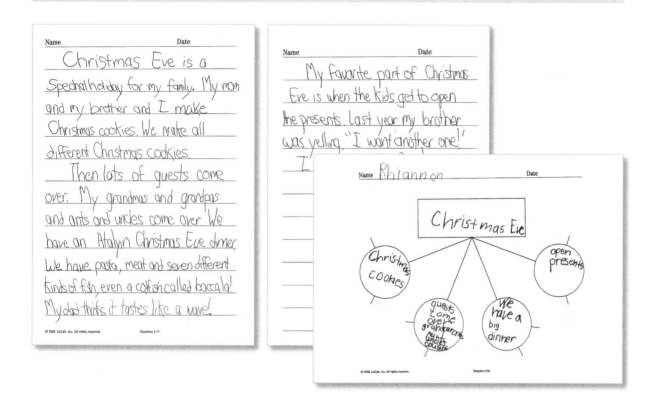

The handwritten worksheets read:

Worksheet 1:
Christmas Eve is a special holiday for my family. My mom and my brother and I make Christmas cookies. We make all different Christmas cookies.

Then lots of guests come over. My grandmas and grandpas and ants and uncles come over. We have an Italyin Christmas Eve dinner. We have pasta, meat and seven different kinds of fish, even a catfish called baccala! My dad thinks it tastes like a wave.

Worksheet 2:
My favorite part of Christmas Eve is when the kids get to open the presents. Last year my brother was yelling, "I want another one!" I

Worksheet 3 (graphic organizer, Name: Rhiannon):
Christmas Eve
- Christmas cookies
- open presents
- guests come over grandparents aunts uncles cousins
- We have a big dinner

- Students fill in the graphic organizer with a big idea and small details, or parts of the big idea.
- Students discuss with a partner their thoughts for each bubble.

Wrap-Up

You did a great job using our organizer. Let's make a plan for tomorrow to use our organizer to write paragraphs.

- Explain to students that you will model writing paragraphs from the organizer, and then they will do it themselves.

DAY 5 Guided Practice

Focused Instruction

Today we are going to write about the big idea in our organizer. We have written about this idea before, so we are comfortable with this topic. However, today we are really going to focus on organizing this idea into paragraphs. We will use our bubbles to help us to do this. We want to make sure that for the idea in each bubble, we put sentences that go with that idea. Now let me show you as I do that from my organizer.

- Recap orally a part of the big idea from a bubble in your organizer and write a paragraph about it.

Independent Practice

Now it is your turn. Stay on the rug until you have talked out your writing enough with your partner. When you are ready, I want you to go off and write a paragraph about a bubble on your organizer. Write paragraphs from as many bubbles as you can during our writing time. Remember to indent or skip a line when you come to a new bubble or idea, showing it is a new paragraph.

- Students use bubbles as a way to organize parts of the big idea.

Wrap-Up

Today you used your organizer to help write your paragraphs. Let's see how some of our classmates wrote their paragraphs.

- Use one or two students' work to demonstrate the writing of a paragraph.

DAY 6 Guided Practice

Focused Instruction

Today I want to show you how you can use paragraphing and punctuation to write fluently, just as we can use them to read fluently. Punctuation and paragraphs are traffic signals on a page. They help us to give readers ideas in a clear and organized way, so I am going to look back at the paragraph I wrote yesterday and make sure I have some punctuation as traffic signals for the reader.

- Model adding punctuation to your paragraph, pointing out how this changes the way the writing sounds.

Independent Practice

Go back to your paragraphs and find places where you can add punctuation to make your writing sound more interesting for the reader. Today let's focus on adding periods at the end of sentences and exclamation marks to show excitement.

- Students reread paragraphs to make sure there are periods at the end of each sentence or exclamation marks to show excitement.
- If students finish this work, they can add another paragraph to their writing.

Wrap-Up

Many of you used punctuation today as traffic signals in your writing. This makes the writing more interesting and clearer for the reader.

- Use one student's work as an example.

DAY 7 Guided Practice

Focused Instruction

Yesterday we added periods and exclamation marks to our paragraphs to make them more interesting. Today we are going to add some more punctuation. We can see if there are places we can add commas, ellipses, and question marks. Since we have already studied this punctuation, we know when to use these marks.

- Model using some other punctuation in your paragraph or model with a student's work.

Independent Practice

Today you're going to add more punctuation to your paragraphs. If you have filled in the punctuation in your paragraphs, you can add another paragraph to your writing and add more punctuation as you go.

Wrap-Up

Turn to the person next to you and share a place where you added punctuation to your paragraphs.

DAY 8 Commitment

Focused Instruction

We have spent the last two weeks looking at paragraphs and punctuation and noticing how they are traffic signals for our writing. Today we are going to look back at an old piece of writing from our notebooks to see if there is a place where we can add punctuation and/or use paragraphs to make our writing clearer.

Independent Practice

- Students choose a piece from their writing notebooks to polish.
- Students add to or change paragraphs.

Wrap-Up

Turn to the person next to you and share a place where you added paragraphing and/or punctuation to help the reader navigate through the text.

DAY 9 Commitment

Focused Instruction

Today we are going to share and celebrate the very grown-up work that we did in this unit. We will share our paragraphed pieces with each other. I also want for us to share how we will take this learning with us into the last part of our year. What will we do to remember to paragraph our writing?

Independent Practice

- Students share and celebrate their writing.

Wrap-Up

- Students share reflections on this paragraphing unit.

The Versatile Reader, the Confident Writer

These two units are a synthesis of an entire year of instruction. Your second graders have been exposed to a wide variety of genres and now they can play in those fields, both as readers and writers. In the following reading unit they will explore the connections between genres, and in the writing unit they will participate in clubs related to their genre preferences. They will feel just right: grown-up and playful all at the same time, the true nature of a second grader.

Making Connections Across Genres: Readers Are Thinkers

STRATEGY

Why Teach This?

- To identify and compare different genres—fiction, nonfiction, poetry, riddles.
- To deepen students' understanding of the similarities and differences of various genres.
- To encourage students to make connections across genres.

Framing Question

- How do readers contrast different kinds of texts?

Unit Goals

- Students will identify and define fiction, nonfiction, poetry, and riddles.
- Students will compare the qualities and features of different genres.
- Students will make connections across genres.
- Students will discuss their features and connections with a partner.

Anchor Texts

Different Genres/Similar Topics:

- *Bear (Watch Me Grow)* by Lisa Magloff and *Little Bear* by Else Holmelund Minarik
- "Doctor Dinosaur" and "Dino Riddles" from *Ranger Rick, How do Dinosaurs Get Well Soon?* by Jane Yolen; *Dinosaurs Before Dark* by Mary Pope Osborne; and "Dinosaur Bone" by Alice Schertle from *Spectacular Science*, selected by Lee Bennett Hopkins)

Theme of Friendship:

- *Frog and Toad are Friends* by Arnold Lobel
- *How to Lose a Friend* by Nancy Carlson and "Making Friends" from *In the Land of Words* by Eloise Greenfield

Unit Assessment Making Connections Across Genre: Readers Are Thinkers			
			STRATEGY
Student name:	EMERGING	DEVELOPING	INDEPENDENT
Identifies fiction, nonfiction, poetry, and riddles.			
Identifies and compares different genre features.			
Identifies and compares themes written in different genres.			
Discusses features and connections with a partner.			

Stage of the Unit	Focused Instruction You will	Independent Practice Students will
IMMERSION 4 days	• read the first chapter in *Dinosaurs Before Dark*; talk about the genre elements (story, chapters, characters who have a problem). • read the article "Doctor Dinosaur" and talk about what students notice in the text (facts, no story, no characters, information). • read "Dinosaur Bone" and talk about what students notice in the text (white space, how the words are positioned). • read "Dino Riddles" and talk about what students notice in the text (no characters, no story, tricky questions, answers).	• browse the fiction, nonfiction, poetry, and riddle book baskets. • browse a book from one genre and discuss why a reader reads that genre.
IDENTIFICATION 1 day	• create a chart that compares the identifying features of each genre: fiction, nonfiction, poetry, and riddles; use the read-aloud books to generate a list of features for each genre.	• identify features from the chart in the books they read independently; discuss with a partner one unique feature they noticed in a book they read.
GUIDED PRACTICE 4 days	• compare a fiction and a nonfiction book with similar themes or topics; use a sticky note on each to mark a feature difference between the books and ask students how they look different.	• work with a partner to compare a fiction and a nonfiction text with similar themes or topics; mark differences with sticky notes.

GUIDED PRACTICE *(continued)*	• compare a poem and a riddle on a topic; use a sticky note on each to mark a difference in their writing; ask students how they sound different. • model comparing two different texts, "A Swim" from *Frog and Toad Are Friends* and "Making Friends" from *In the Land of Words*, and making a connection between them; introduce the phrase "This reminds me of…" to compare the texts. • model using the phrase, "I notice …" to compare and contrast two texts, "A Swim" from *Frog and Toad Are Friends* and a part of *How to Lose a Friend* with a partner; draw connections between the two texts.	• work with a partner to compare a poem and a riddle with similar themes or topics; mark differences with sticky notes. • compare two different texts with a partner and use the phrase "This reminds me of…" to compare them. • use the phrase "I notice…" to compare two texts (of their choice) with a partner.
COMMITMENT 1 day	• compare two texts that you read in this unit and model making connections between them.	• compare two texts that they read in this unit and write one to three paragraphs demonstrating connections between them.
TOTAL: 10 DAYS		

Kinds of Writing

Poems	Letters	Cards
Stories/Fiction	Lists	Signs/Posters
How to…	Biographies	Mysteries
All About	Jokes/Riddles	Newspapers
Maps	Magazines	Short Stories

Writing Topics

Family	Friends	School
Animals/Pets	Vacations	Holidays
Sports	Toys/Games	Special Occasions
Science	Food	Me
Camp	Birthdays	Scouts
Weather	Homes	Jobs
Places to Go	Books	Feelings
History	T.V./Movies	Hobbies

Topic and Genre Chart for student writing notebook.

Writing Clubs: Making Choices in Genre

Why Teach This?

- To identify and compare different genres—narrative fiction, nonfiction, and poetry.
- To deepen students' understanding of a chosen genre.
- To provide students with an opportunity to work collaboratively to develop their writing in a chosen genre.

Framing Questions

- How do writers create pieces that reflect their strengths and interests in genres?
- How can we use collaborative structures to strengthen our writing?

Unit Goals

- Students will work in small groups to explore a shared genre of interest.
- Students will review and reinforce their understanding of a chosen genre.
- Students will utilize a mentor text to guide their writing.
- Students will create an original piece of writing in the genre they are studying.
- Students will provide and receive feedback for generating and revising writing.

Anchor Texts

- *April Bubbles Chocolate on ABC of Poetry*, edited by Lee Bennett Hopkins (for poetry club)
- *Don't You Feel Well, Sam?* by Amy Hest (for narrative club)
- *Sea Creatures* by Sue Malyan, DK series (for nonfiction club)

Unit Assessment Writing Clubs: Making Choices in Genre			PROCESS
Student name:	EMERGING	DEVELOPING	INDEPENDENT
Identifies and compares different genre features for narrative fiction, nonfiction, and poetry.			
Chooses a genre to compose a piece in based on interest and strength.			
Works collaboratively to share and learn about chosen genre.			
Creates an original piece of writing in the chosen genre.			
Works collaboratively to give and receive feedback to peers.			

Stage of the Unit	Focused Instruction You will	Independent Practice Students will
IMMERSION 4 days	• discuss with students what it's like to be in a club and why people join clubs. • read *Don't You Feel Well, Sam?* and discuss narrative elements (story, characters who have a problem, solution and ending). • read *Sea Creatures* and talk about what students notice in the text (facts, no story, no characters, information). • read "Nathaniel Talking" from *In the Land of Words* and talk about what students notice in the text (white space, rhythm, word choice).	• discuss club roles and share positive and negative experiences about being in a club. • browse through a narrative fiction book and identify where they see examples of narrative elements. • browse through nonfiction book baskets. • browse through poetry baskets.
IDENTIFICATION 1 day	• create a chart that compares the identifying features of each text (narrative fiction, nonfiction, poetry); model choosing a genre to write in and give students a genre feature chart for their genre folders.	• identify features for the chart; choose which genre they want to write in.
GUIDED PRACTICE 4 days	• demonstrate coming up with a writing topic in each genre (e.g., for the topic of dogs: *Dogs*, a nonfiction book about caring for a dog, a wondering poem about what my dog thinks about, a narrative about the day I got my dog). • demonstrate using genre planning paper to plan the writing for your chosen genre. • review choosing the right paper for the genre; demonstrate how to create a piece in the genre. • revise according to genre; review genre features and demonstrate using revision paper to add to and revise according to the genre (nonfiction—add a fact box, narrative—craft an ending, poetry—revise line breaks).	• choose a topic to write about that matches the genre they are writing in and share idea with group; reflect on how the club work is going. • fill out genre planning paper to organize their ideas; share their plan with the club; give each writer in the club a compliment and a suggestion. • use genre paper to draft the idea; share with the club; continue assessing how club work went on the genre meeting sheet. • meet with their club to plan revision; use revision paper to revise according to genre.
COMMITMENT 2 days	• demonstrate polishing a piece for publication. • explain a museum share (student pieces on desks, readers go around and read and admire); model how to give positive feedback to fellow authors and reflect on how clubs helped you as a class.	• polish pieces. • celebrate writing with a museum share, complimenting each other on their writing in the different genres. • reflect on what it was like to work in a club; share their learning and love of their chosen genre.
TOTAL: 11 DAYS		

Reflecting on Our Year as Readers and Writers and Planning Ahead

We come to the end of the school year. The windows are open; attention is scattered. We are all eager for summer vacation. We need to measure our growth, as we do with the height marks on the side of a door frame. It is time for our students to admire who they have become—and where they are going next.

Looking Back, Looking Forward: Making Summer Reading Plans

PROCESS

Why Teach This?

- To reflect on the reading students have done throughout the year.
- To make plans for summer reading.

Framing Questions

- How did you grow and change as a reader this school year?
- What are some reading goals you have for the summer?

Unit Goals

- Students will reflect on themselves as readers: favorite books read, favorite genre read, reading activities, strategies learned across genres, reading successes and struggles.
- Students will make plans for summer reading.

Anchor Texts

- *Quest for the Tree Kangaroo: An Expedition to the Cloud Forest of New Guinea* by Sy Montgomery
- *Tar Beach* by Faith Ringgold
- "Where Do You Get the Idea for a Poem?" from *Near the Window Tree* by Karla Kuskin

Unit Assessment Looking Back, Looking Forward: Making Summer Reading Plans			PROCESS
Student name:	EMERGING	DEVELOPING	INDEPENDENT
Identifies qualities of self as a reader.			
Reflects on self as a reader—what has changed in his or her reading life since the beginning of second grade.			
Makes plans for summer reading.			

Looking Back...

Stage of the Unit	Focused Instruction You will	Independent Practice Students will
IMMERSION 1 day	• read *Tar Beach* and discuss the main character's imaginary journey over her city, revisit the word "reflection," and explain how students are going to think back on their journey as readers; model how to talk about a book—what you liked or didn't like about it, your favorite part and character; use the word "because" to support your thinking.	• work with a partner and talk about their journeys as readers and write down at least three favorite books read during the year; focus on what they liked or did not like about the book, their favorite part and character; use the word "because" to support their thinking.
IDENTIFICATION 1 day	• name ways students can reflect on themselves as readers: favorite books read, favorite genres read, book choices, reading activities, strategies learned across genres, reading successes and struggles, what they can do as readers.	• identify a time during the year when reading felt like a struggle and a time when they felt like strong readers; share reflections with a partner.
GUIDED PRACTICE 4 days	• reflect with the class on personal book choices by thinking about the number of books read, certain genres they have read more than others, or an author or series they know really well. • reflect with the class on the different reading activities and genres the class has studied this year; create a class list. • discuss how the understanding of word-attack skills and conventions helped with reading this year; create a class list of these skills and conventions. • discuss the reading comprehension strategy work that helped the class with their reading this year; create a class list of these strategies.	• look over their reading logs to identify the kinds of books they choose to read during independent reading and reflect about their personal book choices. • share with a partner their favorite reading activity and genre studied this year. • work with a partner to reflect on their reading successes and struggles throughout the year. • work with a partner to reflect on the strategies that helped them become better readers and the ones that continue to pose a challenge.

COMMITMENT 2 days	• discuss how the class will share how they have grown as readers by completing a reading interview. Possible questions to include are: What is your favorite genre? How do you choose books to read? What was your favorite reading activity this year? When did reading feel especially good or feel especially challenging to you this year? • make a commitment to read over the summer.	• celebrate themselves as readers; finish the reading interview. • make a commitment to read over the summer.
TOTAL: 8 DAYS		

Looking Forward...

Stage of the Unit	Focused Instruction You will	Independent Practice Students will
IMMERSION 1 day	• discuss how readers think about their reading lives in the future, over the summer, and into the next grade.	• work with a partner and discuss what they feel the most proud of in reading this year and what they will continue to work on.
IDENTIFICATION 1 day	• discuss what summer reading will look like, how you will find the time to read, and what you will choose to read.	• work with a partner to plan what their summer reading will look like. • decorate their summer reading notebook.
GUIDED PRACTICE 3 days	• read "Where Do You Get the Idea for a Poem?" and discuss where many poets find their inspiration for writing poems. • read *Quest for the Tree Kangaroo: An Expedition to the Cloud Forest of New Guinea*; discuss how readers pursue information through reading. • reflect how planning ahead means thinking about themselves as readers and then setting realistic goals for themselves as readers.	• create a list of five possible topics that they would like to read about in a poem. • create a list of five areas of interest they would like to pursue through summer reading. • work with a partner to think about one realistic reading goal they can work on over the summer.
COMMITMENT 2 days	• discuss how they will commit to their reading goal by adding it onto last week's reading interview. • make a commitment to read over the summer.	• add the reading goal to their interview. • celebrate all the great reading work they have done this year.
TOTAL: 7 DAYS		

Looking Back, Looking Forward: Making Summer Writing Plans

PROCESS

Why Teach This?

- To reflect on the writing work done over the school year.
- To make plans for summer writing.

Framing Questions

- How did you grow and change as a writer this year?
- What are some writing goals you have for the summer?

Unit Goals

- Students will reflect on themselves as writers: favorite published piece, favorite writing unit of study, favorite anchor texts, writing successes and struggles.
- Students will make plans for summer writing.

Anchor Texts:

- *Quest for the Tree Kangaroo: An Expedition to the Cloud Forest of New Guinea* by Sy Montgomery
- *Tar Beach* by Faith Ringgold
- "Where Do You Get the Idea for a Poem?" from *Near the Window Tree* by Karla Kuskin
- *Written Anything Good Lately?* by Susan Allen and Jane Lindaman

Unit Assessment Looking Back, Looking Forward: Making Summer Writing Plans			PROCESS
Student name:	EMERGING	DEVELOPING	INDEPENDENT
Identifies qualities of self as a writer.			
Reflects on self as a writer—what has changed on writing life since the beginning of second grade.			
Makes plans for summer writing.			

Looking Back...

Stage of the Unit	Focused Instruction You will	Independent Practice Students will
IMMERSION 2 days	• revisit the word "reflection" and explain how students are going to think back to their year as writers. • model thinking aloud about some of the writing units and pieces from the school year; think aloud about favorite writing-related moments.	• work with a partner and talk about at least one favorite published piece of writing. • work with a partner and reflect on a favorite writing unit or writing activity, and discuss why it was their favorite.
IDENTIFICATION 1 day	• read *Written Anything Good Lately?* and name ways students can reflect on themselves as writers: favorite published piece, favorite genre, favorite writing activity and unit of study, writing successes and struggles, what they can do as writers.	• identify a time during the year when writing felt like a struggle and a time when they felt like strong writers; share their reflections with a partner.
GUIDED PRACTICE 5 days	• reflect on past writing with students by having them reread old pieces and think about what they can do now as writers as compared with the beginning of the year. • reflect with students on favorite writing activity and unit of study from the year and why it meant something to them. • model how to find favorite writing pieces and how to reflect on them by putting a sticky note on the writing to say what it shows they can do as a writer. • model how to choose one piece of writing that shows a time when writing felt hard. • model how to choose one piece of writing that shows your strength as a writer.	• reread past writing and share with a partner what they can do now as writers. • share with a partner their favorite writing activity and unit of study. • reread their writing and find favorite pieces; reflect on them and place sticky notes where it shows what they can do as writers; share their sticky notes with the class to create a class chart. • reflect on and share the strategies they now have when they get stuck as writers; add to class chart. • reflect on and share what made them feel like strong writers; add to chart.
COMMITMENT 1 day	• discuss how they will share how they have grown as writers by responding to sentence starters (e.g., My favorite writing piece was..., The writing activity I liked most...) and then use them to create a reflective paragraph; with the class, make a commitment to write over the summer.	• celebrate themselves as writers; finish the sentence starters and use them to create a short written reflection; make a commitment to write over the summer.
TOTAL: 9 DAYS		

EARLY FALL

LATE FALL

WINTER

SPRING

Looking Forward...

Stage of the Unit	Focused Instruction You will	Independent Practice Students will
IMMERSION 1 day	• discuss places students can write over the summer and the different kinds of writing they can do.	• `work with a partner and make a list of places they can write and all the different kinds of writing they can do over the summer.
IDENTIFICATION 1 day	• discuss what summer writing will look like, finding a time to write and what genres they will try to write over the summer.	• work with a partner to plan what their summer writing will look like.
GUIDED PRACTICE 4 days	• read "Where Do You Get the Idea for a Poem?" and model how to choose some topics you could write a poem about over the summer. • read *Tar Beach* and discuss how writers create imaginary universes to inspire their writing. • read *Quest for the Tree Kangaroo: An Expedition to the Cloud Forest of New Guinea* and discuss how the author might have been pursuing his quest to answer a question by writing this book. • reflect how planning ahead means thinking about themselves as writers and then setting realistic writing goals.	• create a list of five possible topics for poems they would like to write about over the summer. • create a list of three possible imaginary universes you could create to write and write about over the summer. • write a list of five areas of interest they would like to pursue over the summer. • work with a partner and write a goal they would like to accomplish by the end of the summer.
COMMITMENT 1 day	• discuss how they will commit to their writing goals by adding on to last week's written response. • make a commitment to write over the summer.	• record their summer writing goals in their notebooks; add onto last week's written piece by writing down their goals. • celebrate all the great writing work they have done this year.
TOTAL: 7 DAYS		

Circular Seasons: Endings and Beginnings

You will miss these children. And they will miss you. For the rest of their lives, they will remember your name. There should be more of a ritual for you to let go of these children and prepare to embrace the new ones.

In Japan, every fall there is a traditional chrysanthemum festival to celebrate the last blooming before the winter comes. The people journey to view the beautiful flowers and to celebrate the changing seasons. There are special horticulturists who work for a full eleven months of the year to prepare for this festival, creating spectacular chrysanthemum arrangements, which they feature in *uwaya*, serene shelters for the beautiful plantings. In this way, people can contemplate and reflect upon the changing seasons. I wish we had such a thing for the work we do. The seasons go by and then come around again. There is a beauty in that: we know they will always come again. But these, these precious children, they will never come again quite like this. Let these last days of the school year be an *uwaya* for us—a serene shelter for reflection. The work you do with your students is, well, once in a lifetime. Remember this as the seasons of your teaching life begin once again.

Chapter 6

TRACKING STUDENT PROGRESS ACROSS THE YEAR

The C4 Assessment

Assessment is the beginning, the middle, and the end of our teaching. It is the heart of our instruction, the age-old dilemma, the most gratifying, frustrating, and rewarding aspect of our work, because it reveals in stark relief: How are we all doing? Done well, it is not offensive, harmful, hurtful, or unpleasant for children. Done well, it is engaging, reflective, fascinating, and insightful for teachers. Done poorly, it is demeaning, demoralizing, and useless to everyone. Done poorly, it is unhelpful, uninteresting, and slightly boring. We have created rubrics as formative assessments and a yearlong assessment tool we call the C4 Assessment that we believe will lead you to the "done well" column. Done well, assessment is meaningful, as J. Richard Gentry (2008) points out: "....you can loop together assessment and instruction and use both simultaneously to support your students in targeted and powerful ways."

Unit Rubrics as Formative Assessments

Within each unit we have written for this book, we have given you a model assessment rubric such as the following:

Unit Assessment The ARCH: Building a Reading Identity			PROCESS
Student name:	EMERGING	DEVELOPING	INDEPENDENT
Follows routines of reading time.			
Makes book selections independently.			
Identifies personal reading goals.			
Actively participates in a collegial, vibrant community of readers.			

These rubrics can and should be used as formative assessments. By this we mean that you can construct rubrics such as these with your students during the Identification stage of any unit. As you name the expectations for process behaviors, or the elements of a genre, or the type of strategy or convention you would like to see your students use, you can add this list of performance indicators to your rubric. Then you can give the rubric to your students to use during their Guided Practice. If we give students our upfront expectations in writing, and they have helped to form and understand these expectations, we can be sure that they will know what we want them to do as readers and writers. They can use these rubrics as placeholders for our teaching—reminding them on a daily basis what we want them to practice, even when we are not sitting next to them.

By keeping the rubric alongside your conferring conversations with individual readers and writers, you will be able to focus your observations and record your comments on how each student is performing throughout the length of the unit. Using the rubric to supplement your conferring plans will also allow you to refer back on these conversations to plan for future instruction—either for the entire class when you see something that nearly everyone is having difficulty with, or for individual or small-group work.

Unit Rubrics as Summative Assessments

Of course these rubrics can also be summative. You may use them to measure your students' performance at the end of each unit, and you may gather these collective unit assessments to plan and draft your report cards. We believe these rubrics will be extremely helpful on several levels. They will help you focus your instruction towards the expectations listed on the rubric. They will help guide and focus your students practice within any unit of study, and they will allow for self-reflection— for our students and for ourselves. By the end of any unit, we should be able to see what students accomplished, and what we still need to work on.

The C4 Assessment

Rubrics are not the only form of assessment that we would like you to consider. As our entire year has been built around the premise of balanced instruction across Process, Genre, Strategy, and Conventions, we would like to suggest that you consider your students' growing skills and abilities within these four categories. To help you accomplish this task, we have created the C4 Assessment forms seen at the end of this chapter. These forms merge many of the teaching points across the year into collective assessments of students' understanding of Process, Genre, Strategy, and Conventions. The C4A is clear and simple to use, and yet provides a great deal of information for teachers, so that we may differentiate our instruction for all students; for parents so we may share students' growth or challenges; and for schools.

Tracking Our Students Across the Grades

We have designed specific C4 assessments for each grade level. While their format and organization are the same, the content varies as we have given a great deal of thought to the articulation of instruction across the grades. We recommend that these assessment forms be filled out each year, and passed on to the next year's teacher. This will give teachers a clearer sense of their students as readers and writers at the beginning of the year than traditional packaged reading or writing assessments.

Using These Forms

There are many different ways to incorporate these forms into your year. You may choose to:

- use them to conduct a more formal review of student performance at the beginning, middle, and end of the year.

- keep these forms with your other conferring materials and use them to note when students demonstrate progress within a particular unit.

- keep these forms with you as you read through your students' published writing, so you can use their written work as evidence of learning.

No matter which method you use, we ask you to consider how your children are developing as readers and writers inside the Complete 4 components. What have they learned to do as readers and writers? What have they come to understand about genre? What have they learned about reading and writing strategies? What do they now understand about the world of conventions? Our job is to create lifelong readers and writers in our classrooms. Instruction-linked assessment through the Complete 4 is the key to achieving this objective.

Complete 4 Component: Process Second Grade

KEY: **E**=emerging **D**=developing **I**=independent

Student: _____   School Year: _____

CAPACITIES:	BEGINNING OF THE YEAR	MIDDLE OF THE YEAR	END OF THE YEAR
Reads familiar text smoothly (fluency).			
Reads independently for 20 to 30 minutes (stamina).			
Reads at home independently for 10 minutes.			
Sustains book talk independently for 15 minutes (stamina).			
Selects books according to level and interest (independence).			
Explains personal criteria for choosing a book, poem, or story (independence).			
Reads and understands written directions (fluency).			
Writes independently for 20 to 25 minutes (stamina).			
Sustains a selected writing piece over 3 to 5 days (stamina).			
Rereads own writing to add on to it, revise words, or fix spelling (independence).			
Uses pre-writing tools to organize ideas and information (with support).			

ROLES:	BEGINNING OF THE YEAR	MIDDLE OF THE YEAR	END OF THE YEAR
Understands role while meeting in conference with a teacher.			
Is prepared for a conference, with writing ready.			
Transitions from whole-class to Independent Practice without assistance.			
Selects from a variety of paper choices independently.			

Complete 4 Component: Process Second Grade (continued)   KEY: **E**=emerging **D**=developing **I**=independent

Student: _____   School Year: _____

IDENTITIES:	BEGINNING OF THE YEAR	MIDDLE OF THE YEAR	END OF THE YEAR
Expresses ways that he or she has grown as a reader.			
Expresses ways that he or she has grown as a writer.			
Identifies various purposes for reading.			
Uses writing to communicate with others.			

COLLABORATION:	BEGINNING OF THE YEAR	MIDDLE OF THE YEAR	END OF THE YEAR
Hears advice from partner respectfully.			
Shares advice with partner respectfully.			
Makes eye contact with partner.			
Articulates and shares reading experiences with others.			
Asks questions when listening to or reading texts.			
Works collaboratively with peers to comprehend text.			
Leads or participates in discussion about books.			
Responds during conversation by nodding and adding on to ideas.			

Complete 4 Component: Genre Second Grade

KEY: **E**=emerging **D**=developing **I**=independent

Student: _____ School Year: _____

GENERAL	BEGINNING OF THE YEAR	MIDDLE OF THE YEAR	END OF THE YEAR
Recognizes differences in genres of narrative, nonfiction, and poetry.			
Writes in a variety of genres (with support).			
Reads in a variety of genres (with support).			

NARRATIVE	BEGINNING OF THE YEAR	MIDDLE OF THE YEAR	END OF THE YEAR
Identifies the following story elements: character, problem, solution, setting.			
Describes the mood or emotion of a story.			
Compares and contrasts different versions of the same story.			
Writes stories with a clear beginning, middle, and end.			
Writes stories about personal experiences with problem and solution.			
Creates characters, simple plots, and settings in original texts.			
Creates imaginative stories and personal narratives that show evidence of writing process and organization (with support).			

NONFICTION	BEGINNING OF THE YEAR	MIDDLE OF THE YEAR	END OF THE YEAR
Collects data, facts, and ideas from nonfiction texts (with support).			
Connects information from personal experiences to information in nonfiction/informational texts.			
Selects books to meet informational needs (with support).			
Identifies features of nonfiction text (bold print, sidebars, headings, table of contents).			
Recognizes and uses organizational features of text.			
Identifies main idea and details in an informational text (with support).			

Complete 4 Component: Genre Second Grade (continued)   KEY: **E**=emerging **D**=developing **I**=independent

Student: School Year:

NONFICTION (continued)	BEGINNING OF THE YEAR	MIDDLE OF THE YEAR	END OF THE YEAR
States a main or big idea and supports it with own thinking and factual information in a graphic organizer.			
Identifies and interprets facts taken from maps, graphs, charts, and other graphic aids (with support).			
Uses two sources of information in writing an informational text.			
Writes a nonfiction book with graphics and pictures on a topic of interest.			

POETRY	BEGINNING OF THE YEAR	MIDDLE OF THE YEAR	END OF THE YEAR
Identifies common visual characteristics of poetry.			
Recognizes repetition in poetry.			
Recognizes rhyme and rhythm in a poem.			
Attempts repetition in own writing.			
Uses rhythm and/or rhyme to create short poems.			
Writes a poem based on the work of a mentor poet.			
Uses descriptive language in poems.			
Uses white space deliberately to create a poem.			

Complete 4 Component: **Strategy** Second Grade	KEY: **E**=emerging **D**=developing **I**=independent		

Student:		School Year:	
INPUT (The strategies readers use to comprehend text):	**BEGINNING OF THE YEAR**	**MIDDLE OF THE YEAR**	**END OF THE YEAR**
Identifies traits of main and secondary characters.			
Identifies problem and solution and their effect on characters.			
Draws conclusions that summarize the main idea using evidence from the book (with support).			
Makes logical predictions based on details from stories or informational texts.			
Connects at least two texts based on similarities in problem/solution or character.			
Identifies characters in a book and explains how each contributes to the events in the story.			
Recognizes different plots in books by the same author.			
Compares and contrasts information on one topic from two different sources (with support).			
Compares and contrasts characters in literary works.			
Uses previous reading and life experiences to understand literature (with support).			
Uses various strategies to determine unknown words or to clarify confusion in comprehension.			
Draws conclusions and makes inferences about characters (with support).			
Stops reading when a text does not make sense.			
Uses rereading to clarify meaning.			

Complete 4 Component: Strategy Second Grade (continued)   KEY: **E**=emerging **D**=developing **I**=independent

Student: _____   School Year: _____

OUTPUT (The strategies writers use to create text):	BEGINNING OF THE YEAR	MIDDLE OF THE YEAR	END OF THE YEAR
Creates a story plan using plan sheets with pictures and words.			
Generates writing ideas.			
Shows knowledge of story elements by replicating them in own writing.			
Can tell a story in order to prepare for writing a story.			
Uses own experiences and passions to choose writing topics.			
Uses prior knowledge about a topic to add to a story.			
Uses a set of spelling strategies to write unfamiliar words.			
Writes about a character, real or imagined, in detail.			
Lists a sequence of events in a story.			
Writes about a setting in detail.			
Takes notes to record facts from lessons and informational texts (with support).			
Identifies author's purposes and craft in text (with support).			
Uses craft techniques from a mentor author in own writing.			
Generates writing ideas using a mentor author for inspiration.			

Complete 4 Component: Conventions Second Grade   KEY: E=emerging D=developing I=independent

Student: _____   School Year: _____

SYNTAX:	BEGINNING OF THE YEAR	MIDDLE OF THE YEAR	END OF THE YEAR
Recognizes when a sentence does not sound correct in reading 90 percent of the time.			
Recognizes when a sentence does not sound correct in own writing 90 percent of the time.			
Recognizes and writes sentences with subject–verb–object agreement.			
Recognizes and writes sentences with adjectives and adverbs.			

PUNCTUATION:	BEGINNING OF THE YEAR	MIDDLE OF THE YEAR	END OF THE YEAR
Uses periods at end of sentences 90 percent of the time.			
Uses other end punctuation (exclamation points, question marks, etc.).			
Uses internal punctuation (ellipses, quotation marks, commas) 80 percent of the time.			
Uses capital letters for proper nouns and at the beginning of a sentence.			

SPELLING/DECODING:	BEGINNING OF THE YEAR	MIDDLE OF THE YEAR	END OF THE YEAR
Accurately reads and spells familiar sight words.			
Incorporates familiar sight words into writing.			
Makes close approximation of hard words in reading and writing.			
Uses word wall and other print in room to support spelling.			
Recognizes small words inside of larger words when reading.			
Uses knowledge of spelling patters to read and spell challenging words.			
Uses white space and punctuation to read fluently and with expression.			
Organizes topics into chunks or paragraphs.			
Writes sentences in logical order.			

Chapter 7

Essential Reading for the Complete 4 Educator

The Complete 4 for Literacy by Pam Allyn

Pam's book *The Complete 4 for Literacy* introduces us to the idea of the four major components for literacy instruction: Process, Genre, Strategy, and Conventions. She illuminates the components and how they interact throughout the year. In your school communities, we encourage you to form study groups around these components. Begin with Pam's book and study it together to orient yourself. Then each year or each season, select one of the components to focus on. We can use each component to discuss not just whole-class instruction but also how best to confer with individual students, how to work with struggling readers and writers, and how to assess our students. We have prepared a special selection of professional texts to foster your investigation of each of the components.

Writing Above Standard by Debbie Lera

Debbie Lera will help you to frame a year of teaching writing that really helps your students soar using your state standards as a guide. With the Complete 4 as the backbone of her thinking, Debbie takes us on a journey through state standards and how to make them work for us. In the spirit of the Complete 4 and the Complete Year which is all about building flexible frameworks, this book furthers your thinking by helping you to benefit from the structure provided by the standards while attending to the individual needs of your students.

Professional Books on Process

There are wonderful classics in the field of the teaching of reading and writing that help remind us of why process work is so, so critical. Learning routines, talking about books, choosing topics: these activities are the bedrock of a lifetime of success as readers and writers. Remind yourself that process is the key to happiness: how you live your life is as important as what you do with it. The process work is the how.

Here are some of our favorites:

- *Growing Readers* by Kathy Collins (2004)
- *An Observational Survey of Early Literacy Achievement* by Marie M. Clay (2003)
- *Second-Grade Writers: Units of Study to Help Children Plan, Organize, and Structure Their Ideas* by Stephanie Parsons (2007)

Professional Books on Genre

Genre units allow our second graders to try on many hats and be in the world of reading and writing. And genre is power. If you know which genre best suits your purpose, you can communicate most effectively.

Helpful books include the following:

- *Climb Inside a Poem* by Georgia Heard and Lester Laminack (2007)
- *Investigate Nonfiction* by Donald H. Graves (1989)
- *Nonfiction in Focus* by Janice V. Kristo and Rosemary A. Bamford (2004)
- *Significant Studies for Second Grade: Reading and Writing Investigations for Children* by Karen Ruzzo and Mary Anne Sacco (2004)

Professional Books on Strategy

In this book you can see how strongly we believe in the strategic mind of the second grader! The second grader is deeply strategic in his planning and his thinking and his writing. He is comparing genre, using mentor texts, and learning to navigate new media. We need to support our students as they take these large learning steps with units of strategy throughout our year. The following books contain some helpful information on strategy work:

- *After THE END: Teaching and Learning Creative Revision* by Barry Lane (1993)
- *Beyond Leveled Books* by Karen Szymusiak and Frankie Sibberson (2001)
- *Guided Reading* by Irene C. Fountas and Gay Su Pinnell (1996)
- *Second-Grade Writers: Units of Study to Help Children Plan, Organize, and Structure Their Ideas* by Stephanie Parsons (2007)
- *Strategies That Work* by Stephanie Harvey and Anne Goudvis (2000)

- *Teaching for Comprehension in Reading, Grades K–2* by Gay Su Pinnell and Patricia L. Scharer (2003)
- *What a Writer Needs* by Ralph Fletcher (1993)
- *What Really Matters for Struggling Readers: Designing Research-Based Programs* by Richard Allington (2006)

Professional Books on Conventions

We are lucky that these last few years have given us an explosion in interesting, new perspectives on conventions: grammar, punctuation, and syntax. This is the hardest hurdle for us to overcome: Most of us grew up receiving either no grammar instruction or terrible grammar instruction. Grammar and punctuation can all be fun, truly! Conventions instruction is empowering, and students want to be in on the secrets of language.

- *The Fluent Reader: Oral Reading Strategies for Building Word Recognition, Fluency and Comprehension* by Timothy V. Rasinski (2003)
- *A Fresh Approach to Teaching Punctuation* by Janet Angelillo (2002)
- *Mastering the Mechanics: Ready to Use Lessons for Modeled, Guided, and Independent Editing 2–3* by Linda Hoyt and Teresa Therriault (2008)
- *Teaching for Comprehending and Fluency* by Irene C. Fountas and Gay Su Pinnell (2006)
- *Words Their Way: Word Study for Phonics, Vocabulary, and Spelling Instruction* by Donald R. Bear, Marcia Invernizzi, Shane Templeton, and Francine Johnston (2004)

Resource Sheets

Name _____ Date _____

Who Are You as a Reader?

1. I prefer to read:

☐ on the couch

☐ on the beach

☐ on a hammock

☐ at a desk

2. I like best to read:

☐ fiction

☐ nonfiction

☐ poetry

3. My favorite book is:

☐ *Goodnight, Moon*

☐ anything by Dr. Seuss

☐ *I Spy*

☐ Other book: _____

_____

_____

4. I prefer to read:

☐ alone

☐ with a friend

☐ with my class

☐ with my family

☐ in the car

5. My reading role model is:

☐ someone in my family

☐ someone in my school

☐ someone famous

6. I prefer to read:

☐ a magazine

☐ a comic

☐ a series book

☐ a poem

Who Are You as a Writer?

1. **I prefer to write:**
   - ☐ at a desk
   - ☐ on the bed
   - ☐ on a couch
   - ☐ on a rug
   - ☐ in a corner
   - ☐ on a computer

2. **I like best to write:**
   - ☐ fiction
   - ☐ nonfiction
   - ☐ poetry

3. **My favorite topic to write about is:**
   - ☐ my family
   - ☐ my friends
   - ☐ my life
   - ☐ nature
   - ☐ an adventure
   - ☐ how to do something

4. **My writing role model is:**
   - ☐ someone in my family
   - ☐ someone in my school
   - ☐ someone famous

5. **The title of my favorite story or poem I wrote is** _____

_____.

Name _____ Date _____

The Four Prompts Ideas Planner

Writers can use the Four Prompts to help them get ideas. Your writing work today is to look back at some older pieces of writing and think about where you may have gotten your ideas. Write the titles of your pieces in the appropriate boxes below.

I wonder...	I remember...

I imagine...	I observe...

Wondering Plan

Writers are always wondering about the world around them. This is one of the ways that a writer can get ideas. Write some of your wonderings in the wonder bubbles below. Then take an idea from a wonder bubble to write today.

Name _____ Date _____

Remembering Plan

Our memories can give us ideas for our writing. Write a different memory in each one of the boxes below.

I remember when...

I remember when...

I remember when...

I remember when...

I remember when...

I remember when...

I remember when...

Observing Plan

Writers observe the world very carefully. This helps a writer to get ideas. In the boxes below, use your senses to observe the world around you to help you get some new ideas for writing!

I see...	I hear...
I smell...	I touch...
I taste...	I notice...

Name _____ Date _____

Imagination Plan

Writers use their imagination to get ideas. In the cloud below, use your imagination to think about two new ideas. Then write about one of the ideas in the lines below.

_____

_____

_____

_____

_____

_____

_____

_____

_____

_____

Individual Student Word Wall

Aa	Bb	Cc	Dd	Ee
Ff	Gg	Hh	Ii	Jj
KI	LI	Mm	Nn	Oo
Pp	Qq	Rr	Ss	Tt
Uu	Vv	Ww	Xx	Yy
Zz	ch	sh	th	tr

Name _____ Date _____

Stamina Observation

Today we are going to notice the stamina of a good reader/writer. On the left-hand side of the page jot down what you see, and on the right-hand side jot down what you want to try.

Student I am observing_____

What I See	What I Want to Try

Name _____ Date _____

Student Stamina Reading Rubric

I read a book called	Today's date is _____	I read _____ pages	I read for _____ minutes	Next time I will read _____ pages for _____ minutes

RESOURCE 2.10

Name _____ Date _____

Student Stamina Writing Rubric

The title of my writing sample is _____	Today's date is _____	I wrote for _____ minutes	I got to the (beginning, middle, or end) of the page	Next time I will write for _____ minutes and get to the _____ of the page

Writing Strategies for Building Stamina: Strategies for Generating Writing

Reread and Write

This is probably the easiest and sometimes the most fruitful way to begin to build stamina as a writer. Reread your writing and continue to write. Most writers will feel that they can continue by writing what has been left out, or by letting a mentor inspire and influence the entry.

Write/Sketch/Write

Return to an entry, sketch—perhaps vocalizing bits remembered while using a visual cue to prompt further writing—and then write more. Use sketching to show meaning, explain thinking, or stretch thinking, using drawing, diagrams, and/or observations.

Write to the X, or Finish Line

Although this strategy is mostly used to generate writing in the first place, it can also be used for developing writing and assisting you when you are stuck. Talk out the topic, perhaps do some other type of rehearsal, and then mark an X on the page. Then push yourself to write until you reach the X.

Write in the Margins

This strategy is a good tool for looking at your writing in new ways. Reread, make notes, ask questions, and jot this "stuff" down. The strategy may end there or push you to write more.

Free-writing

With free-writing you record your stream of consciousness, unlocking your mind and allowing it to approach the blank page. Free-writing is a way to explore a topic, allowing your thoughts to flow on paper in a conversational way. You can just start writing, or put an idea box on the top of the page to help you get started. Peter Elbow in *Writing With Power* states, "So much writing time and energy is spent not writing.... Freewriting helps you to think of topics to write about.... Finally, and perhaps most important, free-writing improves your writing."

Checking for Meaning Parent Letter

Dear Parents,

Series books provide support for readers in many ways. Their predictable and definitive structures allow readers to develop comprehension strategies more easily.

We are going to read a lot of series books together this month. Please encourage your child to enjoy them, reread them, and notice their patterns. Even if you think they might be a bit easy, don't dissuade your child from enjoying them again. We are using these books to teach important comprehension strategies. Thank you!

Warmly,

RESOURCE 3.1

Author Study Parent Letter

Dear Parents,

In the next few weeks, we are going to study master storyteller and author Tomie dePaola. He is the author and illustrator of more than 100 titles including *Strega Nona*, *The Baby Sister*, and *The Cloud Book*.

If you are visiting a library, please check out a title or two for either in-class use or to add to your home reading stack.

Another great activity would be to visit Tomie dePaola's website at www.tomie.com. Visit this site and read all about his texts, his life, and the questions he is frequently asked by readers. In class, we will be visiting this site as well.

Warmly,

Name _____ Date _____

Author Information

We are learning so much about author Tomie dePaola. Discuss the information we have been learning about him and read biographical information given to you. Write down three or four pieces of information you have learned about his life and his writing.

Tomie Fact 1:	Tomie Fact 2:
Tomie Fact 3:	**Tomie Fact 4:**

Author Comparison:
How Am I Like Tomie dePaola?

(Put a ★ next to the strategies you want to try.)

Name _____ Date _____

Author-Inspired Writing

My Line From Tomie dePaola

RESOURCE 3.5

Name _____ Date _____

Author-Inspired Writing Ideas Paper

Where Does Tomie Get His ideas?	My Idea

Name _____ Date _____

Student Editing Checklist

☐ Did you circle misspelled words?

Did you find the correct spelling of three "no excuse "words?

Did you capitalize:

☐ I's?

☐ First letter of each sentence?

☐ Proper names?

☐ Did you use . ! ? to end your sentences?

☐ Did you reread your piece at least three times (plus a few times with a partner) to be sure it makes sense and says what you want it to say?

Nonfiction Reading Parent Letter

Dear Parents,

We are beginning a very exciting study of nonfiction! Your child will read and write about topics of interest, as well as topics we are learning about in science.

Your child will bring home books from school to read, and I encourage you to check your home shelves and local library, as well, for interesting and engaging nonfiction books that you would like to explore with your child.

Talk about your own interests and passions, and show your child how you might refer to a nonfiction book to learn more about them.

Warmly,

Name _____ Date _____

Nonfiction Reading Graphic Organizer

Fact I learned

My thinking

_____
_____
_____
_____

Picture

Fact I learned

My thinking

_____
_____
_____

Picture

Nonfiction Writing Parent Letter

Dear Parents,

We have just begun a writing unit in nonfiction. Soon your child will be talking to you about topics he or she is interested in and would like to learn more about.

We will research and collect information about topics of interest to your child. Research in second grade is about three things: observing closely, asking questions, and reading. For example, a child writing and thinking about cats could observe a family pet, talk to a neighbor or vet, or look at various cat picture books.

Please talk with your child about his or her interests and help with the research process at home.

Warmly,

Name _____ Date _____

Nonfiction Expert Ideas Paper

What am I an expert at?

Ideas	My Expertise

Name _____ Date _____

Nonfiction Question-and-Answer Paper

Q. _____
_____
_____
_____

A. _____
_____
_____
_____
_____
_____
_____

Name _____ Date _____

Nonfiction Split-Page Paper

My topic: _____

Title of nonfiction text: _____

Fact (something that we know is true)	What does this make me think?

Fact (something that we know is true)	What does this make me think?

Nonfiction Research Question Homework

We are working really hard on our nonfiction writing. We already know a lot about our topics, but we also know that we could find out more information by researching questions we have about our topics. Your job for homework is to research the questions we wrote in class. To find the answers, you may use one or more of the ways listed below.

Interview

Interview someone whom you think would know the answer to one of your questions. For example, if you are writing about soccer, you may want to interview your soccer coach. If you are writing about cats you may want to interview your vet or a neighbor who has had cats for many years. Choose someone who is an expert on your topic.

Internet

Look up your questions on the Internet. You can go to www.google.com and type in the question, and you will get links to lots of websites where you may find the answer.

Books and Magazines

Reference books about your topic could provide answers to your questions. Other nonfiction books may also have the answers. Sometimes magazines may have the answers, too. Some good magazines for kids are *Time for Kids*, *National Geographic for Kids*, and *Your Big Backyard*. You can visit your local library to find these and other magazines.

Observation/Experience

Sometimes you can find information about your topic through observation or experience. We used observation in our class book when we observed our tadpoles. For example if you are writing about dogs, you can observe your dog as he plays in the yard with your sister. Or if you are writing about cooking, you can make your favorite recipe with your mom. After you observe, you will have new information for your topic!

Have fun researching! Remember, your job is to answer the four questions you wrote in class.

Name _____ Date _____

Nonfiction Research Question Homework

Nonfiction Topic _____

Question 1	**Question 2**
Answer:	Answer:
What research method did you use to get your answer?	What research method did you use to get your answer?

Question 3	**Question 4**
Answer:	Answer:
What research method did you use to get your answer?	What research method did you use to get your answer?

Name _____ Date _____

Nonfiction Glossary Paper

Word _____

_____

_____

Word _____

_____

_____

Word _____

_____

_____

Word _____

_____

_____

Name _____ Date _____

Nonfiction Editing Checklist

☐ Did you circle misspelled words? ☐ Did you find the correct spelling of the important content words?	Writer_____ Partner _____
Did you capitalize: ☐ I's? ☐ First letter of each sentence? ☐ Proper names?	Writer_____ Partner _____
☐ Did you use . ! ? to end your sentences?	Writer_____ Partner _____
☐ Did you reread your piece at least three times (and at least once with a partner) to be sure it makes sense and says what you want it to say?	Writer_____ Partner _____

Fluency Reading Parent Letter

Dear Parents,

We are studying fluency in our classroom. Fluency is smooth reading. There are some things that get in the way of smooth reading: difficult punctuation is one, and reading a book that is much too hard is another.

Please ask your child to read a portion of his/her nightly reading aloud to you. Even though we encourage silent reading this year, reading orally, even for five minutes a day at home, will reinforce the skills we are learning regarding oral reading and fluency. In addition, reading aloud to your child is an important way for your child to hear the sound of language, and this will help build his or her fluency more than anything.

Warmly,

Paragraph Noticing Paper

Paragraph	What I notice about it

Name _____

Date _____

Paragraph Graphic Organizer

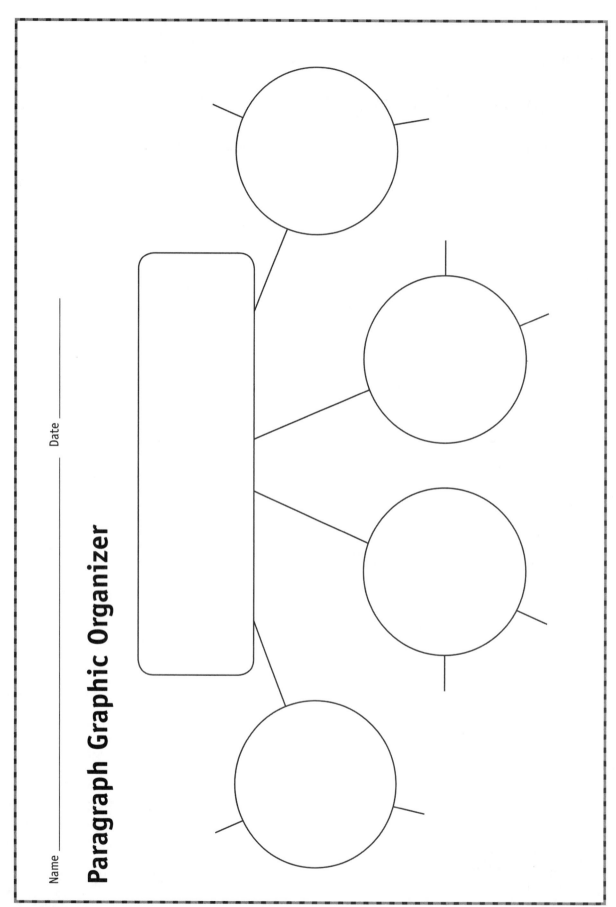

Glossary of Terms for the Complete Year Series

We try to avoid jargon as much as possible, but it is inevitable that a community creates or uses specific terminology to identify important aspects of its work. We want you to feel comfortable with all the language inside this book. What follows are some of the key words we have used throughout this book and throughout the Complete Year series.

Anchor texts These are the books that moor us to the places of our learning. An anchor holds a ship in place, in water that may be moving fast. Texts are like that for us in our teaching. We are in moving water all the time, but great literature anchors us down to our teaching, to our learning, to our goals and outcomes. Anchor texts connect us to the teaching inside our units of study. They keep our teaching on course, steady, focused, anchoring our big ideas, our commitments and indeed, the essence of each unit. Anchor texts may also be used throughout the year in both the teaching of reading and the teaching of writing. For example, one text may be used in a reading unit for retelling, or sensory image, or prediction. The same text may also be used as a demonstration text for writing with detail, strong leads and endings, and the use of dialogue. There are some special texts that can travel with you throughout the year. They are great, lasting titles that transcend any one teaching point. These are considered anchor texts for the year.

Book clubs Working in book clubs allows students to build their collaboration skills and their ability to talk about texts. Book clubs may form from two sets of successful partnerships, or for a variety of teaching purposes. You may group a club according to skill sets or according to interests. Students in a club do not all have to be reading the same book. For example, in a nonfiction unit, the students may meet to discuss editorials or historical writing, using different texts at their own reading levels. You should give clear guidelines for the purposes of a club, its duration, expected outcomes, and how it will be assessed.

Commitment The fourth stage of a unit of study, the Commitment stage, is the bridge from the end of one unit to the beginning of the next one. Look for and make public examples of student work and behaviors that are becoming more integrated into the ongoing work of the individual and the community. This stage asks the question: How is what we have learned in this unit going to inform our learning as we begin the next one? It also requires a response to the question: What have you learned?

Conferences/conferring This is a process for informally assessing your students' progress, and for differentiating your instruction for individual readers and writers. Ideally, you will meet with each student at least once a week in a brief, focused conference session. Stages of a conference are:

- **Preread/Research** (be very familiar with your student's work and processes in advance of the conference)
- **Ask** (pertinent questions relating to your lesson, the ongoing work, and the plans going forward)
- **Listen** (take notes, with attention to next steps)
- **Teach** (one target point)
- **Plan** (what the student will do when you leave the conference: today, tomorrow, throughout the unit and the year)

Conventions The fourth component of the Complete 4, Conventions refers to grammar, punctuation, and syntax. Understanding the conventions of the English language has a direct impact on reading comprehension and writing mechanics and fluency.

Downhill texts These are texts we can rest and relax into—to practice building our stamina or our fluency or to revisit favorite characters, authors, or series. They are books that do not require a great deal of decoding to be done by the reader, as the text is generally below the reader's independent reading level.

Focused Instruction The first part of every day's reading and writing time, Focused Instruction is the short, focused lesson at the beginning of each workshop session in the teaching of reading or writing. Each lesson should build on the ones before it. No lesson is taught in isolation.

Four Prompts In order to help our students learn how to find ideas for writing, we have developed a set of prompts to guide them. They are I wonder, I remember, I observe, and I imagine. You can use these to support your students' writing in any genre.

Genre The second component of the Complete 4, Genre typically refers to a type of text such as poetry, nonfiction, or narrative. Within each of these genres are subgenres, which may include a specific focus on persuasive nonfiction writing, or informational nonfiction writing in nonfiction studies. In a narrative study, the focus might be on the short story, the memoir, or story elements. We want students to focus on how they engage with a particular genre. How do we read a newspaper, for example, and how do we read a poem? How are they different, and how are they the same? We will talk about uses for a genre, the reasons we read inside one genre for a length of time, and how our thinking grows and changes as a result of that immersion.

Guided Practice In the third stage of any unit of study, Guided Practice, we use mentor texts, transcripts, teacher or student writing, think-alouds, role plays, and read-alouds to model exemplary attributes, behaviors, and qualities related to the unit. Over the course of this stage, students are given increasing responsibility for this work. It is generally the longest stage of a unit, as all students need time for practice.

Identification The second stage of any unit of study, Identification, is the time when we begin to develop the common language we will use throughout the study. We identify attributes of a genre, behaviors in a process, qualities of a craft element, rules for a convention or mark. Our thinking is recorded in public charts, student writing notebooks, and our notebook.

Immersion The first stage of any unit of study, Immersion, is the initial period of inquiry during which we surround our students with the sounds, textures, and qualities of a Genre, Process, Strategy, or Conventions focus. We marinate our students in the literature, the actions and reflections, and the attention to detail and conventions that are part of the study. During this stage, students construct a working understanding of the topic under discussion.

Independent Practice Following each day's Focused Instruction, Independent Practice provides time for students to read or write independently and authentically. Students independently read a variety of texts matched to their reading levels. Students also write a variety of texts independently, depending on the unit and their ability levels. They practice the skills and strategies taught in the whole-group sessions. We provide daily lessons to support their work, and confer regularly with the students to assess their individual needs.

Mentor text Somewhat interchangeable with an anchor text, we are more inclined to use mentor text to describe books that have particular appeal to individual students. Mentor texts inspire students' reading and writing, whereas anchor texts are specific texts chosen in advance by the teacher to prepare a unit. So in a poetry unit, one mentor text might be a Langston Hughes poem, "The Dream Keeper," because the student loves it and wants to write like that, whereas another student might choose a Valerie Worth poem because she likes the brevity of her language.

Partnerships At times you may choose to pair children for different reasons and different lengths of time. Partnerships can be very fluid, lasting for just one session, a week, or an entire unit. Partnerships may be based on reading levels, similar interests in particular books or subjects, or because you would like to work with the partners on a regular basis on small instructional reading or writing work.

Process The first of the Complete 4 components, Process asks readers and writers to become aware of their habits and behaviors, and to move forward in developing them. Process units can investigate roles, routines, capacity, or collaboration.

Read-aloud During read-aloud, you read from carefully chosen texts that reflect the reading and writing work the community is doing together. Listening to fluent and expressive read-alouds helps students identify the many aspects of text and develop their own deeper understandings of Process, Genre, Strategy, or Conventions. You may read from a book or short text that illustrates the topic of the Focused Instruction for the day, and encourage students to pursue that thinking in their independent reading and writing. During and at the end of the read-aloud, the whole class may have a conversation relating to the ideas in the story.

Reading notebook *See* Writing Notebook.

Shared reading/shared writing During this activity, you and your students read together from a shared text (on an overhead, chart, or a SMART Board, or using copies of the text). While teachers of younger children use shared reading and writing to help build decoding skills, teachers of older children may use shared reading to teach word analysis, new vocabulary, or punctuation skills. It's also a good way to work with older students on big-picture thinking such as developing an idea about a text, asking questions, or making inferences. Teachers of older students may use shared writing to guide their students toward new writing strategies in a public writing context, or model use of details and elaboration to improve their writing.

Small instructional groups This structure is used to differentiate and direct instruction to the specific needs of a small group of learners. You pull small groups of readers or writers with similar needs to explicitly teach targeted reading and writing skills. You select and introduce the texts for reading and make specific teaching points. You may prompt students in small writing groups to do a short, focused writing exercise based on their needs. These groups are flexible and will change as the year unfolds.

Stages of the lesson Each day, we should work with our students in a whole-small-whole routine. First we bring everyone together for the lesson (see Focused Instruction), then we send students off to practice something we have taught (see Independent Practice), and finally we call them back to join us for a recap and reiteration of our teaching (see Wrap-Up).

Stages of the unit Each unit of study follows a progression of instruction, from Immersion to Identification to Guided Practice to Commitment. These stages provide students with the necessary opportunities to notice, name, practice, and share their learning—all of which contribute to a deeper understanding and application of our teaching (see Immersion, Identification, Guided Practice, and Commitment).

Steady reader or writer This student is making steady progress and meeting appropriate grade-level expectations.

Strategy The third component in the Complete 4, Strategy consists of two types: reading and writing. In reading, Strategy refers to individual or grouped strategies for reading comprehension that impact reading development. These include visualizing, synthesizing, questioning, and inferring. A unit focused on strategy can be embedded in another study or illuminated on its own. Strategy units also include the study of theme, interpretation, building an argument, and story elements. In writing, Strategy refers to craft. This may include the external or internal structures of writing. Units in writing strategy may include structures of nonfiction or narrative texts, a focus on a particular author, or, internally, units focused on the use of repetition, varied sentence length, or the artful use of punctuation.

Strong reader or writer This student is performing above grade-level expectations.

Turn and talk This common technique helps students warm up for their reading or writing work. By asking students to "turn and talk"

to someone in the meeting area to rehearse their thoughts, we give all students a chance to have their voices heard. It is an effective management technique for making sure students are prepared for the work ahead.

Unit of study A one- to six-week period of intensive study on one aspect of reading or writing. The Complete 4 curriculum planning system helps teachers and administrators plan an entire school year in the teaching of reading and writing.

Uphill texts This descriptor refers to a text that is above a student's independent reading level. Sometimes we want our readers to challenge themselves with a harder text. Sometimes readers have very good reasons for why they would like to keep an uphill book close by. Other times, though, we ask them to recognize that the book is too uphill for the task, and that they need to find a level text with which they can feel successful.

Vulnerable reader or writer This describes the reader or writer who struggles to keep up with the demands of the grade level. These are students who need extra support and scaffolding through appropriate texts or individualized or small-group instruction. Our vulnerable readers and writers need special care to feel successful and to flourish in our classrooms.

Wrap-Up The final step in each day's reading or writing time, the Wrap-Up is when we ask our students to return to a whole-group setting for reflection and reinforcement. For example, you may share one or two examples of student work or student behaviors ("Today I noticed..."), or one or two students might briefly share their thinking processes or the work itself.

Writing clubs These are recommended for all ages. Children may create clubs based on common interests, from the block area and writing in kindergarten to mystery writing in fourth grade. Give clear guidelines for the purposes of the clubs, the length of time they will last, the expectations, the outcomes, and how you will assess the progress of each club.

Writing notebook/reading notebook/ writing folder/reading folder These are containers for thinking and tools for collecting ideas, wonderings, observations, questions, research, lists, snippets of texts, and responses to literature. The form of the container is not the important thing; what is important is having containers for student work that make sense to your students and work well for you in terms of collecting and preserving a history of student reading and writing.

Grade 2 Anchor Texts

Early Fall

The ARCH: Building a Reading Identity
- *Abe Lincoln: The Boy Who Loved Books* by Kay Winters
- *Chrysanthemum* by Kevin Henkes
- *Donovan's Word Jar* by Monalisa Degross and Cheryl Hanna
- *Max's Words* by Kate Banks
- *Swimmy* by Leo Lionni
- *Thomas and the Library Lady* by Pat Mora
- *Voices of the Heart* by Ed Young
- *Wonderful Words: Poems about Reading, Writing, Speaking and Listening*, edited by Lee Bennett Hopkins and Karen Barbour
- *Zen Shorts* by Jon Muth

The ARCH: Building a Writing Identity
- *The Art Lesson* by Tomie dePaola
- *Best Wishes* by Cynthia Rylant
- *A Forest of Stories: Magical Tree Tales From Around the World* by Rina Singh
- *In the Land of Words* by Eloise Greenfield
- *The Jolly Postman: Or Other People's Letters by* Janet Ahlberg and Allan Ahlberg
- *The Luckiest Kid on the Planet* by Lisa Campbell Ernst
- *Martin's Big Words: The Life of Martin Luther King, Jr.* by Doreen Rappaport
- *Martina the Beautiful Cockroach: A Cuban Folktale* by Carmen Agra Deedy
- *Mr. Rabbit and the Lovely Present* by Charlotte Zolotow
- *Poetry for Young People: Robert Frost*, edited by Gary D. Schmidt
- *Seeing the Circle* by Joseph Bruchac
- *Show; Don't Tell! Secrets of Writing* by Josephine Nobisso
- *Spiders* by Nic Bishop

- *Written Anything Good Lately?* by Susan Allen and Jane Lindaman

Synthesizing Word-Attack Strategies
- *Diary of a Worm* by Doreen Cronin
- *Dinosaurumpus!* By Tony Mitton
- *My Friend John* by Charlotte Zolotow
- "Sliding Board" from *Did You See What I Saw? Poems About School* by Kay Winters
- "Snow City" from *Good Rhymes, Good Times* by Lee Bennett Hopkins

Building Stamina: Reading Long and Strong
- *Catwings* by Ursula LeGuin
- *Danny and the Dinosaur* by Syd Hoff

Building Stamina: Writing Long and Strong
- *Meet the Authors and Illustrators* by Deborah Kovacs
- *You Have to Write* by Janet S. Wong

Late Fall

Deepening Our Understanding of Fairy Tales
- *Beauty and the Beast, Goldilocks and the Three Bears* by Jan Brett
- *Goldilocks and the Three Bears*, retold by Joan Gallup
- *Little Red Riding Hood* by Heather Amery
- *Little Red Riding Hood* by Jerry Pinkney.
- *Lon Po Po: A Red-Riding Hood Story From China* by Ed Young
- *Rainbow Crow*, retold by Nancy Van Laan
- *The Three Bears, The Little Red Hen*, Byron Barton
- *Twelve Dancing Princesses* by Jane Ray

- "White-Bear-King Valemon," from *The Starlight Princesses* collection, retold by Annie Dalton

Writing Fairy Tales
- *Once Upon a Cool Motorcycle Dude* by Kevin O'Malley
- *Previously* by Allan Ahlberg
- *The Rough-Face Girl* by Rafe Martin
- *Sugar Cane: A Caribbean Rapunzel* by Patricia Storace
- *Twelve Dancing Princesses* by Jane Ray

Making Wise Book Choices
- *Arthur's Loose Tooth* by Lillian Hoban
- *Cam Jansen* by David Adler
- *The Empty Pot* by Demi
- *Nate the Great* by Marjorie Weinman Sharmat

Beginning and Ending Punctuation
- *Don't You Feel Well, Sam?* by Amy Hest
- *A Good Day* by Kevin Henkes
- *The Moon Was the Best* by Charlotte Zolotow
- *My Dadima Wears a Sari* by Kashmira Sheeth
- *Roller Coaster* by Marla Frazee

Enhancing Comprehension Strategies Through Series Books
- Frog and Toad series by Arnold Lobel

Enhancing Craft Strategies: Authors as Guides
- Books by Tomie dePaola:
  - *The Art Lesson*
  - *The Baby Sister*
  - *The Legend of the Indian Paintbrush*
  - *Nana Upstairs and Nana Downstairs*
  - *The Popcorn Book*
  - *Strega Nona*

Winter

Investigating Characters in Reading
- *Chinese New Year's Dragon* by Rachel Sing
- *Jessica* by Kevin Henkes
- *Shortcut* by Donald Crews
- *Skippyjon Jones* by Judy Schachner
- *Stand Tall Molly Lou Melon* by Patty Lovell
- *Tough Boris* by Mem Fox

Investigating Story Elements: Writing Fiction
- *Doctor De Soto* by William Steig
- *A Million Fish . . . More or Less* by Patricia McKissack
- *My Name is Yoon* by Helen Recorvits
- *A Perfect Snowman* by Preston McDaniels
- *Pet Show* by Ezra Jack Keats
- *Spoken Memories* by Aliki
- *Three Snow Bears* by Jan Brett

Using Dialogue Punctuation to Bring Characters to Life
- *Chrysanthemum* by Kevin Henkes
- *The Gift of the Sun: A Tale from South Africa* by Diane Stewart
- *Kiss Good Night* by Amy Hest
- *Owen* by Kevin Henkes
- *Tales of Oliver Pig* by Jean Van Leeuwen.

Growing a Sense of Language and Craft Through Text Study
- *The Moon Was the Best* by Charlotte Zolotow

Exploring Learning Through Reading Nonfiction Texts
- *Almost Gone* by Steve Jenkins
- *Calling All Doves El Canto de las Palomas* by Juan Felipe Herrera
- *Duke Ellington: The Piano Prince and His Orchestra* by Andrea Pinkney
- *Explore and Discover Sharks* by Steven Savage
- *Freedom River* by Doreen Rappaport

- *Frog and Toad Are Friends* by Arnold Lobel
- *Knut: How One Little Polar Bear Captivated the World* by Juliana Hatkoff, Isabella Hatkoff, Craig Hatkoff, and Dr. Gerald R. Uhlich
- *Look to the North A Wolf Pup Diary* by Jean Craighead George
- *Rain* by Honor Head
- *Rosa* by Nikki Giovanni
- *Watch Me Grow Frog* by Lisa Magloff
- *What Do You Do With a Tail Like This?* by Steve Jenkins

Sharing Learning Through Writing Nonfiction Texts
- *All About Rattlesnakes* by Jim Arnosky
- *Did Dinosaurs Live in Your Backyard?* by Melvin and Gilda Berger
- *Father Knows Less, or "Can I Cook My Sister?" One Dad's Quest to Answer His Son's Most Baffling Questions* by Wendell Jamieson
- *It Could Still Be a Fish* by Allan Fowler
- *One Tiny Turtle* by Nicola Davies
- *Why Do Cats Meow?* by Joan Holub
- *Wilma Unlimited: How Wilma Rudolph Became the Fastest Woman* by Kathleen Krull

Rereading Books We Love
- *Calling the Doves/El canto de las palomas* by Juan Felipe Herrera
- *Father Knows Less, or "Can I Cook My Sister?" One Dad's Quest to Answer His Son's Most Baffling Questions* by Wendell Jamieson
- *My Name is Yoon* by Helen Recorvits
- *Over and Over* by Charlotte Zolotow
- *The End* by David LaRochelle

Writing About Reading: Book Blurbs
- *A Boy Called Slow* by Joseph Bruchac
- *Henry and Mudge and the Snowman Plan* by Cynthia Rylant

- *The Magic Treehouse—Day of the Dragon King* by Mary Pope Osbourne

Learning About Nouns and Verbs in Reading
- *Heat Wave* by Eileen Spinelli
- *Kites Sail High: A Book About Verbs* by Ruth Heller
- *Merry Go Round: A Book about Nouns* by Ruth Heller

Learning About Nouns and Verbs in Writing
- *A Mink, a Fink, a Skating Rink: What Is a Noun?* by Brian P. Cleary
- *Nouns and Verbs Have a Field Day* by Robin Pulver
- *To Root, to Toot, to Parachute: What Is a Verb?* By Brian P. Cleary

Revisiting the Writing Ideas We Love
- *If . . . ,* by Sarah Perry
- *In the Land of Words* by Eloise Greenfield
- *Miss Rumphius* by Barbara Cooney
- *My Dream of Martin Luther King* by Faith Ringgold
- *The Three Snow Bears* by Jan Brett

Spring

Learning the Language of Poetry
- *All the Small Poems and 14 More* by Valerie Worth
- "Grounded" from *My Man Blue* by Nikki Grimes
- "How?" from *Spectacular Science*, selected by Lee Bennet Hopkins
- *Laughing Tomatoes/Jitomates Risueños* by Francisco X. Alarcon
- *Sing a Song of Popcorn*, selected by Beatrice Schenk de Regniers, Eva Morre, Mary Michaels
- *Sing to the Sun* by Ashley Bryan
- *White* by Jan Carr

Becoming Poets: Cherishing Words

- *All the Small Poems and 14 More* by Valerie Worth
- *Angels Ride Bikes/Los Angeles Andan en Bicicleta* by Francisco X. Alarcon
- *Ashley Bryan's ABC of African American Poems* by Ashley Bryan
- *Before It Wriggles Away* by Janet S. Wong
- *Carnival of the Animals* by Philip de Vos and Piet Grobler
- *Eats* by Arnold Adoff
- *Finding a Way* by Myra Cohn Livingston
- *Inner Chimes Poems on Poetry* selected by Bobbye Goldstein
- *Seasons* by Charlotte Zolotow
- *Sing a Song of Popcorn*, selected by Beatrice Schenk de Regniers, Eva Morre, Mary Michaels White, Jan Carr,
- *Sol a Sol* by Lori Marie Carlson,
- *Spectacular Science*, selected by Lee Bennett Hopkins
- *Very Best (almost) Friends* collected by Paul B. Janeczko
- *Where the Sidewalk Ends* by Shel Siverstein

Building Fluency Through Phrasing

- "Honey I Love" from *Honey I Love and Other Poems* by Eloise Greenfield
- *Lionel and His Friends* by Stephen Krensky
- CD of *Little Bear's Friend* by Else Holmelund Minarik,
- *My Father's Dragon* by Ruth Stiles Gannett

- "Nathaniel Talking" from *In the Land of Words* by Eloise Greenfield
- *Vacation Under Volcano, Magic Tree House #3* by Mary Pope Osborn
- *Young Cam Jansen and the Library Mystery* by David Adler

Building Fluency Through Punctuation and Paragraphing

- "The Cypress Tree" from *A Forest of Stories: Magical Tree Tales From Around the World* by Rina Singh
- *Family Pictures Cuadros De Familia*, by Carmen Lomas Garza
- *A Little Shopping* by Cynthia Rylant

Making Connections Across Genres: Readers Are Thinkers

Different Genres/Similar Topics::

- *Dinosaurs Before Dark* by Mary Pope Osborn; "Dino Riddles" Reader Riddles, Ranger Rick; "Dinosaur Bone," by Alice Schertle from *Spectacular Science,* selected by Lee Bennett Hopkins
- "Doctor Dinosaur" from *Ranger Rick, How do Dinosaurs Get Well Soon?* by Jane Yolen
- *Watch Me Grow Bear* by Lisa Magloff and *Little Bear* by Else Holmelund Minarik

Theme of Friendship:

- *Frog and Toad Are Friends* by Arnold Lobel
- *How to Lose a Friend* by Nancy Carlson
- "Making Friends" from *In the Land of Words* by Eloise Greenfield.

Writing Clubs: Making Choices in Genre

- *April Bubbles Chocolate an ABC of poetry*, edited by Lee Bennett Hopkins for poetry club
- *Don't You Feel Well, Sam?* by Amy Hest for narrative club
- *Sea Creatures* by Sue Malyan for nonfiction club.

Looking Back, Looking Forward: Making Summer Reading Plans

- *Quest for the Tree Kangaroo: An expedition to the Cloud Forest of New Guinea* by Sy Montgomery
- *Tar Beach* by Faith Ringgold
- "Where Do You Get the Idea for a Poem?" from *Near the Window Tree* by Karla Kuskin

Looking Back, Looking Forward: Making Summer Writing Plans

- *Quest for the Tree Kangaroo: An Expedition to the Cloud Forest of New Guinea* by Sy Montgomery
- *Tar Beach* by Faith Ringgold
- "Where Do You Get the Idea for a Poem?" from *Near the Window Tree* by Karla Kuskin
- *Written Anything Good Lately?* by Susan Allen and Jane Lindaman

Professional References

Allington, R. (2005). *What really matters for struggling readers: Designing research-based programs.* Boston: Allyn & Bacon.

Allyn, P. (2007). *The complete 4 for literacy. How to teach reading and writing through daily lessons, monthly units, and yearlong calendar.* New York: Scholastic.

Alston, L. (2008). *Why we teach: Learning, laughter, love, and the power to transform lives.* New York: Scholastic.

Anderson, C. (2005). *Assessing writers.* Portsmouth, NH: Heinemann.

Anderson, C. (2000). *How's it going? A practical guide to conferring with student writers.* Portsmouth, NH: Heinemann.

Angelillo, J. (2002). *A fresh approach for teaching punctuation: Helping young writers use punctuation with precision and purpose.* New York: Scholastic.

Angelillo, J. (2008). *Grammar study: Helping students get what grammar is and how it works.* New York: Scholastic.

Avery, C. (2002). *And with a light touch: Learning reading & writing & teaching with first graders.* Portsmouth, NH: Heinemann.

Bear, D., Invernizzi, M., Templeton, S., Johnston, F. (2004). *Words their way: Word study for phonics, vocabulary and spelling instruction.* Boston: Pearson Education.

Beaver, J. (2006). *DRA2: Developmental reading assignment.* Parsippany, NJ: Pearson Education.

Calkins, L. (1994). *The art of teaching writing.* Portsmouth, NH: Heinemann.

Clay, M. (1991). *Becoming literate: The construction of inner control.* Portsmouth, NH: Heinemann.

Clay, M. (2005). *Observation survey.* Portsmouth, NH: Heinemann.

Collins, K. (2004). *Growing readers.* Portland, ME: Stenhouse.

Cruz, M. C. (2004). *Independent writing: One teacher, thirty-two needs, topics, and plans.* Portsmouth, NH: Heinemann.

Davis, J., & Hill, S. (2003). *The no-nonsense guide to teaching writing: Strategies, structures, and solutions.* Portsmouth, NH: Heinemann.

Fletcher, R. (1993). *What a writer needs.* Portsmouth, NH: Heinemann.

Fletcher, R., & Portalupi, J. (2007). *Craft lessons: Teaching writing K–8.* Portland, ME: Stenhouse.

Fletcher, R., & Portalupi, J. (2001). *Nonfiction craft lessons: Teaching information writing K–8.* Portland, ME: Stenhouse.

Fountas, I. C., & Pinnell G. S. (1999). *Matching books to readers: Using leveled books in guided reading, K–3.* Portsmouth, NH: Heinemann.

Fountas, I. C., & Pinnell G. S. (1996). *Guided reading.* Portsmouth, NH: Heinemann.

Fountas, I. C., & Pinnell G. S. (2001). *Guiding readers and writers: Teaching comprehension, genre, and content literacy.* Portsmouth, NH: Heinemann.

Fountas, I. C., & Pinnell G. S. (2006). *Teaching for comprehending and fluency: Thinking, talking, and writing about reading, K–8.* Portsmouth, NH: Heinemann.

Gentry, J. R. (2008). *The easy assessment guide: A breakthrough for beginning reading and writing.* New York: Scholastic.

Goodlad, J. (2004). *A place called school.* New York: McGraw-Hill.

Graham, P. (ed.) (1999). *Speaking of journals: Children's book writers talk about their diaries, notebooks, and sketchbooks.* Honesdale, PA: Boyds Mills Press.

Graves, D. (1989). *Investigate nonfiction.* Portsmouth, NH: Heinemann.

Hahn, M. L. (2002). *Reconsidering read-aloud.* Portland, ME: Stenhouse.

Harvey, S., & Goudvis, A. (2008). *Strategies that work: Teaching comprehension to enhance understanding, second edition.* Portland, ME: Stenhouse.

Harwayne, S. (1992). *Lasting impressions: Weaving literature into the writing workshop.* Portsmouth, NH: Heinemann.

Heard, G. (1999). *Awakening the heart: Exploring poetry in elementary and middle school.* Portsmouth, NH: Heinemann.

Heard, G., & Laminack, L. (2007). *Climb inside a poem.* Portsmouth, NH: Heinemann.

Hindley, J. (1996). *In the company of children.* Portland, ME: Stenhouse.

Hoyt, L. (2008). *Mastering the mechanics, grades 2–3: Ready-to-use lessons for modeled, guided, and independent editing.* New York: Scholastic.

Hoyt, L. (2004). *Spotlight on comprehension: Building a literacy of thoughtfulness.* Portsmouth, NH: Heinemann.

Kaufman, D. (2000). *Conferences and conversations: Listening to the literate classroom.* Portsmouth, NH: Heinemann.

Keene, E., & Zimmerman, S. (2007). *Mosaic of thought: Teaching comprehension in a reader's workshop, second edition.* Portsmouth, NH: Heinemann.

Krashen, S. (2004). *The power of reading: Insights from the research, second edition.* Portsmouth, NH: Heinemann.

Kristo, J., & Bamford, R. (2004). *Nonfiction in focus.* New York: Scholastic.

Laminack, L. (2007). *Cracking open the author's craft: Teaching the art of writing.* New York: Scholastic.

Lane, B. (1993). *After the end.* Portsmouth, NH: Heinemann.

Lera, D. (2009). *Writing above standard: Engaging lessons that take standards to new heights and help kids become skilled, inspired writers.* New York: Scholastic.

Le Guin, U. (1998). *Steering the craft: Exercises and discussions on story writing for the lone navigator or the mutinous crew.* Portland, OR: The Eighth Mountain Press.

McLaughlin, M., & DeVoogd, G. L. (2004). *Critical literacy: Enhancing students' comprehension of text.* New York: Scholastic.

Miller, D. (2002). *Reading for meaning: Teaching comprehension in the primary grades.* Portland, ME: Stenhouse.

Parkes, B. (2000). *Read it again! Revisiting shared reading.* Portland, ME: Stenhouse.

Parsons, S. (2007). *Second grade writers: Units of study to help children plan, organize, and structure their ideas.* Portsmouth, NH: Heinemann.

Pearson, D., & Gallagher M. (1983). "The instruction of reading comprehension." *Contemporary Educational Psychology,* 8(3), 317-345.

Pinnell, G. S., & Scharer, P. (2003). *Teaching for comprehension in reading, grades K–2.* New York: Scholastic.

Prescott-Griffin, M., & Witherell, N. (2004). *Fluency in focus: Comprehension strategies for all young readers.* Portsmouth, NH: Heinemann.

Rasinski, T. (2003). *The fluent reader: Oral reading strategies for building word recognition.* New York: Scholastic.

Ray, K. W. (2002). *What you know by heart: How to develop curriculum for your writing workshop.* Portsmouth, NH: Heinemann.

Ray, K. W. (1999). *Wondrous words: Writers and writing in the elementary classroom.* Urbana, IL: NCTE.

Ray, K. W., & Laminack, L. (2001). *The writing workshop: Working though the hard parts (and they're all hard parts).* Urbana, IL: NCTE.

Rich, M. (2007, November 19). Study links drop in test scores to a decline in time spent reading. *New York Times,* pp. E1, E7.

Roser, N., & Martinez, M. (2005). *What a character! Character study as a guide to literacy meaning making in grades K–5.* Newark, DE: International Reading Association.

Routman, R. (2002). *Reading essentials: The specifics you need to teach reading well.* Portsmouth, NH: Heinemann.

Ruzzo, K., & Sacco, M. (2004). *Significant studies for second grade. Reading and writing investigations for children.* Portsmouth, NH: Heinemann.

Samway, K. D., & Taylor, D. (2007). *Teaching English language learners: Strategies that work, K–5.* New York: Scholastic.

Silvey, A. (1995). *Children's books and their creators.* Boston: Houghton Mifflin Company.

Stead, T. (2006). *Reality checks: Teaching reading comprehension with nonfiction K–5.* Portland, ME: Stenhouse.

Strunk, W., & White, E. B. (1999). *The elements of style* (4th ed.). New York: Longman.

Szymusiak, K., & Sibberson, F. (2001). *Beyond leveled books: Supporting transitional readers in grades 2-5.* Portland, ME: Stenhouse.

Szymusiak, K., & Sibberson F. (2008). *Day-to-day assessment in the reading workshop.* New York: Scholastic.

Taberski, S. (2000). *On solid ground: Strategies for teaching reading K–3.* Portsmouth, NH: Heinemann.

Weaver, C. (2006). *The grammar plan book: A guide to smart teaching.* Portsmouth, NH: Heinemann.

Welty, E. (1984). *One writer's beginnings.* Cambridge. MA: Harvard University Press.